INDIA'S DEVELOPMENT AFTER INDEPENDENCE

INDIA'S DEVELOPMENT AFTER INDEPENDENCE

Edited by
B.M. JAUHARI

GYAN PUBLISHING HOUSE
NEW DELHI–110 002

INDIA'S DEVELOPMENT AFTER INDEPENDENCE

(Economic and Reference)

Rs. 690

ISBN : 81-212-0777-0

Published in 2002 in India by
Gyan Publishing House
5, Ansari Road, Darya Ganj
New Delhi-110002
Phones: 3282060, 3261060, Fax: 3285914
E-mail: gyanbook@vsnl.com
Visit our website at: http://www.gyanbooks.com

Laser Typesetting : A.S. Printers, Delhi
Printed at : Chawla Offset Press, Delhi

This Volume is dedicated to the memory of Great Indians, who fought for our Independence and who initiated the process of Economic Development so as to ensure Economic Freedom to masses

CONTENTS

SECTION–IV

Science, Education and Technology–Future Perspective

PREFACE

It was on August 15, 1947 that the British rulers transferred the political power to Indians (A Tryst with Destiny). We became a sovereign nation on 26 January, 1950, with the adoption of our Constitution. We carved out a path for building up a strong, vibrant, a truly Sovereign Democratic Republic. Development plans were adopted in order to ensure economic and social freedom to masses. During past half a century we have seen wars and peace, ups and downs, triumphs and tragedies, national losses and sacrifices, national crisis and international upheavals, developmental plans and great achievements, social tensions and religious fundamentalism, nationalist forces and divisive elements, successes and failures, strong polity and weak governments, changing priorities and adherence to old notions, a dream come true and a blurred vision.

Many knowledgeable, authentic and reliable volumes were published on the occasion of Golden Jubilee of our independence. But an indepth study on all the aspects of our national life is perhaps not yet available. Hence this volume, which touches upon all the areas and includes works of experts in their respective fields. It is a small effort with a definite purpose.

For the convenience of our well informed readers, the book is divided into four sub-sections—Economy of India, Polity, Constitution and the Parliamentary Democracy, Social Organisation—Cultural and Moral values, and Education, Science and Technology.

I express my deep sense of gratefulness to all the contributors whose great and sincere efforts have indeed enriched, embroidered and adorned this volume.

I am greatly indebted to Dr. B. Satyanarayan Reddy former Governor of Uttar Pradesh and Orissa, Mr. Abid Hussain former Indian Ambassador to US, Mr. N. Vittal, Central Vigilance Commissioner, Prof. Y.K. Alagh former Vice-Chancellor of Jawaharlal Nehru University, New Delhi and Prof. S.S. Mohapatra former General Secretary, All India Congress Committee for their very kind and generous guidance, help and assistance.

Finally I express my respects to Prof. J.K. Mathur, Dr. A.K. Khare, Shri H.M. Jauhari, Dr. M.K. Jain, Mr. P.K. Pandey, and Mr. Mukesh Jain, Mr. Devendra Rai and Mr. M.M. Johri lent a great help in the preparation of the manuscript and they deserve special appreciation. I must also thank Mr. R.P. Goel for neatly typing the important papers selflessly and M/s. Gyan Publishing House, New Delhi for making the volume available to all of us.

January 14, 2002.

B.M. Jauhari

LIST OF CONTRIBUTORS

In his very informative chapter, Mr. N. Vittal highlights the achievements during the last fifty plus years of economic planning in India, but expresses his displeasure over the weaknesses. He has high hopes about the future of India—the youth power, science and technology and the will of the people to solve the problems. In support of his argument, he quotes 'holy scriptures' very extensively.

In their work on "Growth of Income and Consumption in India", Prof. Shri Prakash and Dr. Shalini Singh, deal with the two important aspects of the national economy. This is a highly technical work and is based on mathematical models.

In his article, Prof. A.K. Jain deals with the need of widening direct taxes base in the new Millennium. He discusses in details about the need, effects and challenges of this measure with reference to Indian Economy.

Justice V.M. Tarkunde, in his article, examines the new Economic Policy with reference to the concept of *Swadeshi*. In support of his argument, he takes the help of various opinions on the subject. Indianisation of the policy is very necessary, he rightly concludes.

New Economic Policy and the entire reform process needs foreign direct investments in Indian Economy in larger and larger amount. The article makes an indepth study of possibilities and prospects, utilization and limitations of our policy Pertaining to F.D.I. The authors of this article Monita, Shailesh and Nitin have rightly created their place in this volume by their labour and herculean effort in the field.

Dr. I.C. Dhingra, in his article, describes the utility of

both the private and public sectors and advocates the necessity of State Control in different aspects of public life.

In his work on 'Development of Power Sector after Independence', Mr. Raj Kumar deals with the generation and distribution of power and the problems of the Sector.

Dr. M.K. Jain takes into account the gains and losses of nationalization in India and the need for privatisation under new policy measures.

Prof. S.K. Singh discusses at length about the financial sector reforms—their need and rationale. He comes out with a number of suggestions.

Prof. S.A.R. Bilgrami takes into account the export performance of Indian agriculture with reference to the emerging World Trading System. The author also describes the challenges and prospects.

Dr. Dev Raj tells very extensively about public sector banks, banking and financial sector reforms in India and the future threats.

Mr. Madan Verma traces the historical development of Indian Economy, glorious past, problematic immediate past and the present position of challenges and opportunities.

Dr. B.M. Jauhari and Ms. Monita Mohan in their work discuss the need for employment generation under the present reform process and the need for enlarging the employment opportunities for the growing population. The task, though, challenging must become a national priority.

Prof. H.M. Jain, in his article, describes the crisis of the nation-state in India and its impact on our polity, Constitution and the Parliamentary Democracy and urges upon leaders to tackle it tactfully and sincerely.

Dr. Subhash Kashyap discovers a new role for youth, and education in the social transformation and takes the help of holy scriptures in support of his argument. If the nation is to progress, the youth must be empowered and given their due role.

Prof. H.M. Jain in his second article deals with Pandit Jawaharlal Nehru and the Constitution making in India and traces the historical developments related to it. Pt. Nehru was a genius, a Statesman and a true Indian in letter and spirit.

Dr. M.K. Jain, in his article on parliamentary democracy deals with the role of Parliament in India and rightly discusses Parliament as an institution of national and social transformation. Our Parliament is great.

Dr. B.M. Jauhari, in his second article, describes the social composition and social crisis as a result of economic reforms and considers reforms as an important tool of social change if put in right perspective. According to him, the second stage of economic reform should include the real factors. Such a shift is nationally desirable.

Dr. Afroz Ahmad, in his very timely contribution on 'Water—a Looming Crisis', takes into account the availability of water resources in developing countries and also examines the Indian scene very vividly. He comes out with recommendations for water resource use, conservation and management.

Dr. M.C. Bhartiya and Dr. Ravindra Kumar in his work, expresses utter dismay and disgust on the decline of cultural and moral values in independent India and suggests the need for the re-generation and restoration of moral values in individual, social and national interest.

Mr. Deepak Jain, in his article describes extensively about the environment, the need for education and training and the management of environment in India, especially when we are recasting our policies under a global concern and national needs.

Dr. Anurag Saxena and Mrs. Monika Jauhari in their article truly examine in details the role of science, technology and education in the national transformation. They also take into account the perspectives and the path ahead. The article rightly fits into the present requirements of education and, therefore, assures great relevance and importance.

Prof. R.L. Varshney deals with the role of management, education, and challenges before the managers under the new economic dispensation in India. The role of a manager assumes new responsibility.

The father of plans in India, Mr. Tarlok Singh, in his contribution, tries to rediscover the role of social sciences for the year 2000 and after. He suggests for a wider and greater role of social sciences in nation-making, youth-making, social and national transformation.

Dr. C.L. Jain, in his article, depicts India—in the new millennium—its environmental health and the importance of education for Indian community.

Section–I

Economy of India–From Nationalisation to Privatisation

Section-I

Economy of India-From Nationalisation to Privatisation

1

ECONOMIC REFORMS IN POST-INDEPENDENCE INDIA

N. Vittal

It is surprising that Socialism and Communism which are based on altruism ultimately could not prove to be very effective in comparison to the enlightened self-interest of capitalism. In the 53 years, since independence, we adopted socialist policies and the dirigist approach. The net result was we had what Rajaji called the permit-licence raj, 1991 brought about a U-turn economic policy. In the last one decade or so we have been trying to re-orient our policies and also link our economy more closely with the global economy. Nevertheless half a century is a good landmark in the life of a country. Although it is a very small period in the life of a nation, it is very large chunk of an individual life.

I do not know whether our objective is only to look at the past 53 years since our independence or draw lessons, take our bearings today and project where we would be in the future. I think a mere exercise in looking at the past may give us probably insights and the 2020 vision which has been called the Granny glasses of hind sight. An exercise of learning from the past and trying to use those lessons to build on our strengths and overcome our weaknesses would have the advantage of helping us to perform better in the future. We have two broad issues to examine. The first is, will socialism continue to be relevant in the future? The second is can socialism be taken advantage of in building a new India?

As I see it, the first lesson we learn, is that the focus on socialism led to the emphasis on reducing inequalities of income. This attempt was made at one stage by progressive taxation measures and later on poverty alleviation measures. We had land reforms in the early years of independence and a number of constitutional amendments can be traced to these measures. But when it comes to the ground realities, we find that only in State like West Bengal have the reforms been carried out to the fullest. In many other States, perhaps, the original objectives of the land reforms process have not been achieved. In between, during the time of Nehru, there was an attempt at co-operative farming. Vinobha Bhave tried to carry on the Gandhian tradition of the *Bhoodaan* Movement. But these Gandhian or socialist ideas were not successful.

However, on the agricultural front the great success of India has been in internalising the modern technology of Green Revolution. From being a country, which was dependent on import of food grains, we became self-sufficient in food grains. Even this claim can be challenged. If we take the principle that every one should have at least 2400 calories per day of food, we find that many may not qualify because at least thirty per cent of our people continue to live below the poverty line. They may not be able to have two square meals a day. Nevertheless, the fact remains that Green Revolution was a success. It became a success because a suitable technology was available. There was a systematic attempt to make even the illiterate farmers understand the benefits of the new technology by thousands of demonstration farms. Once the farmer accepted the new technology, inputs by way of hybrid seeds, irrigation water, pesticides, fertilisers were made available. Finally, there was a price support mechanism, which ensured that the Green Revolution was a success. An equally comparable success has been the White Revolution. Thanks to the vision and leadership of Dr. Kurien and Tribhuvan Das

Patel at Amul in Anand in Gujarat, India today has become the biggest producer of milk. A doubt can be raised at this stage whether in the context of economic liberalisation the co-operatives which were consciously promoted for achieving the milk revolution will be threatened. Dr. Kurien has been vigorously fighting a battle with his back to wall to protect the special position of the co-operatives, but we do not know what the future is going to be.

On the industrial front, the 53 years of liberalisation with the doses of socialist policies and the permit-licence raj, it had one advantage. We diversified our industrial base. However, this diversification was at a cost. Most of our industries are not of global standards. Today, as India links to the global economy very closely, the Indian industry is going through a painful process of readjustment. Nearly ninety per cent of the Indian industry in the private sector is in the favour of family owned companies. These companies are making attempts to adjust to the new situation. In the early years of liberalisation of 1991, the trend was for the joint ventures. But as one of my industrialist friend says having a joint venture with a multinational is like having a breakfast with a tiger. You can have breakfast with a tiger, but thereafter the tiger will have you for breakfast. In recent times, I find that the Indian industry is learning to adopt different strategies to survive. The first was engaging international consultants like McKinsey to get ideas about how to focus on their core competencies and shed unrelated diversification. There is also a wave of mergers and acquisitions and there is an attempt to build on size. But will the Indian industry be able to overcome the twin challenges today of the multinationals, namely, being up-to-date in technology and at the same time being large in size.

It is here that I think the emerging knowledge economy gives an opportunity to Indians. The new knowledge economy opens new horizons, particularly, for the first generation technocrat entrepreneurs especially in the field of information technology. We should be able to build up on this front. It is a healthy sign that the government have recognised the significance of information technology. The Prime Minister has called IT as India's tomorrow. The recommendations of the Task Force of the Information Technology are before the government. Let us hope that as we move on to the 21st Century, Indians will be able to make a mark in the new knowledge-based economy, industries like Information Technology, Internet-based start ups, Telecommunications and so on. At the same time, traditional industries must be able to gear up and come up to global standards.

The other important fact is that India has also become a member of WTO and is a signatory to some of the agreements like information technology agreement, global telecom agreement and agreements relating to intellectual property rights, financial sector reforms and so on. These are going to drastically change the face of Indian business and industry and in the process we hope that the Indian industry will be able to survive.

The emerging era is the era of technology. Here if we look back at the legacy of socialistic control, two trends become obvious. Those technologies in which India did not have any opportunity to borrow or buy technology, it was able to develop on its own. Areas like Atomic Energy, Nuclear Power, Missile Technology and Space Technology fall in this category. India has been able to build a competent set of technocrats who are able to take on the challenges of foreign technology. When Cray was reluctant to provide Supercomputers, Rajiv Gandhi's inspired leadership showed that we can develop the technologies by ourselves. Pitroda brought the telecom revolution in this country and showed how, in a developing country, concepts of access to telecom services can enhanced by innovations like the STD booths, which have become an essential part of the rural scene throughout the country today.

While India has mastered strategic technologies, it failed because of its socialist policies and the licensing raj in commercially useful technologies owing to restrictions on import of technology and foreign equity. Consequently, Indian companies ended up buying obsolete technologies. Indian industry suffered both from the problem of uneconomic sizes and also of obsolete technologies. These are the problems that have to be overcome today. Fortunately, with a visionary leader like Dr. Mashelkar championing the cause for a patent literacy mission, India must be able to build on its technological strengths.

The last decade of twentieth century also saw a lot of talk about liberalisation based on the Washington consensus. This in turn has led some of the elite insisting on our following the Washington consensus to the letter. Objections are raised by those who champion the cause of the poor that we must have reforms with a human face. The first stage of reforms resulted, for instance, in sectors like telecommunications, power, roads and ports being open to the private sector. However, except in telecommunications and to some extent in power, there has hardly been any improvement. The debate will continue about the future course of reform. At the same time, we come across an interesting phenomenon of a political consensus emerging so far as the reform is concerned. Murasoli Maran, in one of his talks, traced this devolution in a beautiful way. He said that when Indira Gandhi came back to power after Emergency, in 1980, she introduced reforms by accident; then in Rajiv Gandhi time, we had reforms by stealth where concepts like broad banding of licenses were introduced. Narasimha Rao's was the period where we had reforms by crisis. Finally we had coalition governments and we are having reforms by consensus. This, perhaps, is the strength of the Indian democracy. So we need not feel that as a country on the path of reforms we are in any way standing to lose, compared to the tiger economics of south-east Asia, which were the range and the models to emulate in the late 1980s and 1990s . The 1997 crisis of South-East Asian countries have brought out the fact that perhaps by sheer accident India might have chosen the right path thanks to its democracy and a cautious approach for reforms.

Nevertheless, I had always held that we appear to be a

country afraid to make a choice. We choose the middle of the road, but the middle of the road is the most dangerous place to be on the road. I would, therefore, suggest that as we look forward, we should focus on the following as a strategy for what can be called as the second-generation reforms.

There is a lot of debate in the media about the second-generation reforms. Issues focussed in the second-generation reforms are :

* Opening up of the insurance sector
* Reforms in the banking sector
* Reforms in infrastructure
* Regulatory agencies in different sectors like telecommunication, Power and so on

Is the current agenda for second-generation reform adequate? I am afraid, that the second-generation reforms, which are now being discussed, suffer from the following drawbacks, which also form the basis of the criticism of the first-generation reforms :

* The prime focus is on attracting foreign investment. The Indian entrepreneur may feel that he is given a second class treatment.
* The basic approach seems to be guided by the Washington consensus to open up the economy for global trade.
* The opponents of reforms always point out that the reform agenda is of interest only to the elite. The common man and the poor are completely overlooked in the process.

In this context, is it possible to seriously think of a second generation of reforms, which will achieve all the goals of the current promoters of reform and at the same time satisfy the pro-poor critics of current reforms? A new approach based on following three points may succeed.

* Zero tolerance of corruption

* Increasing tenfold the velocity of government operations
* A focus on productivity to make the investments already made in different sectors yield the promised benefits.

The first item of vital importance, in the second-generation reforms should be a frontal attack on corruption. The Prime Minister has already given a lead to the country by calling for zero tolerance of corruption. The Mahbub-Ul-Huq Centre at Islamabad in its Human Development in South Asia Report 1999 has pointed out that if corruption levels in India were reduced to those in the Scandinavian countries, investment rates could rise annually by some 12 per cent and GDP growth rate by almost 1.5 per cent each year. After all, the promoters of second-generation reforms are talking about attracting foreign direct investment and promoting growth. Why not focus on corruption and practise zero tolerance so that the common man also who is an everyday victim of the menace of corruption in our country can breathe more easily? In this way the second-generation reform can become more popular.

A three-point strategy can be a broad framework for such an onslaught against corruption. The first is to simplify the rules and regulations so that the scope for corruption is eliminated. The second is to empower the public so that they know their rights and can have access to information. In this context, the need for a Freedom of Information Act becomes very vital.The third is effective and prompt punishment of the corrupt.

Here I would draw attention to a weakness currently hurting the power structure of Lok Sabha and Rajya Sabha as of today in carrying out the second-generation reforms wherever any new law has to be enacted. While the ruling coalition has the majority to pass a bill in the Lok Sabha, in the Rajya Sabha it does not have the necessary majority to carry out its will. This will mean that every legislative measure will have to be the result of a political compromise. The danger of the baby being thrown out with the bath water in such compromises cannot be ruled out.

Is there a way out? I think there must be. All that is needed is for the government to decide that the main thrust of the second-generation will not depend on passing laws but effective implementation through executive action. For example, even without a Freedom of Information Act, every department can declare what information it will make available openly to the public. Once the departments take this initiative, people will become automatically empowered and there will be greater transparency.

That brings us to the second point of the second generation of reforms, namely, a total attack on red-tape and delay in our system. We must aim at a tenfold increase in the velocity of government transactions. If every department of Government of India and all State governments were to take a simple decision that whatever is the transaction time taken today to handle cases will be brought down to ten per cent of the time taken, there will be a dramatic increase in the velocity of business transactions. A focus on using IT extensively in governmental systems will automatically result in the increase of velocity of business in government tremendously. Automatically this will also reduce the scope for corruption. In today's global context, investment is attracted where there is greater velocity in decision-making. Time is money in today's world. The objective of the current champions for second generation reforms for attracting foreign direct investment will thus be served more effectively. Incidentally, the domestic entrepreneurs as also the citizens will stand to benefit.

A major issue that is always discussed in the second-generation reforms is that we need a very large amount of capital upfront especially to improve our infrastructure. We do not have this capital and therefore we have to go in for foreign investment or assistance from multilateral agencies. But have we ever thought whether we use whatever infrastructure we have, effectively? For instance, in successive five-year plans, the irrigation engineers used to get large amounts allocated for irrigation projects. There was always a difference between the area claimed to have potential for irrigation and the actual area irrigated. Why not in the second stage of reforms focus on issues like this and examine whether from whatever infrastructure we have created, are we getting optimum promised results? This can be in the area of irrigation, telecommunication, power—generation etc. Everybody knows about the transmission losses of the order of 22 per cent in power sector. A focus on productivity must be the third point of the second-generation reforms. I wonder whether the champions of reform believe in the *mantra* of the Washington consensus and the pro-poor critics of reform will come together to implement the second stage of reforms on the lines I have indicated.

Having crossed the half-century mark as a nation and as a Republic and looking to the future, I think we should take a quick stock about our strengths, weaknesses, opportunities and threats. Our strengths are that we have proved that we can be multi-ethnic, multi-lingual, multi-cultural society and still have the coherence of a single nation. The manner in which the country has responded to the threat of Kargil shows that the nationalistic spirit has come to stay. The second strength of India is our boisterous and vigorous democracy. We have had 13 elections and frequent changes of governments lately and when we compare ourselves with other nations that became independent along with us, that India can be proud of the fact that even though when universal adult suffrage was introduced there might have been criticism and doubting Thomases. Today the inherent correctness of the choice we made has been proved. When it comes to the third strength, the strength of our technologies whether at the mass level as the Green Revolution or the White Revolution or at the higher-end as in the Information Technology or strategic technologies like Defence and Atomic Energy.

On having entered the 21st Century we find

opportunities arising because it is a knowledge economy we are entering and our one billion strong population itself provides and excellent market and even the thirty per cent of the people who are below the poverty line provide an opportunity. Dr. Prahlad has been finding out that the entrepreneurs should look at the poor people themselves as a market opportunity. He pointed out the successful operation of rural co-operatives leading to the White Revolution, the success in Madurai of the Arvind Eye Camps where India can provide world class medical services at a competitive cost. Dr. Pratap Reddy who has contributed to the development of the concept of corporate hospitals has said that India can provide world class healthcare at 1/6th of international cost. In fact, India can emerge as a great service centre of the global economy if we are able to have policies by which we would consciously encourage services like, health services, It enabled services and even repair and maintenance of aircrafts and high technology instruments and so on. Threats, of course, are always there and the threat of corruption has already been pointed out how if you could only focus on reducing our corruption to that of Scandinavian countries, our GDP will go up by 8 per cent and foreign investment will go up by 12 per cent. The threat of conflict with our neighbour Pakistan is a perennial threat. Added to that are the threats of militants and low intensity conflict, which we face in various parts of the country. But we must be able to overcome this because if we are able to build on the strength of our people, our market potential then automatically it will lead to prosperity which in turn will be helpful in overcoming many aspects of militancy. In fact, if we look at the militancy in our border-states, we can trace them to high corruption on one side and frustration of the unemployed youth on the other. With the check on corruption and generation of employment opportunities by intelligent economic policies, we should be able to indirectly strike at the root of the militancy also.

Ultimately, therefore, the furture is in our hands. We should be able to follow the old Rig Vedic dictum of keeping our minds open to all ideas that can come up and see how we can build on these good ideas. *Aano bhadrah kritavo yantu vishwalah.* In shaping the policies we can do nothing better than following the age-old advice of the *Taitreya Upanishad.* Let us come together, let us enjoy together, let our strengths come together, let there be brightness of knowledge, let there be no misunderstanding or hatred. That way lies progress.

Sahanavavlu sahanaubhunaklu sahaviryam kara va vahai Tejasvinam aditamastu ma vid visha vahai, Om shanti shanti shanti.

our minds open to all ideas that can come to and see how we can build on these good ideas. [illegible] In shaping our policies, we can do nothing better than following the age-old advice of the [illegible]: Let us come together, let us enjoy together, let our strengths come together, let there be brightness of knowledge, let there be no misunderstanding or hatred. That way lies progress.

[illegible]

2

GROWTH OF INCOME AND CONSUMPTION IN INDIA

Shri Prakash
Shalini Singh

Explaining Macro Consumption Behaviour by Micro Theory

Conventional theory relates consumers' behaviour to allocation of income among different uses. Consumers are supposed to allocate income between consumption and savings. The same choice confronts the decision makers at macro level also. Importance of decision lies in the determination of fractions of income to meet consumption and savings needs. Budgeted consumption expenditure is allocated among numerous expenditure categories or commodity groups. However, consumers' behaviour may be analysed either at individual household level or at macro level. There have been several commodity specific demand or consumption studies for India. But aggregate consumption functions have been estimated only as a part of macro econometric models of the Indian economy. Thus, the estimation of aggregate consumption functions *per se* has remained neglected, by and large. This study is an attempt to estimate the aggregate consumption function for India in the macro context. The macro analysis may focus on aggregate consumption function to determine total consumption expenditure when national income is given. The aggregate consumption function is generally a part of macro econometric models, though the macro models may focus mainly on the determination of such national aggregates as income and its sectoral components, imports, exports, etc. Aggregate consumption function may, therefore, be specified as a part of macro econometric model, needing macro economic theory for its explanation. Even if the aggregate consumption function alone may constitute a single equation model, the model is implicitly a part of some macro model.

Aggregate consumption function relates total consumption expenditure functionally with national income (Intriligator, p. 8, 1980). Consumption decisions at macro level may be treated as the decisions of all consumers taken together as one entity. Aggregate function may then be treated as the sum of individual consumption functions to keep it amenable for the application of micro theory of consumers' behaviour (For Different Assumptions and Aggregation Procedures, See, Wallis, 1973; Cramer, 1973).

Alternatively, aggregate consumption function may be treated as a special case of the typical demand function of micro theory of consumers' behaviour. The micro theory postulates the households or individual consumers to choose that combination of two or more goods, including services, from all combinations available at the prevailing prices, that will maximize the utility function subject to the constraint of given income. If, however, all prices, except the price of the good under consideration, and income are held constant, a special demand function for a specific good will be obtained. Similarly, if all prices are held constant and quantities of demand for all goods and services taken together are related to income, a special demand function will be obtained (Intriligator, p. 208, 1980). This function is defined as the *Engel curve.* Engel curve describes the relationship between any given trait of consumers' behaviour with income, ceteris paribus (Cramer, p. 26, 1973). Therefore, if the behaviour of all consumers in the market and their demand for all goods, taken together, are related to aggregate of their incomes, one moves from micro to macro Engel curve.

Consumer's behaviour involves a diversified series of choice making decisions. The exercise of choices results in outcomes that emerge as the presence or absence of attributes like the ownership of durable goods or expenditures incurred on hobbies, habit forming intoxicants and/or luxuries. These traits may not be universally associated with all consumers. Thus, it may be assumed that consumers face two-fold choice: allocation of the current income between consumption and savings. This implicitly assumes allocation decisions to be dichotomous. If choice is envisaged to be dichotomous, it may facilitate probabilistic measurement of consumers' choices. Functions like logit or probit may also be specified as aggregate consumption function for estimation from given data if the variables are measured or interpreted in probabilistic terms.

Dichotomous choice of income allocation between savings and consumption treat the decision process to be discrete and hierarchical as against the traditional theory's stipulation of these choices to be in continuum. The choices generally revolve round the following questions:

(i) how much to spend on current consumption?

(ii) how much to save for future? But these choices about consumption and savings are decomposable into sub choices. Consumers have to choose simultaneously or hierarchically to decide:

  (a) which of the available goods and services to consume and which of them to leave out of consideration,

  (b) how much quantities of the goods and services chosen for consumption to purchase, and

  (c) which quality or brand of each selected consumption goods/service to prefer wherever such choices are available.

Branded goods command higher prices than the unbranded ones and greater the reputation of the brand and/or the market share of the producer, greater is likely to be its price. Consumers generally associate high prices with high quality. Price differentials may be assumed to reflect the quality differentials. Tastes and preferences, including habits and hobbies, price differentials and incomes may be considered as the main determinants of consumers' choices. The consumers' choices may differ from lower to higher income groups and from one year to another as aggregate income changes with time.

Choices pertaining to savings become operationally meaningful if savings are carried forward into future, or these converted into investment. The choice of portfolio and determination of the quantity of its component becomes important. The savers and investors will have to decide:

(i) how much savings are to be kept liquid through investment in short term instruments like Savings Accounts with the banks and/or post offices,

(ii) what proportion of savings should be invested in short/long run fixed or recurring deposits,

(iii) what proportion of savings should be invested in equity shares, bonds, mutual funds, NSCs, NSS and other Securities, and

(iv) what proportion of savings should be allocated to fixed income yielding debentures, etc.

Two types of macro consumption and savings decisions are to be distinguished: sum of all households' decisions and sum of outcomes of decisions of the government and their agencies, public sector undertakings and autonomous institutions, corporate houses and organisations. The overall outcome of consumption decisions of all individual households may be defined as "aggregate private final consumption expenditure". Outcome of consumption decisions of second group of entities may be defined as "public consumption." Aggregate private savings and investment may similarly be distinguished from public and institutional savings and investment. This study analyses the aggregate private final consumption function. The variate values, therefore, relate to aggregate or average expenditure incurred by all households on consumption of all goods and services. Similarly, aggregate or average income is the sum of incomes accruing to all households. But this study has used the aggregate of disposable private incomes. Disposable income is estimated by deducting income tax and other charges paid directly to the government and its agencies from net GNP at factor cost. Aggregate consumption is the sum of expenditure incurred by all consumers and aggregate income is the sum of earnings of all spending units. These earning and spending units may coincide with entire population of the country.

Assumptions

Levels and patterns of consumption and income are assumed to be inter and intra-group invariant. Thus, highly marked inter and intra-group differences of both consumption and income are overlooked. It is more realistic to assume that differences both between earning and spending units within and between groups cancel out in averaging or aggregating. The assumption is relevant for the analysis of aggregate time series which generally does not provide information about inter-personal or inter-group diffenences in population. The assumption implies that the income and consumption aggregates at any given point of time represent the decisions of all earning and spending units whose tastes and preferences are similar. Differences in levels, commodity composition and structures of consumption of different groups will remain hidden. Sum of aggregate savings and consumption equals aggregate of individual incomes. Aggregate income may, therefore, be the most decisive determinant of consumption. But aggregate consumption expenditure and its proportions in income will vary with the changes in aggregate income through time. Aggregate consumption function describes the relationship between aggregate consumption and aggregate income. Aggregate savings are complements of total consumption expenditure in aggregate income. The consumption function may, therefore, be treated as equivalent to the savings function (Crimer, 1971).

Models and Methodology

An aggregate consumption function, even if it is specified as a single equation model, has generally some macro economic model as its framework. The aggregate consumption function is distinctly different from micro consumption functions and it requires a different theoretical framework. Alternative theoretical underpinnings have naturally been developed for the analysis of aggregate consumption function. This study focuses on the analysis of aggregate final private consumption function for the Indian economy during a period of 47 years from 1950-51 to 1996-97. The Indian economy has traversed a long distance along its growth path during this period. Structural breaks from the past trends may, therefore, be expected.

Alternative theoretical paradigms have been evaluated for possible approximation of aggregates consumption function for the Indian economy. Keynes' consumption function is one of the alternatives examined empirically in the study.

Keynesian Model

If savings and consumption dichotomy is postulated in Keynesian framework for the determination of aggregate income, fractions of income allocated to consumption and investment directly contribute to effective demand. But consumption constitutes the single largest component of effective demand. Savings may then be treated as residual income left after meeting consumption needs. It may, however, be noted that, besides consumption and investment, there are various other factors like imports, exports, government expenditure, changes in stocks, taxes and subsidies that affect effective demand. Negligence of these components of effective demand in specifying investment as and exogenous factor and postulating it as the difference between income and consumption for purposes of identification of aggregate consumption function is an approximation for empirical testing of the abstract Keynesian model. Keynes' model is, in fact, the first model that furnished the definition of an aggregate or macro consumption function (1936, pp. 96-98). The following system of simultaneous equations may describe the Keynes' macro economic model:

$$Y(t) = S(t) + C(t)$$

$$= I(t) + C(t) \quad ...(1)$$

$$C(t) = C[Y(t)] \quad ...(2)$$

$$S(t) = I(t) \quad ...(3)$$

where Y, S, C, I and t represent income, savings, consumption, investment and time respectively. This is the simplest form of the Keynesian model in which consumption function is the only behavioural relation. The aggregate consumption function causally relates current consumption to current income. In this specification identification of the consumption function is straight forward. Relation 1 is the definitional identity, indicating investment as second component of effective demand. Investment is an autonomous and exogenous variable. Investment is, therefore, related neither to consumption nor to income. Relation 3 may either be postulated as an equilibrium condition, or Keynes' postulation may be invoked to designate it as a definitional identity. All variables of the system relate to the same time period. The model stipulates both marginal propensity to consume (MPC) and income elasticity of consumption to be positive but less than unity. This virtually amounts to *a priori* restrictions on parameters of the linear and log linear functional forms of aggregate consumption function.

Friedman's Permanent Income Hypothesis

Friedman's function represents an ultimate stage of conceptual refinement of macro consumption function ever since its introduction by Keynes. Friedman's function is based on four very strong assumptions to analyse aggregate consumption in terms of micro theory of consumers' behaviour. Friedman's postulations generated raging controversy due partly to inter-relatedness of his thesis. Direct empirical verification of the Friedman's main hypothesis is amenable to alternative interpretations in the context of other components of his thesis. None of these alternative interpretations of the empirical results may be conclusive. This makes his assumptions and postulations highly debatable.

Friedman first assumes expenditure on consumer durables as investment in capital goods on following counts:

(i) like capital goods, consumer durables render services to their users over a period of time. Annual services utilized by consumers may be treated as consumption. Like capital goods, consumer durables also depreciate in value and this depreciation may be treated as annual consumption;

(ii) purchases of consumer durables may partly be financed from savings. Thus, expenditure on durable consumer goods is similar to investment. Friedman's theory is thus different from macro definition of consumption.

Friedman assumes both income and consumption to consist of permanent and transitory parts. Income and consumption is thus defined as follows:

$$Y(i) = Y(pi) + Y(Ti) \qquad ...(4)$$

$$C(i) = C(pi) + C(Ti) \qquad ...(5)$$

where i refers to i-th consumer to entrap the thesis in micro consumption theory, p and T denote permanent and transitory components of these two variables respectively.

An important characteristic of the standards of living and patterns of consumption is that consumption is highly flexible upwards but it is downward rigid. Consumers generally prefer to wait before moving from lower to higher consumption levels. They tend to adopt such levels and patterns of consumption as may be sustainable by their regular incomes. But regular income may be the floor of actual total income expected to accrue through time. As against permanent income, transitory income may accrue only occasionally. The transitory income is, in fact, random in nature. People, however, have some notion about the preferred way to spend transitory income as and when they get it.

Consumers distinguish between the problem of allocation of regular and transitory incomes between permanent and transitory consumption. Transitory consumption cannot be related to the permanent income. But people do expect their permanent incomes to rise on yearly basis. They may, therefore, raise their permanent consumption gradually in correspondence with regular incremental incomes. This hypothesis constitutes a radical departure from the conventional theory of consumption. Since relations 4 and 5 are definitional identities, identification and measurement of one component will facilitate the derivation of other as a residual.

Friedman's third assumption relates permanent consumption functionally to permanent income alone:

$$C\ (pi) = f\ \{Y\ (pi)\} \qquad ...(6)$$

Friedman uses his fourth assumption to specify the functional relation as follows:

$$C\ (pi) = m\ Y\ (pi) \qquad ...(7)$$

where $0 < m < 1$. It implies that the slope of consumption function is positive but less than unity. The assumption is based on theoretical reasoning about consumers' behaviour. It is also assumed that there is no other functional relationship whatsoever among the four variables defined in the model.

The same restriction has been imposed on MPC by Keynes. But unlike Keynes, Friedman hypothesizes the permanent income elasticity of permanent consumption to equal unity :

$$n = d \log C(pi)/d \log Y(pi) = (Y/C)\ (dC/dY) = 1 \qquad ...(8)$$

where n is income elasticity of consumption.

This postulation may not be satisfied by empirical estimates of elasticity. Incidentally, income elasticities of consumption, estimated from cross section data on the basis of permanent income hypothesis, have been found to be much lower than the aggregate long run elasticity of consumption estimated from time series data (Cramer, 1973).

Following facets of Friedmanian consumption function are noteworthy:

(i) aggregation over consumers requires movement from micro to aggregate consumption function,

(ii) Friedman's function is without an intercept term. Empirical estimation of such functions requires the shifting of origin to the means of variate values.

Friedman postulates permanent consumption to be uniquely related to permanent income alone. This eliminates the theoretical need to capture the influence of other exogenous variables, excluded from the function, on the dependent variable. This reduces the intercept to zero.

Partial Adjustment Hypothesis

Dynamic models involve expectations or lags and expectations or lags may be incorporated in aggregate consumption function both on theoretical and empirical grounds. Production of goods, and hence, generation of Income involves time. It is rational to assume that there is one period gap between income generation and its spending. The assumption makes current consumption depend on past income:

$$C(t) = a + b\,Y(t-1) \qquad \text{...(9)}$$

Relation 9 implies that consumption reacts to the changes in income with a lag of one time period. To many consumers, specially non-wage/salaried self-employed ones, current income is unknown till the end of the year. Then, payment of incomes from profits, dividends, interest, bonus etc., while based on annual accounting concept, is considerably delayed.

Such time lags are alomst institutionalized in National Income Accounts.

An alternative specification defines consumption as a function of weighted sum of current and preceding year's income (Cramer, p. 191, 1973). It implies one part of consumption to depend on current income and the rest on lagged income.

As a variant of models. proposed for empirical testing, partial adjustment hypohtesis may, therefore, be empirically evaluated. Lagged dependent variable can directly be introduced in the function as an additional determinant. Brown (1952) assumed consumers' inertia, notalgia and habit persistence as the base of following model:

$$C(t) = a + b\,C(t-1) + g\,Y(t) \qquad ...(10)$$

Though aggregate consumption depends on income, yet there may be a difference between actual and desired degree of adjustment of consumption to changes in aggregate or permanent income. The degree of actual adjustment of aggregate or permanent consumption to the changes in aggregate income or its permanent component may be only a fraction of the desired change. Income or consumption expectations are realized only partially rather than fully. Koyck's assumption of geometrical decline in co-efficients and his transformation mechanism may also be used to simplify the function. Relation 10 is also compatible with adaptative expectation and partial adjustment hypothesis:

$$C(t) - C(t-1) = k\,\{C(t) - C(t-1)\} \qquad ...(11)$$

where C(t) is the desired/expected level of consumption. Relation 11 suggests that the actual change in consumption from one year to another is only a fraction of the desired change. Frictions, psychological inertia and nostalgia about the past, habits and institutional barriers to full-fledged adjustment of consumption to changes in aggregate income or its permanent component permit only partial adjustment. Then, the instinct to make sure that change in aggregate income or its permanent component is not temporary, and hence, change in p£ermanent consumption is really warranted also accounts for this lag in adjustment, where k is the co-efficient of adjustment. The adjustment co-efficient will satisfy the following inequality:

$$0 < k \leq 1 \quad ...(12)$$

Algebric manipulations of the relevant relations will furnish the following linear and log-linear forms of the consumption function (Wallis, 1976):

$$C(T) = a + b\,C(t-1) + g\,Y(t) \quad ...(13)$$

and $\log C(t) = a + b \log C(t-1) + g \log Y(t)$ ...(14)

OLS has been used to estimate the parameters of the functional relations under consideration. Results furnished by OLS estimates do not warrant the derivation of GLS estimates of the preferred functions.

Data Base

Time series of aggregate income and consumption expenditure in constant 1980-81 prices have been used as the data base. Implicit mid-year population estimates have been obtained as the ratios of the current income and income in constant prices for the years of the period of observation. Similarly, the implicit deflator has been obtained as the ratios of the values of current income and income in constant prices for the corresponding years. These data may be used to further supplement the results of this study in the subsequent exercises. All the data have been taken from the various issues of National Accounts Statistics, CSO, Ministry of planning, Government of India, New Delhi.

Empirical Evidence

Results of empirical testing of hypotheses associates with the models outlined above with the data of Indian economy have been presented sequentially.

Indian masses have already gone through the revolution of rising expections during the struggle for political independence due mainly to (1) importance attached to the programmes of socioeconomic uplift of masses in political agenda, and (2) nearly unanimous belief that under-development of Indian economy and poverty of the people was the consequence of colonial exploitation. This belief has been founded on logical thrusts and empirical evidence provided by Dadabhai Naoroji in his book *Un-British Rule in India* (Prakash, 2000) as well as the day-to-day experiences of the people.

National leaders and the masses looked forward to political independence as the means to lift India from its shoe-strings through sustained development of its economy and the emancipation of the poor. This required improvement in the living conditions of the masses. This called for the implementation of well-designed programmes of economic development and poverty amelioration. The launching of First Five Year Plan in 1951 and implementation of successive plans was thus the realisation of these long cherished dreams about development. Implementation of these plans of development has resulted in an alround development of India. This assertion may be tested by evaluating the growth performance of the Indian economy. Annual compound growth rates have been derived from OLS estimates of linear regression equation :

$$\log Y = a + b T + u \quad ...(15)$$

where Y is any dependent variable growth of which is to be estimated, T is time and u is random disturbance. Development performance of Indian economy over a period of 47 years from 1951 to 1997 is tabulated below :

Table 2.1
Growth of Real Income and Consumption in India

Variable/ Period	*1951-97*	*1951-60*	*1961-70*	*1971-80*	*1981-90*	*1991-97*
Income	1.77	1.57	1.19	1.53	2.19	2.57
t-value	61.86	21.29	5.72	9.72	22.55	12.21
Consumption	1.55	1.40	1.34	1.37	1.98	2.00
t-value	69.06	14.07	19.32	9.79	52.45	16.77

Table 2.2
Significance of Difference between overall and Decadel Growth of Income and Consumption

Variable/ Period	*1951-97*	*1951-60*	*1961-70*	*1971-80*	*1981-90*	*1991-97*
Income						
t-value	—	5.33	19.22	6.62	17.06	30.64
Consumption						
t-value	—	6.45	9.21	8.06	19.46	20.47

Table 2.3
Significance of Differences between Growth of Income and Consumption

Variable/ Period	*1951-97*	*1951-60*	*1961-70*	*1971-80*	*1981-90*	*1991-97*
t-value	6.21	2.29	–0.75	1.07	2.16	2.67

Table shows that national disposable income at factor cost in 1980-81 constant prices has been growing at a low but statistically significant and consistent annual compound rate of 1.77 per cent. Contrary to the postulation of the critics of Nehru-Mahalanobis growth strategy that despite the growth of real per capita income, living standards of Indians have not changed much, above results show considerable impact of this gradual but consistent growth of real income on real consumption both in absolute and per capita terms. Real consumption has, in fact, grown consistently and steadily at a slightly lower but statistically significant annual compound rate of 1.55 per cent during the entire observed period. Income elasticity of aggregate consumption, derived from growth rates of consumption and income, equals 0.8996 which is numerically significantly lower than unity. This supports the Keynes' postulation that income elasticity of consumption tends to be lower than unity:

$$0<(d \log C/d \log X) <1 \qquad ...(16)$$

Satisfaction of this inequality by income elasticity of consumption may make marginal propensity to consume, MPC also to satisfy the same inequality:

$$0<(dC /dX) <1 \qquad ...(17)$$

where d is differential operator, C is aggregate consumption and X is aggregate income.

Less than unit marginal propensity to consume implies that the aggregate consumption will never be too high to converge towards the saturation point which may induce consumers to save their entire incremental income. At the micro household level, there will always be inadequately satisfied want for some or the other goods, or want for some new goods will emerge to claim a fraction of incremental income to consumption. It is only at saturation/satiety point that MPC may converge towards zero. In that case, entire incremental income may be saved. At the other end of the spectrum, MPC can equal or exceed unity only when currently low consumption levels do not permit full satisfaction of even the demand for necessities. Then, howsoever low the income and consumption levels may be, these will never be too low to completely eliminate at least the precautionary motive to save for future. Similarly, howsoever high the proportion of savings income may be, a fraction of incremental income is likely to be saved. Hence, marginal propensity to save will also be less than unity but greater than zero.

Savings and consumption behaviour complement each other to keep both marginal propensity to save and consume within the stipulated bounds. Lower than unit marginal propensity to consume may keep income elasticity of consumption also numerically below unity.

Whereas minimum consumption needs are guided mainly by requirements of physical survival, urgency to enhance or maintain standards of current consumption of conveniences, necessity to meet socio-cultural requirements, expenditure on consumption above the minimum level is guided mainly by habits, hobbies and the urgency of wants for luxuries of conspicuous goods for keeping up with the peers, provided that the total expenditure does not violate income constraint. Psychological urges and motivations guide only a part of consumption expenditure. Keynes may be in consonance with reality only partially in designating his law governing numerical bounds of MPC as psychological. As against this, among the transaction, precautionary and speculative motives, psychological urges and motivations may play a much more decisive role in the determination of savings than what Keynes envisaged.

However, Cramer considers the reasons advanced by Keynes for lower than unit value of income elasticity of consumption as less convincing than those advanced by him to support his thesis about marginal propensity to consume being less than unity. The fact is that statistically incremental values directly affect averages at which elasticities are calculated.

The Keynesian postulation about the numerical value of marginal propensity to consume is directly supported by the value furnished by estimates of linear aggregate condumption function for the entire observed period:

C=10508.55+0.6953X, (t=90.85) R-Square=0.9946 ...(18)

The t tests reveal this numerical value of MPC to be significantly above zero but lower than unity.

Growth During Sub-periods

Rates of growth of real income and consumption have, however, varied greatly from one period to another. Variance of growth in different periods is not surprising as forty seven years is a pretty long time. Structural changes are bound to occur during such a long period of observation. This postulate has been examined by testing the significance of differences between the growth rate of the composite period and rates of sub-periods of much shorter duration of one decade except the last sub-period which comprises of only seven observations.

Both income and consumption have been growing at statistically significant annual compound rates during all these sub-periods. The table reported above shows that annual compound growth rates of both income and consumption declined from first to the second decade. The decline may partly be attributed to changes in development strategy in Second Five Year Plan, but was mainly owing to two consecutive years of crop failures during mid-sixties on the one hand, and the failure of rapid industrialization during second and third plans to sufficiently alter the structure of Indian economy on the other. India continued to be dominated by primary production in general and agriculture in particular. Thereafter the pace of growth of both real income and consumption registered significant rise during the eighties and nineties. This may probably be attributed to the impact of new economic policy on growth. However, income has been growing consistently faster than consumption in all periods except the sixties when the growth of consumption was significantly higher than that of real income. This may probably be accounted by the fact that the sixties recorded significant declines in agricultural output in two consecutive years, slowing the pace of growth on income. But at low income and consumption levels, slow growth of income could not contain the growth of consumption, especially that of necessities which dominated the consumption baskets then. But the differences between the corresponding growth rates of these two variables have not only varied significantly through time, but these differences between the corresponding growth rates of income and consumption have been statistically significant also barring the decades of sixties and seventies.

It seems that acceleration of the pace of development in general and growth of income in particular unleashed the race for satisfying the pent up demand for necessities and conveniences among the poor and luxuries, especially consumer durables, among the better off segments of consumers. Then, acceleration of the momentum of growth during eighties and nineties further accelerated the movement towards consumerism. Two consecutive phases of globalisation and liberalization have radically changed economic structure of India when the ownership of white consumer durables like televisions, refrigerators, coolers, washing machines, automobiles is no more confined to the microscopic minority of the very rich.

These facets of growth have been duly reflected in income elasticities of consumption, derived from the ratios of growth rates of aggregate consumption and aggregate income:

Table 2.4
Income Elasticities of Consumption Derived from Growth Rates

Variable/ Period	*1951-97*	*1951-60*	*1961-70*	*1971-80*	*1981-90*	*1991-97*
Income Elasticity	0.9012	0.8917	1.1301	0.8954	0.9041	0.7782
t-Values (difference from unity)	2.15	2.33	1.141	2.47	2.53	2.87

Income elasticities of consumption are substantially lower than unity for all but one sub-period. Income elasticity equals unity for the second sub-period, implying that consumption has changed proportionately with income during this period probably for reasons that have already been discussed. If income and consumption levels are so low as do not permit the meeting of even the minimum consumption needs of the masses, both marginal propensity to consume and income elasticity may equal or even exceed unity. This seems to have been the case in the second decade of development of the Indian economy. This hypothesis may hold true for the poorest of the developing economies and such poor people of other developing economies whom the abysmally low income levels permit only meeting of the minimum consumption needs of un-diversified subsistence. It means that Keynes' prediction of income elasticity and marginal propensity to consume being lower than unity becomes true only if subsistence or starvation thresholds have already been crossed.

Other facets of the pattern of growth has been that (i) acceleration of deceleration of growth of income and consumption is statistically significant, and (ii) growth of income is significantly higher than that of consumption in all periods except one.

Income Elasticity of Consumption

Real aggregate consumption has been regressed on real aggregate income to derive income elasticities of consumption directly form log-linear form of the consumption function. Estimates of these functions are reported in the table below:

Table 2.5
Aggregate Log-linear Consumption Functions

Variable/ Period	*1951-97*	*1951-60*	*1961-70*	*1971-80*	*1981-90*	*1991-97*
Intercept	0.4213	0.4273	0.2441	0.5122	0.4513	1.0844
Elasticity	0.89	0.8961	0.9341	0.8774	0.8937	0.7730
t-slope	122.7	23.67	6.26	17.04	28.74	44.86
t-diffi. unit	14.04	2.74	0.44	2.38	3.40	13.18
t-diff. com. period	—	0.17	5.03	2.72	0.49	17.01
R-squarred	0.9970	0.9859	0.8305	0.9732	0.9904	0.9975

Note: t-values relate to the significance of (i) slope, (ii) difference between estimated elasticity and unity, and (iii) difference between elasticities of the composite period and sub-periods.

Above results establish that :

(i) income elasticity of per capita aggregate real consumption is significantly lower than unity in all periods except the sixties. These results are in consonance with those derived from the ratios of rates of growth of aggregate real consumption and income,

(ii) decadal income elasticities are significantly different from the elasticity for the composite period for all periods except two. Numerical values of income elasticity for sixties and eighties are statistically equal to that of the composite period. The period of sixties is marked by the lowest growth of income and consumption, whereas eighties are marked by considerable acceleration of growth of real income and consumption. Elasticities for these two periods are different from those derived from the ratios of growth rates also,

(iii) decadal elasticities differ greatly among themselves, range of variation being 0.77-0.93. But these variations are qualitative well within a narrow band, while numerical values remain significantly below unity,

(iv) decadal elasticities, by and large, tended to hover around the elasticity of the composite period. This may suggest the near constancy of its value, decadal variations notwithstanding.

Log-linear aggregate consumption function has fitted the data very well. This function has, in fact, yielded slightly better results than those yielded by the linear and two forms of semi-log-linear functions. Therefore, log-linear function may be preferred to other functional forms.

Temporal Shifts in Functional Relation

Significant differences between (i) decadal and composite period growth rates, and (ii) income elasticities of consumption may suggest that either the structure has been changing or aggregate consumption function has been shifting through time. The hypothesis has been directly tested by incorporation of time, T as an additional determinant of aggregate consumption in the log-linear functional form for the composite period:

$$\text{Log } C = 1.3371 + 0.6976 \log X + 0.0035\, T \qquad \ldots(19)$$

(t=11.31) (t=3.26) R-Square=0.9976

Coefficient of multiple determination has improved by 0.001 after introduction of time as an additional determinant consumption. The coefficient of time, parameter of temporal shift in the function (Schultz, 1938), is statistically significant at one per cent probability level. The significance of the coefficient of time may be interpreted in the light of the fact that practically all economic variables, specially income, are likely to be significantly related to time in a planned developing economy like the Indian one (Prakesh, 1977). Relation 19 is quite likely to be afflicted by multi-collinearity.

Multi-collinearity could have reduced the shift parameter to non-significance. Improvement in the coefficient of multiple determination and the significance of shift parameter, therefore, show that time is not a superfluous variable in this function. Incidentally, linear aggregate consumption function also lends strong support to the thesis of structural breaks or temporal shifts in the relation:

$$C = 9807.70 + 0.5988\ X + 497.1933\ T \qquad ...(20)$$

$$(t=8.20) \qquad (t=36.17) \quad R\text{-Square}=0.9946$$

Aggregate consumption function may be taken to have been shifting upwards to the right through time. Besides other implications, these results may imply that the steady growth of income has been consistently raising the living standards of the masses since the beginning of the First Five Year Plan. The consumption baskets might have also been diversified under the impact of change in tastes and preferences that usually occur with the growth of income and/or structural breaks in the trends. This is unlike the development experience of the erstwhile USSR where emphasis was laid on the production of capital and heavy goods for accelerated growth and the living standards of the moves were artificially kept low (Myrdal, 1955). This also refutes the oft repeated criticism that the Nehru-Mahalanobis strategy of development, underlying the Indian development plans most of the time, did not allow either the economy to grow rapidly or consumption standards to rise (Also see, Prakash, 1996, Prakash and Singh, 1999).

Experiment with Semi-log Functions

Semi-log functions are also suggested as alternative functional forms for the analysis of the relationship between income and consumption. Either of these functional forms may furnish better results than the log-linear functional form if consumption expenditure alone or income alone is subject to non-linearities:

$$C = a + b \log X \qquad ...(21)$$

and

$$\log C = a + b\ X \qquad ...(22)$$

Income elasticity varies inversely with the already attained consumption standards if relation 21 is specified. This function may, therefore, be appropriate for the analysis of the consumption of necessities for which income elasticities will decline continuously as saturation points are approached. In consumption function 22, income elasticity varies directly with income. Hence, this function may be useful for analysis of the consumption of luxuries and conspicuous goods, specially the highly priced consumer durables. We have no reason to believe that either consumption alone or income alone suffers from non-linearities. Besides, the study does not analyse necessities alone or luxuries alone. Hence, these functions are not considered to be appropriate for this study. Accordingly, results of empirical estimation of these functions are not reported here.

Influence of Population

Indian population has recorded an explosive growth since independence. Population is estimated to have crossed 1 billion mark in May 2000. Population has, in fact, grown at a statistically significant annual compound rate of 0.938 per cent from 1951 to 1997. As both income and consumption are directly affected by population growth, results may be required to be corrected by population growth. Results, corrected for population growth, are reported in the following table:

Table 2.6

Growth of Income and Consumption Net of Population Growth

Period/Growth Rate	*1951-97*	*1951-60*	*1961-70*	*1971-80*	*1981-90*	*1991-97*
Population	0.938	0.825	0.76	0.98	0.929	0.79
Growth Net of Pop.						
Income	0.832	0.745	0.43	0.55	1.261	1.78
Consumption	0.612	0.575	0.58	0.39	1.051	1.21

Population growth has had negative impact on the growth of both income and consumption. Growth of per capita income and consumption will, therefore, be considerably lower than the corresponding growth of income and consumption in absolute terms. In other words, annual compound growth rates of per capita income and per capita consumption are likely to be significantly lower than the corresponding growth rates of aggregate income and consumption in absolute terms. This implies that either population should explicitly be introduced as an additional determinant into the functional relations or scale effect of population may be neutralized by measuring the variables in per capita terms. The second alternative has been preferred.

Analysis of Aggregate Per Capita Consumption

Only log-linear form of aggregate consumption function has been estimated from time series of per capita consumption and per capita income. The hypothesis of upward temporal shift in the function has again been tested. The OLS estimates of these two functions are reported hereunder:

$$\log C = 0.6268 + 0.7781 \log x \quad (t=50.37) \quad \text{R-square}= 0.9826 \qquad ...(23)$$

$$\log C = 0.6977+0.7547 \log x+0.0002\, T \qquad ...(24)$$

$$(t=11.13) \qquad (t=0.35) \qquad \text{R-square}=0.9826$$

where c and x are per capita consumption and per capita income respectively. The function fits the data extremely well. But the neutralization of scale effect of population size reduces the explained proportion of variation by 1.44 per cent in comparison to the variation explained by the function in absolute terms. Income elasticity of consumption in per capita terms is reduced by as much as 11.92 per cent in comparison to income elasticity of consumption in absolute terms. These results highlight the quantitative dimensions of the impact of population growth on aggregate consumption.

But the consumption function in per capita terms, as against the function in absolute terms, does not shift significantly through time. The statistical non-significance of the coefficient of T and invariance of the coefficient of multiple determination after introduction of time as an additional determinant highlight the superfluousness of time as an explanatory variable in this function. It may partly be the consequence of multi-collinearity. It implies that Time as an additional explanatory variable in the function in absolute terms has captured the influence of population on consumption. Income elasticity, furnished by the function in per capita terms without the shift variable, may be regarded as quite stable. Incidentally, the difference of 0.2281 between unity and income elasticity, given by this function, may be taken as the income elasticity of savings. This savings rate is highly in agreement with the observed savings rate in the Indian economy. This function is obviously more satisfactory than all other functions discussed earlier. The function is, however, seriously afflicted by significant auto-correlation, value of rho being as high as 0.438 and that of Durbin-Watson d being only 1.12. The calculated value of d is less than the table value of d(1). Thus, auto-correlation is significant at five per cent probability level.

Significance of auto-correlation is not surprising. Most of the functions, estimated from time series data, are likely to be affected by auto-correlation. Auto-correlation may arise from (i) either omission of one or more significant determinants of consumption from the function, (ii) or mis-specification of function, (iii) or transformation of structural equations into their final form prior to estimation of the parameters. Serial correlation of the errors may also be introduced in solving the dynamic systems (Cf. Wallis, pp. 89-91, 1973). First and third causes may be examined together as explicit factors of auto-correlation in this case.

Partial Adjustment Hypothesis

Partial adjustment hypothesis is, therefore, tested for this function. The estimated consumption function is reported below:

$$\log c = 0.4058 + \underset{(t=6.04)}{0.5349} \log x + \underset{(t=2.76)}{0.3212} \log c\ (t-1) \qquad \ldots(25)$$

R-square= 0.9845, Rho= 0.116, d=1.77

Introduction of lagged consumption as an additional determinant of per capita consumption has freed the function from auto-correlation. Explained proportion of variation has also been raised marginally, while the coefficient of both per capita income and lagged consumption are highly significant at one per cent probability level. Whereas the short run income elasticity of consumption is only 0.53, long run elasticity is as high as 0.788. Thus, long term elasticity is significantly lower than unity as well as income elasticity of 0.8973 which is furnished by log-linear consumption function. The difference between these two elasticities is as much as 0.1093 which almost equals the difference between income elasticities furnished by consumption functions in absolute and per capita terms. The lagged function seems to be superior to all the preceding functions. Average length of adjustment lag is only 0.4759. As the adjustment coefficient is much lower than unity, adjustment process is expected to be quite rapid. Consumers take only two years in completing as much as 89.7 per cent of total desired change in per capita consumption in respone to changes in per capita income.

Permanent Income Hypothesis

The pivotal problem in empirical testing of permanent income hypothesis is the identification and measurement of the permanent and transitory components of per capita income and consumption. Aggregation of individual consumption functions may make transitory component of consumption indistinguishable from the disturbance term in the function:

$$c(t) = m \times (pt) + U(t) \qquad ...(26)$$

where c(t) = c (pit) and × (pt) are the observed aggregate per capita consumption and income. Friedman assumes that conceptually permanent income is subjective. His empirical approach makes his function identifiable with the distributed lag model. He assumes consumers' behaviour to be characterized by partial or incomplete adjustment of consumption with changes in permanent income. He further assumes that permanent income coincides with consumers' income expectations. But income expectations are continuously revised in the light of past experiences. Process of revision of income expectations make adjustment of actual to expected income incomplete. Therefore, actual change is only a fraction of the desired change:

$$y(pt) = m \{y(t)+(1-s)\ y\ (pt-1)+.........\} \quad ...(27)$$

Permanent income may then be expressed as the weighted average of past incomes, while the weights, having a sum of unit, decline geometrically. Friedman estimated the time series of y(pt) from first seventeen terms of the infinite series on the right hand side. He then fitted his consumption to US data for 47 years from 1905 to 1951.

Koyck's transformation makes Friedman's consumption function resemble the partial adjustment model except for the presence of intercept in the distributed lag models. But the theoretical underpinnings of these two models are quite different.

Bodkin's Refutation of Friedman's Thesis

Bodkin tested Friedman's hypothesis that transitory income does not affect either permanent or transitory consumption. His multiple regression equation was estimated from the data of 1400 households of war veterans who received back payment of war time insurance. This bonus, being entirely unexpected windfall gain, operationally approximates the concept of transitory income. The results showed that (I) marginal propensity to consume out of transitory income is not zero, and marginal propensity to consume out of transitory income is greater than the propensity to consume out of total income which contained both permanent and transitory components. These findings are at variance with Friedman's postulations. But such data as these are hard to get. But usually available data may hardly be expected to throw up results that will refute Friedman's theses or assumptions (Cramer, p. 153, 1973). According to such views, Friedman's hypotheses, like the true theory, are difficult to either prove or refute by empirical evidence.

Friedman's Thesis in Indian Context

Validity of Friedman's thesis has been examined with Indian data. Time series of per capita *Permanent Income* and *Per capita Permanent Consumption* for a period of 47 years from 1951 to 1997 has been consutrcted.

The study is based on annual time series data which is unlikely to contain seasonal variations. Cyclical variations have been smoothed out by three years moving averages of the observed values of aggregate per capita income and aggregate per capita consumption. This leaves only trend and random errors in the series. Estimates of per capita aggregate income and per capita aggregate consumption have then been derived from two separate linear regression equations of these variables on time. These values are now free from random component also. This series of aggregate per capita income and per capita consumption may be taken to converge towards their respective permanent components. These trend values may be taken to reflect the income and consumption expectations of people on the basis of their past experiences.

For testing the validity of Friedman's theses, four different aggregate per capita consumption functions have been estimated from this specially constructed time series. OLS estimates of these functions are tabulated below:

Table 2.7

Function/	*Intercept*	*Coefficient of*		*R-squarred*
		Income	*Lagged Cons.*	
Linear	314.83 (t=80.23)	0.6241 (Very High)	—	1.0
Log-linear	0.6673 (t=75.37)	0.7657 (t=249.7)	—	0.9993
Linear Lagged	32.0898 (t=2.51)	0.8228 (t=9.5)	0.1347 (2.63)	0.9960
Log-linear Lagged	0.0213 (t=8.9)	1.0364 (3901.5)	–0.0399 (–192.62)	1.00

These results show that :

(i) Intercept in all four functions is significantly different from zero. This contradicts Friedman's thesis that permanent consumption is not affected by any variable except permanent income. Friedman, in fact, assumes permanent consumption to be proportional to permanent income, coefficient of proportionality being positive but less than unity. As intercept is hypothesized to capture the influence of such factors on the dependent variable as have been excluded from the function, non-zero intercepts in all these four functions refute Friedman's thesis of permanent consumption being a function of per capita income alone.

(ii) Friedman's postulation of income elasticity of permanent consumption being unit is also refuted as 0.7657 value of income elasticity, furnished by second function, is significantly lower than unity.

(iii) Elasticity of permanent consumption with respect to permanent income is lower than the long term income elasticity of total consumption with respect to total income. This result is similar to that of Bodkin (Quoted from Cramer) regarding MPC. It implies that 2.2 per cent of total observed consumption is financed from transitory income which is not in consonance with Friedman's thesis that transitory income is not related to any other variable of the system. Another implication is that households save relatively more from permanent than transitory income, while there is a tendency to spend more from transitory than real income. These interpretations may correspond to peoples' tendency to spend more on non-regular purchases of such semi-durables as clothes and shoes, occasional items of expenditure like tours and travels, and consumer durables when windfall gains accrue to them as transitory incomes.

(iv) Estimated marginal propensity to consume satisfies inequality stipulated by Friedman.

(v) As the proportion of variation explained both by linear and log-linear forms of Friedman's function equal unity and almost unity, introduction of second determinant in these two relations may not improve its value. But the coefficient of multiple determination in linear function declines from unity when lagged permanent consumption is introduced as additional explanatory factor, while the coefficient in log-linear form of lagged permanent consumption function is negative, thus violating a priori restrictions on the coefficient of adjustment. Therefore, both these functions are not acceptable on statistical grounds.

Main Findings of the Study

The major findings of the study are listed below:

(1) Real aggregate income and consumption have grown steadily through time. Basic objective of raising the living standards of Indians through planned development of the Indian economy seems to have been effectively realized, through one would have liked the economy to achieve greater degree of growth.

(2) Rapid population growth has, however, lowered the growth of real per capita aggregate income which, in turn, has lowered the impact of income on real aggregate per capita consumption.

(3) Aggregate consumption, both in absolute and per capita terms, is a function of income.

(4) adjustment of real aggregate consumption, absolute as well as per capita, to the changes in real aggregate income is spread over several periods.

(5) Adjustment of consumption to the changes in income is, however, quite rapid. Approximately 90 per cent of the total desired change in consumption in

response to changes in real income is accomplished within two years.

(6) Income elasticity of consumption is significantly lower than unity. Whereas short run income elasticity is only 0.54, long run elasticity is much higher than this, having a value of 0.79. But both these values are quite lower than unity.

These results highlight the fact that short and long run responses of consumers to the changes in real per capita income are quite different. The response pattern probably highlights the fact that, as consumption levels are downward rigid, consumers raise their standard of living only when they are sure that incomes have risen permanently. This reflects the psychological cautions approach of consumers to change their levels and patterns of consumption. Besides, both marginal propensity to consume and income elasticity satisfy Keynes' postulations.

Results of this study, however, do not lend empirical support to Friedman's theses that (i) permanent consumption is a function of permanent income alone. This is refuted by significant intercepts in Friedman's functions; (ii) income elasticity of permanent consumption is significantly lower than unit on the one hand, and long term income elasticity of total consumption with respect to total income on the other. Consumers spend 2.2 per cent more from transitory than permanent income; (iii) people tend to save more from permanent than transitory income, refuting Friedman's assumption that transitory income and transitory consumption are not related to any other variable of the system. These findings controvert Cramer's assertion that Friedman's theses cannot be invalidated empirically. But Indian data are in dissonance with Friedman's assumptions and theses, and our results are in contradistinction to the prediction of Friedman's theory.

REFERENCES

1. Bhattacharya, N. (1975), *Studies on Consumer Behaviour in India.* In Bhattacharya, N. and Iyenger, N. S. (Editors) Iyengar, *Survey of Research in Economics-Econometrics,* ICSSR, N. Delhi.
2. Brown, T.M.(1952), *Habit Persistence and Lags in Consumer Behaviour, Econometrica,* Vol. XX.
3. Cramer, J.S. (1973), *Empirical Econometrics,* North Holland.
4. Friedman, Milton (1957), *A Theory of the Consumption Function,* Princeton University Press.
5. Intriligator, M.D. (1980), *Econometric Techniques, Methods and Models,* Prentice Hall of India, N. Delhi.
6. Meenakshi, J.V. (1996), *How Important are Changes in Taste?* A State Level Analysis of Food Demand, *Economic and Political Weekly,* Dec.14.
7. Murty, K.N. (1997), *Trends in Consumption and Estimates of Income and Price Elasticites of Demand for Major Crops in Semi-Arid Tropics of India, A Compendium Progress* Report 123, SEPD, ICRISAT, Patancheru, India.

3

NEED FOR FURTHER WIDENING THE DIRECT TAXES BASE IN THE NEW MILLENNIUM

Dr. Anil Kumar Jain

Introduction

Since Independence, the Indian Government has tried to use taxation for achieving various socio-economic objectives. For this purpose, it tried to make the tax-system integrated and broad based on the recommendations of Professor Kaldor. Although it is natural in a developing economy that indirect taxes would contribute a large share of total tax collections, having wider coverage, but it is equally important that the structure of direct taxes be so geared as to help in achieving horizontal equity (equal treatment of equals) and vertical equity (unequal treatment of unequals). Its coverage should be increased with the passage of time so as to ensure its increasing contributory share in total tax revenue. However, changes in various tax measures were introduced in such a great hurry that the direct tax system in India got overloaded with numerous provisions at providing incentives and disincentives. These were serious violations of horizontal equity. These violations, together with inefficient administration and large scale evasion, resulted in slow progress of the direct taxes and declining share of direct taxes in total tax revenue of the Union Government.

The gross tax revenue of the Central Government from direct taxes was Rs. 176 crore in 1950-51 which increased to Rs. 292 crore in 1960-61, to Rs. 869 crore in 1970-71, to Rs. 2,997 crore in 1980-81 and further to Rs. 11,030 crore in 1990-91, (Table 1). However, this increase in absolute revenue from direct taxes was much slower as compared to the increase in revenue from indirect taxes. Accordingly, the share of direct taxes in total tax revenue declined from 43.5 per cent in 1950-51 to 32.6 per cent in 1960-61 to 27.1 per cent in 1970-71 to 22.7 per cent in 1980-81 and further to 19.2 per cent in 1990-91. Part of the reason for such a state of affairs could also be attributed to the relatively slower growth in the number of taxpayers. The total number of income tax payers was only 30.12 lakhs in 1970-71 which constituted less than half a per cent of India's population. The number of income tax payers increased to 45.94 lakhs in 1980-81 and slightly more rapidly to 75.65 lakhs in 1990-91 (Table 2) but still this number constituted less than one per cent of India's population. While it is true that indirect taxes are more effective way of reaching semi-subsistance population and their burden is felt less by taxpayers on account of tax being camouflaged in the price of the product, the fact remains that a more effective way of imparting justice and equity to the taxpayers in the long run can only be through increasing reliance on direct taxes.

The fiscal situation, which was under strain throughout the 1980s, assumed alarming proportions in 1990-91, with a sharp deterioration in different parameters of deficit. The macro imbalances were reflected in the form of increasing budgetary and fiscal deficits. Increased external and internal borrowings led to a rise in interest burden, decumulation of reserves and double-digit inflation. The Gulf Crisis of 1990 worsened the situation further. Therefore, when the Congress Government assumed office in June, 1991, the economy was left with no soft options and there was hardly any time to contemplate. Therefore, the Government immediately started undertaking measures towards macro-economic stabilization. Obviously, comprehensive tax reform had to be an essential part of any such programme of stabilization and structural reforms. Accordingly, a Tax Reforms Committee was appointed under the chairmanship of Dr. Raja J. Chelliah. This Committee submitted its Report in January, 1993. It was guided by the basic objective of restoring the Indian tax system to its primary function of generating revenues in an efficient and equitable manner.

Guided by the recommendations of the Tax Reforms Committee, the Government undertook a number of measures to reverse the declining share of direct taxes in total tax revenue. Among the various measures undertaken towards this end, one of the important steps has been to widen the tax base. The Government realised that unless the tax base of income tax is increased, many other measures might not bear fruit. This study attempts to review the various measures undertaken by the Government to widen the income tax base during the past decade or so. These measures comprise:

(1) Presumptive Scheme of computation of income for persons engaged in retail trade, etc.,

(2) Introduction of Estimated Income Method of Assessment for certain categories of taxpayers,

(3) Enlarging the scope of deduction of tax at source,

(4) Obligatory filing of Income Tax Return based on certain economic indicators,

(5) Providing for Penalty for non-filing of returning of income,

(6) Compulsory quoting of Permanent Account Number/GIR in certain categories of transactions, and

(7) Compulsory mention of Bank Account Number in Income Tax Return.

Effects of Measures to Widen Tax Base

Various steps undertaken by the Government since 1991 to widen the tax base of direct taxes has resulted in a positive effect in several areas. The number of income taxpayers was only 70.27 lakhs at the end of March, 1990. This number increased to 106.65 lakhs towards the end of 1996 and further to 180 lakhs by April 1, 1999 (Table 2). In view of the sharp increase in the number of taxpayers in the recent past, the Government is planning to revise the target for number of taxpayers by the end of March, 2000 to 250 lakhs. While it is true there has been an increase in the number of new assessees as a result of surveys, the fact remains that the income tax base has considerably increased since the introduction of One-by-six economic criteria scheme, quoting of PAN for high value transactions and quoting of Bank Account Number in the return of income.

The gross tax revenue from direct taxes has also increased with the passage of time. The gross tax revenue from direct taxes which was Rs. 11,030 crore in 1990-91 increased to Rs. 33,559 crore in 1995-96 and is expected to be Rs. 56,135 crore in 1999-2000 (Table 1). Consequently, the share of direct taxes in total gross tax revenue of the Central Government has improved from 19.2 per cent in 1990-91 to 30.2 per cent in 1995-96 and further to 33.5 per cent in 1998-99.

The scheme of deduction of tax at source has also yielded rich dividends. The total collection from tax deducted at source was Rs. 6,209.5 crore in 1992-93. It increased to Rs. 9,603.7 crore in 1994-95 and further to Rs. 15,334.3 crore in 1996-97. Thus, within a span of five years, yield through TDS has become two-and-a half times. The break up of TDS reveals that tax collections from TDS in the case of companies increased from Rs. 2,321.2 crore in 1992-93 to Rs. 5,138.9 crore in 1996-97 and for non-company assessees it increased from Rs. 3,888.3 crore to Rs. 10,195.3 crore during the same period.

Challenges ahead and the Ways Out

One of the immediate challenge before the Income Tax Department due to a sharp increase in the number of taxpayers in the recent past is that workload has considerably increased, without a corresponding increase in the strength of assessing officers and the supplementary staff, it would be difficult for the Income Tax Department to cater to the increased workload. The total working strength of officers in 1996-97 was 3,930 out of which 3,169 officers were deployed on assessment duty ad 761 officers were engaged in non-assessment duty. We think that it would be difficult with the existing strength of officers to handle more than 20 million cases, bearing in mind the varied and complicated nature of work involved in the assessment work. In 1998-99, about 2.3 lakh new cases came up for assessment before the Central Board of Direct Taxes (CBDT). The total number of cases to be tackled during the financial year, including backlog, was 4.58 lakh. Of this, only 2.16 lakh cases were disposed off. Limited manpower is said to be the main constraint in speedy disposal of cases. Therefore, the CBDT has decided to select only high revenue yielding cases for assessment, against the earlier practice of random selection. An Official Press Release (Reported in *Financial Express*, 11 June, 1999) has pointed out that, under the new policy initiative, all returns will now be accepted under Section 143(1) except a very limited number of returns and that from 1999-2000 onwards mere filing of returns will complete the assessment process in majority of cases. Cost-effectiveness seems to be the overwhelming consideration behind such an approach.

However, we do not agree this approach. Table 3 gives data with respect to the cost of collection of direct taxes from 1991-92 to 1999-2000. The percentage cost of collection of direct taxes was 2.41 in 1987-88. This percentage declined to 1.65 in 1991-92 and to a low of 1.27 in 1996-97. For the year 1999-2000, the percentage cost of collection is expected to be 1.52. While it is true that the cost of collection of direct taxes is higher as compared to the cost of collection of indirect taxes like customs and excise, but we should remember that there is a basic difference in the nature of direct and indirect taxes. While in the case of direct taxes there is hardly any forward shifting and consequently there is a constant tug of war between tax collectors and taxpayers, there is nearly complete forward shifting in respect of indirect taxes in India. We think that stress should be laid on correct assessment and not quick assessment and on more effective and efficient administration. Indian experience in respect of Summary Assessment, yields from Presumptive Tax Scheme and Estimated Income Method Scheme has been far from satisfactory. Therefore keeping long-term goals in mind, there is an urgent need to increase the strength of the assessing officers, with necessary complementary and supplementary staff. Together with this there is need to introduce the system of 'accountability' in Income Tax Department.

The increasing use of e-commerce through Internet is likely to pose serious challenge to the Income Tax Department in the near future. Under electronic transactions it becomes very difficult to prove transactions because flow of information is in electronic form. This problem is further complicated when the flow of information is across the borders, more so when transaction is routed through three countries or more. The present taxation laws, based either on business connection or permanent establishment, do not provide for a solution to the problem of taxation of internet transactions. To tackle this challenge, there is an urgent need to explore all the possibilities which should enable the Indian Government to receive information of internet commerce. The suggestion of the CBDT to form an International organisation with the participation of various countries needs to be implemented at the earliest because it would help in detecting commercial or financial transactions on the internet.

There are at present several areas in the economy such as self-employed persons like lawyers, doctors, chartered accountants, small shop-keepers, coaching and tuition centres, beauty parlours or fashion designing, etc. where income is being earned and spent. Extensive external surveys and use of information technology needs to be made to bring such potential taxpayers into the tax net.

While there is need to strictly implement the six economic criteria to catch hold of the potential taxpayers, we think that under the present circumstances such reliance cannot be placed on 'voluntary compliance'. Some element of compulsion is necessary. Therefore, the government needs to take advantage of modern information technology. To begin with, the Income Tax Department should first match the telephone directory of each of the notified cities with the taxpayer base of that city and issue notices to those who have not filed their tax returns. The Government should explore the possibility of adding some new economic criteria for mandatory filing of income tax returns. One such economic criteria could be the owning of a Personal Computer and the facilities of e-mail and Internet attached to it.

We also think that there is need to further extend the scheme of Tax Deduction at Source to newer and newer areas so that together with increased revenue, the number of potential tax evaders may be minimised. To begin with, the information regarding payments made by companies to the Chartered Accountants, lawyers, Doctors, etc. may be obtained and they may be asked to deduct tax at the rate of ten per cent on all payments made to such persons beyond Rs. 10,000 in a year.

Table 3.1

Share of Direct Tax Revenue of the Central Government in Total Tax Revenue

(Rs. Crore)

Year	*Gross Tax Revenue from Direct Taxes*	*Gross (Total) Tax Revenue*	*2 as percentage of 3*
1	2	3	4
1950-51	176	405	43.5
1955-56	171	485	35.3
1960-61	292	895	32.6
1965-66	598	2,061	29.0
1970-71	869	3,206	27.1
1975-76	2,205	7,609	29.0

1	2	3	4
1980-81	2,997	13,179	22.7
1985-86	5,620	28,671	19.6
1990-91	11,030	57,577	19.2
1995-96	33,559	111,224	30.2
1996-97	38,895	128,762	30.2
1997-98	48,280	139,221	34.7
1998-99	49,854	148,700	33.5
1999-2000	56,135	167,526	33.5
2000-2001	59,235	176,860	—

Source: (1) Indian Public Finance Statistics
(2) Receipts Budget (1999-2000), Government of India.

TABLE 3.2
Number of Income-tax Payers in India

Year	*Number (in Lakh)*
1970-71	30.12
1975-76	37.96
1980-81	45.94
1985-86	54.86
1986-87	62.61
1987-88	65.25
1988-89	68.11
1989-90	70.27
1990-91	75.65
1991-92	78.44
1992-93	86.39
1993-94	102.06
1994-95	102.85
1995-96	106.65
1996-97	116.43
1997-98	145.00
1998-99	180.00
2001-02	210.00

Source : Annual Reports of the Ministry of Finance, Government of India for different years.

TABLE 3.3

Cost of Collection of Direct Taxes

(Rs. Crore)

Year	*Revenue Collection from Direct Taxes*	*Cost of Collection*	*3 as percentage of 2*
1991-92	15,294	253	1.65
1992-93	18,097	296	1.63
1993-94	20,298	335	1.65
1994-95	26,971	388	1.44
1995-96	33,559	492	1.47
1996-97	38,895	494	1.27
1997-98	48,280	715	1.48
1998-99	49,854	766	1.53
1999-2000	56,135	856	1.52
2000-2001	59,235	940	—
2001-2002	—	1070	—

Source: Figures upto 1996-97 have been taken from the Report of the Comptroller and Auditor General of India, Union Government (Direct Taxes) for different years and later figures from Budget Documents.

Conclusion

While various measures undertaken by the Government during the Post-Reform period deserve appreciation, there is need to implement such measures strictly and extend their scope. We think that there is an urgent need for reforms and improvement in the administration of direct taxes, even if it might mean increase in the cost of collection in the short-run. There is a need to lay adequate emphasis on achieving horizontal equity, i.e., equal treatment of equals in the long-run. The strength of the Income Tax Department needs to be considerably increased to cater to the new challenges and to be in a position to develop a tax-system which would really be broad-based.

TABLE 3.4

[illegible] Cost of Collection of Direct Taxes

Year	[illegible]	[illegible]
1986-87	13,?38	[illegible]
[illegible]	[illegible]	[illegible]
1987-88	[illegible]	[illegible]
1988-89	21,4??	2??
1989-90	[illegible]	1??
[illegible]	[illegible]	[illegible]
1990-91	35,280	215
1991-92	[illegible]	[illegible]
1992-93	[illegible]	[illegible]
1993-94	[illegible]	[illegible]
[illegible]	[illegible]	[illegible]

Source: [illegible]

Conclusion

[illegible]

4

GLOBALISATION VERSUS SWADESHI

V.M. Tarkunde

The new economic policy, characterised by liberalisation and globalisation of industry and finance, initially met with opposition from a large number of economists in the country, probably by a majority of them. It was condemned, in particular, by those who have leftist leanings. By now, however, it appears that most of the economists who were initially opposed to the new policy have begun to support it. That is probably due to the fact that the policy has resulted in some benefit even to the poor people in rural areas. The benefit is limited in extent, but that is natural in view of the fact that the policy has only recently been adopted. It is significant that the economic betterment in rural areas, however limited, has been experienced throughout the country. It is experienced in areas of rain-fed dry farming as well as in the economically retarded States in the Hindi heartland.

The new economic policy was being followed in a limited way from about 1980. When there was a crisis in the international balance of payments in January, 1991, it was openly and fully adopted, apparently on the advice of the World Bank and the IMF which gave a large loan to India to tide over the financial crisis. It was then alleged by a large number of economists and social thinkers that the Indian Government adopted the new economic policy under the pressure of the IMF and the World Bank, who were allegedly interested in promoting the interests of affluent countries at the expense of countries like India. We were among the few persons of leftist leanings who rejected the pressure theory and pointed out that the new policy can be supported on merit as it is more advantageous than the policy that was being previously pursued.

Since its open adoption in January 1991, the new economic policy was resolutely followed for about one and a half year. Thereafter, it has been followed by fits and starts, largely because the Central Governments in the country were weak and unstable and also because the prevailing economic stagnation in the USA and the European Community raised doubts about the new policy and strengthened the *Swadeshi* lobby. Another factor which may have affected the pursuit of the new economic policy was the fear that powerful multinationals would establish their hold in India as a result of liberalisation and globalisation. More recently, the economic regression in the Asian countries like Taiwan, South Korea, Indonesia and others, which had made remarkable economic progress as a result of a policy similar to the one recently adopted in India, has again revived the doubters. We shall presently consider whether any of the above considerations justifies the abandonment or modification of the new economic policy. Before doing so, some facts may be observed with regard to the economic progress made in rural India since 1980 when the new policy began to be adopted on a limited scale.

Since 1980, the income per acre of both irrigated and non-irrigated agricultural lands in all parts of the country, including economically backward States like Bihar, increased at the average rate of three per cent per year. For the first time, the increase in agricultural income throughout the country was higher than the increase is population which was taking place at the rate of a little less than two per cent per year. The increase was mainly the result of improvement in the terms of trade of agricultural products, which was the consequence of the new economic policy. The increase of the income to owners of agricultural land resulted in more private investment in agriculture and also in the increase of wages of agricultural labourers. What is more, there was also an increase in non-agricultural employment in rural areas, which was a consequence of the increased demand of goods and services by agriculturists. Because of the weak and hesitant pursuit of the new economic policy after the middle of 1993, the rate of economic improvement in rural areas was reduced to some extent, but recent investigations have shown that the economic improvement continues at a reduced rate even after the open but hesitant adoption of the new economic policy.

Many articles of economic scholars have appeared in the last two or three years describing the limited but definite economic improvement in rural areas as a result of the new economic policy. We shall quote from two of the latest articles which appeared in the *Economic and Political Weekly* of July 18-24/25-31, 1998. C.H. Hanumantha Rao in his article titled "Agricultural Growth Sustainability and Poverty Alleviation", after referring to the improvement in the terms of trade for agriculture, observes: "The rise in agricultural wages itself is attributable mainly to the rise in demand for labour in non-agricular activities notably construction and services... This may indeed explain why, across the countries of east and south-east Asia, rural poverty reduction bears a stronger correlation with overall economic growth than with agricultural growth *per se*... The employment generated from growth as well as from the officially sponsored poverty alleviation programmes, apart from their direct and immediate impact by way of increasing the incomes of the poor, have important indirect and long-term effects in terms of improving the socio-economic status of the poor. For example, Employment Guarantee Scheme in Maharashtra has immensely contributed to empowering women, thus triggering-off desirable changes at the household as well as at the village level."

Another economist, J. Mohan Rao, in his article titled "Food, Agriculture and Reforms", in the same issue of the *Economic and Political Weekly,* refers to the paradox of slow growth of employment in urban areas and a much more rapid growth of employment in rural areas in the period from 1977 to 1991 and observes: "This paradox seems to spell, as we argue further below, a radical change in the rural labour market, i.e. a transition from surplus labour to full employment" This author further observes: "A number of authors have noted that the principal factor associated with the rise in wages has been a perceptible rise in the non-farm share of rural employment. As much as seventy per cent of the increase in the rural labour force between 1977-78 and 1989-90 was absorbed in the rural non-agricultural sectors even though the average share of the latter was only about fifteen per cent of the rural labour force at the beginning of the period" (p. 1957). The author has further observed that if the new economic policy is more resolutely pursued, the improvement in the rural economy would be more rapid.

We shall now turn to the factors which, apart from the weakness of the Central Governments, come in the way of a resolute pursuit of the new economic policy.

The doctrine of *Swadeshi* means that the Indian people should purchase goods made in India, even if they are poorer in quality and higher in prices than foreign goods available in the market. During the earlier days of British rule, when the foreign government was bent upon restricting Indian industry and promoting the sale of British goods in India, the programme of *Swadeshi* was justified. From 1920, the British Government changed its policy and decided to promote Indian agriculture as well as Indian industry, though the intention of the government was that Indian industry should play a role subordinate to British industry. Since India did not have a normal economic growth during British occupation, a policy of deliberately prohibiting the import of foreign goods and encouraging of production of similar goods in India was justified for a couple of decades after Independence. However, the continuation thereafter of the same policy hindered the growth of Indian industry because the restriction of imports from abroad resulted necessarily in the restriction of the export of Indian goods to foreign countries.

The advantage of free foreign trade was clearly brought out, as early as in 1976, by Adam Smith, who is regarded as the father of economics as a social science, in his famous book, *The Wealth of Nations*. While India followed the *Swadeshi* policy of "import substitution" right from the attainment of independence, some other Asian countries adopted the opposite policy of "export promotion" and soon they outstripped India in economic growth. In view of the far more rapid economic growth of Asian countries like Taiwan, South Korea, Hongkong, Singapore, Indonesia and Malaysia, the Indian government slowly began to change its policy from about 1980 and openly adopted the new economic policy from January, 1991. After all this experience, to go back to the *Swadeshi* cult, described usually as the policy of import substitution, is obviously suicidal to India's economic growth.

It is observed that those who follow the *Swadeshi* cult are usually opposed not only to the import of foreign goods, but also to the import of foreign capital for industrial investment in India. Now the import of foreign capital for industrial investment is far more beneficial to us than the import of foreign goods. This is because, firstly, industrial investment of foreign capital leads to the employment of both skilled and semi-skilled Indian labour. Secondly, the import of foreign capital for industrial investment usually brings in an improved technology, advantage of which can be taken by other industrialists in the country. Those who follow the cult of *Swadeshi* object to foreign capital because the profits made as a result of the capital go abroad. They forget that we are short of capital and if foreign capital is not invested in Indian industry, we shall have to seek foreign loans for our industrial (including infrastructural) development and we will have to pay interest at the commercial rates on the foreign loans, irrespective of whether the concerned industries make any profit or not. This will be a big burden on the economy without getting the benefit of superior technology. All developing countries welcome foreign capital and it is only the *Swadeshi* fad in our country which opposes it.

It may be noted that foreign capital should be allowed to be invested even in industries which are at present included in the small-scale sector. A major proportion of our exports, such as cloth and garments, cut diamonds prepared from imported rough diamonds, tanned leather and leather goods, carpets, etc. are all in the small-scale sector. If foreign investment is not allowed in this sector, improved technology will also not be available to us and our export markets would slip out of our hands to producers in other countries.

Believers in *Swadeshi* are particularly opposed to foreign capital being invested in consumer goods industry. There is, for instance, an organised opposition to Pepsi and Coca Cola. The question, however, is why our consumer goods industries, which are not nascent industries and should not require protection, should be expected to be unable to compete successfully with imported foreign goods or goods manufactured in India by foreign capital. Competition with such goods is necessary for promoting the efficiency of Indian industries, and that is obviously beneficial to Indian industrialists as well as Indian consumers. While it is true that foreign capital is more urgently required for some heavy industries, it is not a wise policy to prevent foreigners from investing their capital in all industries, irrespective of whether the investment is in the production of capital goods or consumer goods. Of course, we should give preference to investment of foreign capital in our infrastructure rather in consumer goods, but that is the policy which the Government of India is already pursuing. But to prohibit the investment of foreign capital in consumer goods industries and to undertake a campaign such as the one for destroying bottles of Coca Cola and Pepsi is clearly wrong. It may lead to foreign capital being scared away from India.

Fear of Multinationals

There is a huge concentration of capital in the hands of multinationals and concentration of capital implies concentration of power. It is obvious that concentration of power, whether economic or political, is harmful to the democratic way of life. The apprehension against multinationals has, therefore, a good deal of justification.

The danger of multinationals should, however, not be exaggerated. Even before the present information revolution, Japan exemplified that comparatively smaller industrial units can compete profitably with large-scale multinationals. Due to the facilities created by the information revolution, it is now possible for small-scale industries to compete successfully with multinationals. By now, the advantage of scale, which is the main advantage of multinationals, has been greatly minimised. There is a growth of technologically efficient small-scale industries in the Western world. This phenomenon is widely observed and many articles have recently appeared on the subject. To take one instance, N.S. Siddharthan, in his article, "Approach to Science and Technology Plan", in the *Economic and Political Weekly* dated 22-2-1997, has observed : "The current technological revolution possesses seemingly paradoxical characteristics of globalisation as well as decentralisation. All that an individual or a firm needs for globalising are a personal computer, a modern, a telephone and e-mail facilities. With these instruments, an individual can have access to computers in any part of the world. E-mail and internet facilities will grant an individual access to diverse information channels dealing with numerous fields and disciplines. However, to gain entry to global information inflows, one need not seek affiliation with large organisations. One can globalise through the computer in the privacy of one's home. In this sense, the information technology has encouraged several small and medium firms to take advantage of the computer and e-mail facilities to globalise (develop linkages with other firms, jointly develop or obtain designs, adopt computer aided designs and computer aided manufacturing) and enhance their international competitiveness.....Furthermore, the current technological revolution is not confined to a given sector, product or a process. It cuts across nations and sectors. Its range of influence could extend from marginal dry land farmers and handloom weavers to giant multinationals and sophisticated aircraft manufacturing firms.... Yet another feature of the current technology is the absence of scale economy advantages in several spheres of manufacturing. The earlier technologies favoured mass production of a product with a given specification. This feature favoured large-scale production and consequently promoted the growth of giant corporation. The current technology favours flexible manufacturing systems, support frequent changes in the product specifications and product-mix. These consumer-oriented manufacturing applications of the computer aided technology favour small and medium sized high-tech firms. The growth and proliferation of small and medium high-tech firms in the engineering, auto components, electronics and instrument sectors have transformed the industrial organisation of these sectors. The share of the smaller firms in value added and in employment has grown significantly even in the developed countries". The author says that our government should adopt a policy which would "enable India to participate in the decentralising revolution".

It would be recalled that Jayaprakash Narayan was in favour, not of technologically backward cottage industries, but small-scale industries conducted with the most modern technology. This was not possible in his lifetime. It has now become possible, and the Government of India should take serious note of the possibilities of highly efficient small-scale industries for replacing or restricting multinationals.

As shown above, the doctrine of *Swadeshi* has now become a fad and the apprehensions of multinationals are also exaggerated. Another factor which has recently come to the help of those who are opposed to the new economic policy is the industrial recession in all the advanced East-Asian countries. However, India has the advantage that its currency is not yoked to the dollar, but is based upon a basket of foreign currencies. Moreover, we have not yet extended the convertibility of the rupee to the capital account. We can thus shield the recession of the kind experienced by the East Asian countries, provided we ensure that foreign capital which may come to India is invested for long-term industrial development.

What India now requires is a stable government which will pursue the new economic policy, coupled with the realisation that it is the duty of the State not only to develop the physical infrastructure (such as power, communications, etc.), but also to make adequate investment in schemes of poverty alleviation, primary and secondary education, provision for sanitation and health services to the poor, and make the investment effective by decentralisation of power in favour of the *panchayat* system in the rural areas and ward committees and municipalities in towns and cities.

Economic Ideals of Radical Humanism

Before dealing with the issue of globalisation versus *Swadeshi*, it is desirable to clarify my approach, which I believe is shared by other Radical Humanists or at least by most of them, to the primary problem of poverty, ignorance and the miserable living conditions of the vast majority of the Indian people. In the absence of such a clarification, the readers may carry the impression that we the Radical Humanists are supporters of unbridled capitalism, which certainly we are not. Radical Humanists agree with the other leftists that capitalism is a defective and highly unjust economic system, but we have been of the view that the alternative to capitalism is not the wholesale nationalisation of industry as advocated by communists under the influence of Marxism, but a co-operative economy in which the economic pursuits of production, distribution and exchange would be carried out mainly through appropriate co-operative institutions. As early as in 1947, M.N. Roy stated that an appropriate humanist-democratic alternative to capitalism was a co-operative economy and not the nationalisation of all industries.

In my opinion, there are two main drawbacks of the capitalist system. In the first place, capitalism regards a human individual as an economic animal. Capitalist competition means that each man works for himself, without caring for the social good. Adam Smith, the father of capitalism, advocated the doctrine that social good is automatically advanced when every man works only for himself. This view is not only belied by experience but morally reprehensible and is contrary to the spirit of co-operation which must be the basis of social existence. Secondly, the functioning of a free market in a capitalist society necessarily increases economic disparities between the rich and the poor. The purpose of the market is to supply goods and services, not in accordance with the needs of the people, but in proportion to their purchasing power. The result is that the poor are always at a disadvantage in a market economy. The terms of trade being against the poor and in favour of the rich, the functioning of the market normally results in increasing economic disparities. This does not necessarily mean that in a market economy, while the rich get richer, the poor become poorer. What happens in an affluent society is that the economic advancement of the poor is at a much lower rate than that of the rich. In countries like India, where the population goes on increasing, the market economy may result in the poor remaining stagnated in poverty and ignorance, while a minority of the well-to-do experience economic betterment.

In the years 1947-48, M.N. Roy made two seminal observations, one in relation to political democracy and the other in relation to the economic system. Regarding political democracy, Roy observed that political parties are essentially undemocratic institutions, if democracy means rule "by and of the people and not "rule" for the people." He anticipated that the party system will result in a concentration of power in the hands of a successful political party or parties, and also that the struggle for power between political parties will bring about a divorce between morality and political practice so that the latter will be unprincipled and opportunistic.

In the economic system, he observed, as mentioned earlier, that a co-operative economy is the appropriate alternative to the unjust capitalist system. Although previously there were few takers for the two suggestions made by Roy, their acceptability has grown in the course of time. Political practice in India has become so unprincipled and opportunistic that no single party is really liked by the Indian people. Roy's idea of a partyless democracy appears now, to have more feasibility than when it was mooted. It is likely that Roy's ideas about the co-operative economy will also have the same fate. In the past, about twenty years back, people used to regard co-operatives as inefficient and corrupt. That is no longer the public attitude. In fact, the cooperative movement is now spreading not only in the spheres of finance and distribution of goods but also in the sphere of production. Housing to the middle-classes in many cities in the country is now being increasingly provided by co-operative societies. The milk supply in the country is being managed by cooperatives for the most part. Sugarcane production in Maharashtra is almost entirely a co-operative enterprise. Co-operation in the economic sphere being a sound idea, there is every reason to assume that it will occupy an increasing space in our economic life. It appears that there is a sizeable co-operative development in other countries also. It is not possible to discuss here as to how large enterprises can function on co-operative lines and how efficiency can be increased by competition between co-operatives supplying the same or similar goods.

Since nobody can lay down a blueprint for the future, one cannot be sure whether and when a co-operative economy will replace the prevailing capitalist system. Even if it does so, it will take a long time before that ideal is realised. In the meantime, ways and means must be found to ensure that capitalist development is so moulded as to serve, as far as possible, the interest of the deprived majority. For that purpose, Radical Humanists have been advocating ever since India's independence that the Indian Government must divert a sizeable part of public revenue for the alleviation of poverty and for the provision of primary, secondary and vocational education as well as adequate health services to the rural and urban poor. Alleviation of poverty requires employment generation on a large scale. Now, all the primary requirements of the people, such as food, water, shelter, clothing, education and medical aid can be supplied through the development of industries and undertakings which are labour-intensive. Employment can be generated on a large scale by undertaking schemes for improvement of agriculture, watershed management, reforestation, construction of houses and roads, supply of clothing, provision for education and improvement in social hygiene and provision of medical aid. This is obviously the best way of reducing poverty, promoting education and improving public health. Resources required for this programme can be met by the states by reducing the expenditure on the bureaucracy and defence and by economising on wasteful government expenditure. Decentralization of power (*Panchayats* and Ward Committees) will facilitate the implementation of this programme.

The above programme will not only meet the needs of the underprivileged majority but will also increase their purchasing power so as to provide a sound base for a rapid economic development in a regime of liberalisation which logically includes globalisation. The increased availability of resources will enable the State to convert itself into a Welfare State by providing security to the people against all calamities caused by various contingencies such as unemployment, poverty, accident, physical disability, widowhood, illness and old age. If in the meantime, a cooperative economy is built up, there will be greater economic and social equality, a far better cultural climate, and possibly a reduction in unemployment, but the necessity of a Welfare State will still remain in order to take care of the people in the various vicissitudes of life and thereby promote distributive justice. The economic ideal of Radical Humanism should be a cooperative economy in a Welfare State.

Why Globalisation?

Having dealt broadly with the ideals of Radical Humanists in the economic sphere, we can now turn to the merits of the present policy of economic-reforms including the problem of globalisation. After attainment of Independence, the Indian Government under the leadership of Jawaharlal Nehru was mainly concerned with bringing about a rapid development in agriculture and industry. The policy adopted for industrial development was that of "import-substitution", which meant that instead of importing goods from abroad, we should try to produce the same goods in our country. Thus import-substitution has essentially the same meaning as *Swadeshi*. Other countries which became free from imperialism at about the same time as India, and which were economically as backward as India, successfully followed the normal policy of exporting the goods which they could export and importing the goods which they needed. However, they tried at the same time to produce as far as possible the goods similar to the imported ones and thereby increased their industrial production. The countries which followed the latter policy, which is often described as the policy of export-led development, improved their economic condition much faster than India. Some of them like Taiwan, Korea, Singapore and Hongkong became "Asian Tigers", so named because of their spectacular economic growth. There were some other countries also had a similar economic development, though less rapid than that of the Asian Tigers, such as Indonesia and Malayasia. Compared to these countries, India remained in economic backwardness. While these countries had an annual economic growth of between five and ten percent of the GNP, India's growth rate remained at about 3.5 per cent which came to be ridiculed as the "Hindu growth rate". Obviously, the method of export-led economic promotion followed by other countries was far superior to the policy of *Swadeshi* adopted by India.

A change in India's economic policy was initiated in 1980s by the Government of Rajiv Gandhi. He started spending substantial sums for poverty alleviation by various schemes, which were to some extent on the lines mentioned above except that education and health continued to be neglected. As a result of this policy change, the annual economic growth rate of India increased from 3.5 per cent to about 5.3 per cent. However, the additional investment for poverty alleviation was undertaken without enforcing economy in other government expenditure. In the result, India's economic debt went up by 400 per cent and this led to an economic crisis in January 1991 when India did not have sufficient foreign currency to meet its current international financial obligations for more than two to three weeks. India had to seek a huge loan from the International Monetary Fund (IMF) and this led to the adoption by India of what is called the new economic policy.

The new economic policy consisted of some structural adjustments as well as liberalisation and globalisation of Indian economy. India agreed to bring down its annual fiscal deficit, which was as high as 7.5 per cent of its GNP. It devalued the rupee to a substantial extent. It decided to liberalise the Indian industry by removing the numerous permits and licences to which it was subject. It accepted the policy of globalisation which meant reduction in the high custom duties which had been imposed on the import of goods. India also decided to invite foreign capital for its industrial development. This change of policy was adopted by the Indian Government in consultation with the IMF and the World Bank and was presumably a part of the scheme under which the requisite loan was granted to India.

A hue and cry against the policy was raised by Indian leftists because they believed that in adopting this policy, the Indian Government had yielded to the demands of the IMF and the World Bank. These critics overlooked the fact that there was not a single item in the new economic policy which India should not have adopted voluntarily for overcoming the economic crisis of virtual insolvency and for bringing about a more rapid rate of economic growth. The reduction in fiscal deficit only meant that India should, as far as possible, live within its means. In substance, fiscal deficit consists of the excess of national expenditure over national income. Continuation of fiscal deficit must result in an increase in India's indebtedness. Surely, the decision to adjust annual national expenditure to the annual national income was necessary and appropriate. The rupee was obviously over-valued and its under valuation was quite necessary. It is generally agreed that the permits and licences which were required to be procured by Indian industry, were unnecessary and coercive and were also a source of corruption. There can be no dispute that the end of the "licence-permit raj" was beneficial to Indian industry.

The controversial question is that of globalisation of the Indian economy. In practice it consists of two parts: one, the gradual reduction of the protection given to Indian industry from foreign competition by a high wall of import duties, and two, the inviting of foreign capital for India's economic development.

In my editorial on "impediments to Economic Progress: Fad of Swadeshi and Fear of Multinationals", I had pointed out that foreign competition is desirable both for improving the efficiency of Indian industry and for enabling Indian consumers to got better quality goods at reasonable prices. About the second aspect of globalisation, the import of foreign capital, I referred to the obvious fact that while we have an abundant and increasing labour-force, we do not have adequate capital to bring about the necessary economic development by providing employment to the increasing number of workers. What is more, foreign technology will come to the country along with foreign capital and that will result in technological development similar to the development seen in countries like Taiwan, South Korea and other Asian Tigers. Earlier, I had welcomed foreign capital not only in consumer industries but even in small-scale industries, which produced most of the goods which we exported such as cloth and clothing, cut diamonds, tanned leather and leather goods, carpets, etc. We had to compete with other countries, which also exported similar goods. Increase in exports was vital for our economic development. It with the help of foreign technology, our competitors improved the quality or reduced the prices of those goods, our exports were bound to suffer. Foreign capital in our small-scale industry will bring in foreign technology, and that will result in our ability to compete successfully with other countries and increase our exports.

Response to Mr. Rath's Criticism

In this open letter, Mr. Bhagabat Prasad Rath has criticised my views mainly on the ground that globalisation will result in the Indian economy being dominated by the multinationals. While I do not wish to under estimate the harm that may be caused by multi-nationals, it is essential that the harm should also not be exaggerated. China has imported foreign capital which is more than twenty times the capital imported in India and there is no evidence that the Chinese economy is dominated or dictated by multinationals.

Moreover, Mr. Rath has over-looked the fact mentioned by me that the growth of multinationals has received a setback as a result of the computer-based information revolution. Several small and medium scale industries are growing in developed countries; they are successfully competing with multinationals by taking advantage of the computer, the e-mail and internet facilities. Several articles by experts have appeared in the press explaining how the "advantage of scale" previously enjoyed by multinationals has been greatly minimised as a result of the new computer-based technology. I referred to an article of N.S. Siddharthan who has pointed out that the industrial development of the future will be in the direction of globalisation and decentralisation at the same time. By decentralisation he means the gradual withdrawal of multi-nationals. In a subsequent article published in *The Economic and Political Weekly*, the same author, N.S. Siddharthan, has observed that during the last ten years, the monopoly of multinationals in international industrial production has been reduced from 65 per cent to 57 per cent.

Moreover, multi-nationals can grow in India even if we revert to the old *Swadeshi* policy which was followed by our government from 1947 to 1991 and which proved on the whole a failure. In fact, in his open letter, Mr. Rath has referred to Larsen and Toubro as one of the internationals. Now, Larsen and Toubro has become an Indian company and I remember that I was involved in 1942 in a trade union of its workers in a factory situated near the Bombay sea-shore. It is, therefore, not right to oppose globalisation on the ground that it will result in Indian industry being dominated by multinationals.

Mr. Rath has expressed horror at my suggestion that foreign capital should be allowed even in small-scale industry in India. He fears that millions of workers will lose their job if foreign capital makes its entry into small-scale industry in India. The fear is misplaced. Foreign capital is not supplied only by multinationals. Investment of foreign capital does not necessarily mean invitation to multinationals. I have seen quite a few small-scale industries in India, which are being run with foreign collaboration. They have increased employment instead of reducing it. Multinationals have nothing to do with them.

Mr. Rath has referred to the Asian Tigers and several other countries, which had invited foreign capital and which ran into economic recession. Economists have already explained how the present recession started in these countries. The reason was that portfolio capital, which is commonly used for gambling on the stock exchange, and which was received by the banks of these countries, was wrongly employed by them in real estate and other long-term investments. Portfolio capital, as distinguished from industrial capital, is necessarily volatile and it may be withdrawn at any time and shifted from one country to another for stock exchange operations. Inability to pay back the portfolio capital which was wrongly employed in long-term investments was the main reason behind this recession which has travelled from the borrower countries to the rest of the world. Obviously, the recession is not likely to be permanent and there is every reason to hope that industrial development will be revived when the recession comes to an end. Even today, in spite of the industrial recession, the Asian Tigers and other countries who had entertained foreign capital rank much above India in the Social Development Index annually prepared by the United Nations.

Reference is also made to several African and Latin American countries which are in a bad financial condition. Unless one knows the economic history of each of these countries, one cannot comment on the causes of its present economic difficulties. Mr. Rath has mentioned the economic distress of those countries without showing whether their present economic condition is the result of liberalisation or globalisation.

Then there is reference by him to the enormous economic disparities in developed countries. There is no doubt that these disparities do exist and they are likely to increase in the future. While it is true that these disparities are a social evil, it is also true that the poor people in developed countries have experienced economic betterment, although the rate of their economic growth is very much lower than the rate at which the income of the richer sections of their societies has increased. For instance, it is estimated that in Great Britain at present, more than 55 per cent of the people are well-to-do, while the condition of the remaining 45 per cent is also better than before. Of course, this excludes the unemployed who have to live on the dole.

While dealing with the problem of globalisation versus *Swadeshi,* we should not forget that we had a long era in which the *Swadeshi* Policy was followed. It lasted for at least thirty years after independence. Did we make any satisfactory economic progress during that period? Did the poor people in India experience any relief till Rajiv Gandhi started his populist and profligate policy in 1980 which resulted in India's virtual bankruptcy? With that experience in mind, it is not possible to prefer *Swadeshi* to the present policy of economic liberalisation and globalisation.

5

ROLE OF THE STATE AND ECONOMIC PLANNING

I.C. Dhingra

There is an old saying: "Comparing the principles of Christianity with the practices of Islam and *vice-versa,* you can prove anything". This is nowhere more true than in the case of state intervention in the economic system.

The debate among economists on the role that a government can usefully play by manipulating market forces had been going on at least since Adam Smith divined the working of an 'invisible hand' in the market. In more recent years the leading opponents of government interference have been the group of monetarists who have closely followed Milton Friedman's *laissez faire* economic philosophy and also some international organisations, notably the IMF and the World Bank. On the other hand, a large number of economists, including the majority of neo-Keynesians, especially those working on the development problems, have attempted to emphasize the positive role that governments can play in growth and development through planning and through intervention in the economy at both macro and micro levels. The principal advocates of this economic philosophy among international organisations have been most Regional Economic Commissions of the United Nations as well as UNCTAD.

Arguments in Support of State Intervention

The principal arguments in support of State intervention in economic system arise basically from market failures and can be summed up as follows:

Ignorance and Lack of Information

This will be especially important for investment decisions where the lifetime of capital goods is long and where the indivisibility of capital makes for "lumpy" investment.

Obstacles and Bottlenecks

A system of market prices may, because of the economic structure of a developing economy, require large and destabilising price changes to achieve useful results. Obstacles and bottlenecks of all kinds may exist. Resources may be immovable. Perhaps there is even perverse ("backward-bending") response to price changes by labour, farmers and small business. All these constraints may make supply so inelastic that large price changes are needed to bring in small adjustments. Such changes can only be administered by the State and cannot be left to the push and pull of market forces.

Further, the market mechanism is not as effective in the UDCs as the developed countries because the latter are provided with much greater social overhead capital and with a wider array of complementary factors of production and intermediate goods which make it possible for private enterprise to react to market indicators. If the poor performance of the market mechanism in developing countries were due mainly to the lack of social capital, government would be able to create favourable conditions by increasing investment in social capital, which would provide base for private enterprise to invest in directly productive activities.[1]

Divergence between Social Costs and Benefits

There often exist divergences between the private and social costs and benefits of investment projects. The private entrepreneur is quite naturally concerned only with the cost incurred by him on a project, and with the income received in deciding whether or not to embark on it. He is not expected to, nor does he in practice attach any weightage to what are called *externalities* of his activities, namely, the side-effects (positive or negative) of his operations on the rest of the economy. Important examples of externalities of investment projects are: the effect on employment and on the pattern of production; contribution to a balanced development of industries and regions and to an equitable income distribution through the choice of investment projects and technology;. environmental considerations and the effect on foreign exchange outlays and earnings when growth is constrained by BOP considerations. These side-effects of investment have important long-term implications for the development of a country and should be accorded adequate weightage in the allocation of resources although they fall almost entirely outside the sphere of interest of individual entrepreneurs. The government can attempt to deal with externalities either by way of taxes and subsidies (taxing the pollution, subsidising pollution abatement); by regulation (prescribing certain activities); or within a legal framework (letting those injured sue and possibly taking action that lower the costs of such private suits).[3]

Environment

In many cases, market mechanism is found incapable of adding to efficiency. Making the polluter pay will not rectify the damage that has already been done to the environment. Environment, in fact, constitutes the weakest point in the discourse of market led growth and state withdrawal. One cannot let natural resources be freely exploited endlessly, especially when the market system does not even provide ways of internalising the costs—present or future.

Monetary Control

No progress can be made without a sound monetary and banking system. Savings have to be mobilised and credit controls manipulated to suit the changing conditions. Only the State can undertake this task.

Mobilisation of Resources

Only the State can mobilise the resources—domestic and external—required for financing the various development and infrastructure needs on such a large scale. This may be beyond the capacity of individual entrepreneurs.

Skill Formation

Development needs a high level of skill formation. Skills can be developed only by investing in the SOC and building up the infrastructure consisting of different services. No individual can provide this type of investment. The responsibility devolves upon the State.

Balanced Development

It is the State which can lay down a balanced development programme of agricultural, industrial and other economic activities with a view to bring about the maximum welfare of the largest number of people.

Poverty and Deprivation

The State may be called in to deal with poverty and deprivation. This is an issue of central concern to a UDC like India. Further, the State may be looked upon as an agency that acts paternalistically to ensure certain basic rights to its citizens such as the right to basic education and primary health. By the same token the paternal role of the State may be extended to encompass strict legislation and enforcement against drugs and liquor. The State may also intervene to protect the interests of the future generations in terms of issues like environmental degradation and global warming, a concern that is simply unlikely to be addressed by the market.[5]

Welfare State

The concept of State has undergone a radical change. The modern State is a Welfare State. This contemplates a reduction in inequalities of income and wealth, a re-distribution of land ownership and property ownership by fixing land ceilings and urban property ceiling, provision of employment, participation of labour in the management of industry, etc. All these and many other similar functions can be performed only by the State. These cannot be left at the hands of the private enterprise.

In short, the dominant view has been that the modern State is an indispensable instrument of economic development and that it should undertake activities that would compensate for "market failure"—market failure is perceived as the inability of markets to allocate optimally resources over time, that is, for investment because of the 'miopic' nature of markets. What the modern State can achieve through a process of aggressive and judiciously selective intervention is amply demonstrated by dramatic success stories in East Asia. There is a remarkable similarity between the government activities undertaken by the East Asian countries and those undertaken by the United States in a comparable period of its development. There are few examples on the other side of success without government involvement.

Forms of State Intervention

Government intervention is needed. The debate is not over 'Whether state intervention' but 'how much' and 'what type' of role. We may distinguish between four different types of roles of a modern State, *viz.*, (i) regulatory role, (ii) promotional role, (iii) entrepreneurial role, and (iv) planning role.

The *regulatory role* of government may include :

(a) determination of the conditions under which individuals or groups would be permitted to enter certain lines of business or avail of public facilities and scarce resources;

(b) regulating the conduct of industrial or business ventures in operation through legislation or laying down rules and standards for management to abide by;

(c) controlling the accrual and disposal of business income; and

(d) regulating the relationship between different segments or interest groups in the economy so as to protect legal rights or resolve conflicts of interest.

The *promotional role* of the government may include : (i) promoting education, (ii) promoting technology, (iii) supporting the financial sector, (iv) investing in infrastructure, (v) preventing environmental degradation, and (vi) creating and maintaining a social safety net.

The *entrepreneurial role* of the government may involve its participation in business through public ownership and management of industrial and commercial undertakings.

The *planning role* of the government involves allocation of scarce resources according to national priorities, and is exercised through the instrumentality of economic planning.

Development planning fulfils various functions. By providing an analytical framework of the economy's structure, it allows the policy makers to evaluate the prospects for, and constraints upon, economic growth and structural change. By assembling a consistent and integrated set of relationships for the whole economy, it enables the policy makers to identify the direct and indirect effects of particular policy changes.[7] Planning is believed to be an answer to the inability of the price-mechanism to ensure growth, efficiency and equity,[8] although the ability of economy to draw an 'optimal' plan has been widely debated. In a famous debate between Oskar Lange, Abba Lerner, Ludwig von Mises and Friedrich Hayek during the 1930s and 1940s, the planners (Lange and Lerner) argued that (a) because of the ubiquitous imperfections in most markets, no market economy could ever in practice attain the Utopian norm of perfect competition, but that (b) by using computers to stimulate the outcome of a perfectly competitive economy and legislating to compel the production of the resulting quantities of inputs and outputs (or their relative prices), a planned economy could achieve Utopia.[9] Hayek and Mises pointed out that though such kind of planning might be theoretically feasible in a world where information about resources, technology, and the myriad actual and possible production processes and tastes of consumers could be costlessly acquired by the central planning authority, in the real world it would be impossible. Moreover, if it were possible to acquire the information, it would be impossible speedily to solve the resulting system of millions of simultaneous equations.

Government Failure

Economic planning has had its heyday during the *fifties and the early sixties* of the last century among the development economists the world over and the policy-makers. Drawing up of a Five Year Plan became the norm of developing economices; donors of foreign aid as well as World Bank almost insisted on such plans.[11] It came to be said, "we are all planners now". The *seventies* saw the world economy in crisis. Stagflation and intense social distortion became the destiny of the first world. The second world was unable to maintain its pace of growth as planning faced difficulties in coming to grips with an intensive phase of development which needed fine-tuning in many ways. During the same period the third world's development dream too was seen to have turned sour. All these developments were treated as failures of planning and interventionism, or what came to be known as *government failure.*

Causes of Government Failure

Major causes of government failure have been identified as follows[12] :

(i) Individuals may know more about their own preferences and circumstances than the government.

(ii) Government planning may increase risk by pointing everyone in the same direction—government may make bigger mistakes than markets.

(iii) Government planning may be more rigid and inflexible than private decision-making since complex decision-making machinery may be involved in government.

(iv) Governments may be incapable of administering detailed plans.

(v) Government controls may prevent private sector individual initiative if there are many bureaucratic obstacles.

(vi) Organisations and individuals require incentives to work, innovate, control costs and allocate efficiently; the discipline and rewards of the market cannot be easily replicated within public enterprises and organisations.

(vii) Different levels and parts of government may be poorly coordinated in the absence of the equilibrating signals provided by the market, particularly where groups or regions with different interests are involved.

(viii) Markets place constraints on what can be achieved by government, for example, resale of commodities on black markets and activities in the informal sector can disrupt rationing or rather non-linear pricing or taxation schemes. This is the general problem of "incentive compatability".

(ix) Controls create resource-using activities to influence those controls through lobbying and corruption— often called rent-seeking or directly unproductive activities in the literature.

(x) Planning may be manipulated by privileged and powerful groups which act in their own interests and further, planning creates groups with a vested interest in planning, for example, bureaucrats or industrialists who obtain protected positions.

(xi) Governments may be dominated by narrow interest groups interested in their own welfare and sometimes activities hostile to large sections of the population. Planning may intensify their power.

(xii) Some industries are more attractive at different points of time. But governments have proven to be singularly incompetent in targeting winning horses. The Japanese lost billions of yens in a government inspired programme to entre into mainframe computers, Europeans lost millions in an EEC attempt to create competitiveness in high definition television. It is best to leave these decisions in the hands of private sector managers.

On-going Debate on State Versus Markets

Economists, by and large, appear increasingly convinced that a system of detailed central planning in a huge diversified economy is counter-productive. Hayek and Mises won their round of debate, while Lange and Lerner had to beat a hasty retreat.

Under this condition, the ideologies of the market, private enterprise, rational expectations and supply side economics gained respectability. All economic ills came to be ascribed to government failures and faulty macro economic and sectoral policies. Market forces, free from government action, came to be recognised as the necessary means to promote economic growth and efficiency in resource allocation and utilisation. Public sector and state enterprises were disappearing and privatisation appeared on the agenda of most, if not all, countries. To talk of the State intervention began to attract the same kind of disdain "as would a person playing a 75 rpm record with 1920s music at a party". *The Economist* called it a "bloodless revolution".

During the *eighties* the role of government started shrinking. But it was soon realised that the free markets were not magically solving the problems of the poor or of development. Free markets have weak institutional foundations in UDCs and thus tend to malfunction or not even exist.[13] Peasants and the poor did not benefit from the numerous economic reforms undertaken in the decade of *eighties* and *nineties*.

Towards the *end of eighties* a consensus was emerging in favour of what came to be known as *market-friendly* approach to development, that stressed the complementary ways markets and governments can pull together. The beginning of the *nineties* saw the emphasis being shifted to the *govern the market* or 'market-plus', plus implying social obligations role of the State, where government intervenes actively to promote investment and the growth of national private enterprise.[14] To this approach has been added the rider that the markets should be *people-friendly*. People-friendly markets are those which are accessible to all who wish to participate in them, in which all participants have a fair chance of benefiting from such participation. Functioning of a friendly market is essential for evaluation of efficiency. In the absence of such a market the system becomes blind to costs and efficiency and leads to enormous wastage of resources, ultimately resulting in waste of growth potential.

Functions of the State Addressing Market Failure Improving Equity

<table>
<tr><td>Minimal Functions</td><td colspan="3">Providing Pure Public Goods
■ Defence
■ Law and order
■ Property rights
■ Macro-economic management
■ Public health</td><td>Protecting the Poor
■ Anti-poverty programmes
■ Disaster relief</td></tr>
<tr><td>Intermediate Functions</td><td>Addressing Externalities
■ Basic Education
■ Environmental protection</td><td>Regulating Monopoly
■ Utility regulation
■ Anti-trust policy</td><td>Overcoming Imperfect Social Information
■ Financial protection
■ Consumer protection</td><td>Providing Insurance
■ Redistributive pensions
■ Unemployment insurance</td></tr>
<tr><td>Activist Functions</td><td colspan="3">Co-ordinating Private Activity
■ Fostering markets
■ Cluster initiatives</td><td>Redistribution
■ Asset redistribution</td></tr>
</table>

Source: World Development Report 1997.

The *mid-nineties* were witness to the emergence of a synthesis paradigm of a 'socially responsible maket economy'

(SRME) tailor-made to suit the politico-socio-economic conditions of a country. The paradigm has been considered necessary for avoidance of both "government excesses" and "market excesses" and for ensuring more equitable distribution of the fruits of economic growth. The ultimate goal of SRME is the joint maximisation of the people's welfare reconciling and satisfying the interests of all sections of the economic players. These include not only the consumers but also producers, traders and wage-earners as well as non-wage earners.

As we have moved into the *21st century*, the case for active state intervention is becoming more assertive and definite. Even it is being argued[15] that the East Asian meltdown could have been avoided only if the state had played a more activist role.

In this paradigm the government's role may be defined to include the following: *One*, it has to be an umpire; it has to ensure fair and vigorous competition in the marketplace *Two*, its legal system must make sure that contracts are honoured. *Three*, it has to guarantee law and order and political stability. *Four*, it has to provide fiscal and monetary policies, which keep inflation low and growth high. *Five*, it has to provide those public goods which the private sector cannot—universal education, health and in many cases, physical infrastructure. Even when the private sector is capable of providing infrastructure, the government has to play a crucial role in determining infrastructural needs and in providing transparent rules and mechanisms to ensure that the private sector does its job fairly and honesly. *Six*, the government has to provide a safety net for the poor and the vulnerable since in every society ten to twenty per cent of the total population always fails. *Finally*, the state alone can do standard-setting, whether on water quality, building codes, pollution limits, use of urban spaces, or school curricula. Like the traffic controller on public street, the government would have the power the responsibility to effect discipline and not the prerogative to take the driver's seat.

The various functions of the state can be tabulated as in Chart above.

The debate on the respective roles of the state and the market thus goes on, as Deepak Nayyar puts it[16], "we have not yet reached the end of the history. There is much appeal in the proposition that neither the market nor planning are complete in themselves nor are the two irreconcilable, inveterate foes, which are mutually exclusive."

Their respective roles should be determined by the comparative advantage of each,[17] besides, the relationship between the two has to be highly supportive and non-antagonistic.

Meanwhile, however, and understandably, as a natural corollary, there has developed what can be called *plan weariness* in many parts of the world, not excluding India. 'Economic reform' is the key phrase. But even to get away from planning, as Prof. Sukhmoy Chakravarty puts it, one has to know what it has achieved.[18] Or in the maxim of J.M. Keynes, we have to "study the present in the light of the past for the purposes of the future."

REFERENCES

1. Miguel Urrutia and Setsuko Yukawa (eds.): *Development Planning in Mixed Economies*, United Nations University, 1988. Also, V.V. Bhatt: *East Asian Miracle*, World Bank, 1993.
2. Bhaskar Datta (ed.), *Welfare Economics*, OUP, New Delhi, 1995.
3. Joseph E. Stiglitz, *The Economic Role of the State*, Basil Blackwell, Oxford, 1989.
4. Dolly Arora, "Politics, Markets and Social Concerns: Liberalisation and Reorganisation of Space", in *The Indian Journal of Public Administration*, Vol. XLII, No. 3, July-September, 1996.
5. Pulin B. Nayak, "The State and The Market", *EPW*, Vol. XXXI, No. 4, January 27, 1996.
6. Joseph E. Stiglitz, "An Agenda for Development in the Twenty-First Century", *Annual World Bank Conference on Development Economics 1997*, World Bank, 1998.

7. Anis Chowdhury and Colin Kirkpatrick, *Development Policy and Planning An Introduction to Models and Techniques,* Routledge, London, 1994.
8. Griffin and Enos, *Planning Development,* p. 21.
9. Pranab K. Bardhan and John e. Roemer (eds.): *Market Socialism,* OUP, New York, 1993.
10. Cf. Deepak Lal, *The Hindu Equilibrium,* Vol. I, Clarendon Press, Oxford, 1988, pp. 234-35.
11. T.N. Srinivasan, "Development Economics: Then and Now", in Jan Willem Gunning *et al* (eds.): *Trade, Aid and Development,* MacMillan, London, 1994.
12. Nicholas Stern, "The Economics of Development", *Economic Journal,* September, 1989.
13. Robert Klitgaard, *Adjusting to Reality, Beyond "States Versus Market"* in *Economic Development,* ICS Press, California, 1991.
14. This gave rise to the concept called "Command capitalism", that is capitalism with government intervention. See Callum Henderson: *Asia Falling? Making Sense of the Asian Currency Crisis,* McGraw, 1998.
15. Arjun Sengupta, "Market mechanisms", *The Times of India,* August 6, 1998.
16. Deepak Nayyar, "Globalisation: The Past in our Present", *Presidential Address* delivered at the Annual Conference of the Indian Economic Association on December 28, 1995.
17. Sukhmoy Chakravarty, *Development Planning: The Indian Experience,* OUP, Oxford, 1987, p. 3.
18. Cf. Subroto Roy and William E. James (eds.): *Foundation of Indian Political Economy,* Sage, New Delhi, 1992.

7. Anil Chowdhury and Colin Kirkpatrick, Development Policy and Planning: An Introduction to Models and Techniques, Routledge, London, 1994.

8. Griffin and Enos, Planning Development, p.24.

9. Pranab K. Bardhan and John e. Roemer (eds.), Market Socialism, OUP, New York, 1993.

10. Deepak Lal, The Hindu Equilibrium, Vol. 1, Clarendon Press, Oxford, 1988, pp. 24-26.

11. R.M. Sundrum, "Development Economics: Then and Now," in Lin Wiliem Gunning et al (eds.), Trade, Aid and Development, MacMillan, London, 1991.

12. Nicholas Stern, "The Economics of Development", Economic Journal, September, 1989.

13. Robert Klitgaard, Adjusting to Reality, Beyond 'State versus Market' in Economic Development, ICS Press, California, 1991.

14. This gave rise to the concept called "Corporate capitalism" that is capitalism with government intervention. See Callum Henderson, Asia Falling? Making Sense of the Asian Currency Crisis, McGraw, 1998.

15. Arjun Sengupta, "Market mechanisms", The Times of India, August 6, 1988.

16. Deepak Nayyar, "Globalisation: The Past in our Present", Presidential Address delivered at the Annual Conference of the Indian Economic Association on December 28, 1995.

17. Sukhamoy Chakravarty, Development Planning: The Indian Experience, OUP, Oxford, 1987, p. 3.

18. Subroto Roy and William E. James (eds.), Foundations of India's Political Economy, Sage, New Delhi, 1992.

6

DEVELOPMENT OF POWER SECTOR AFTER INDEPENDENCE

Raj Kumar

India has surpassed fifty years of independence. We have entered new millennium. Still the power remains the most important aspect in meeting the developing needs of the country. In fact the infrastructure of the country to a large extent is based on the growth of this sector. The present century has concentrated on the development of energy as the input to infrastructure. India needs constant ten per cent growth to ensure the momentum of seven per cent growth in over all growth in the economy. The ratio of growth rate of demand of power of GDP in the First Five Year Plan was as high as 3.06 in the First Five Year Plan, increased to 5.11 in Third Five Year Plan and reduced to 1.55 in the Seventh and Eighth Five Year Plan. Though the growth of power generation capacity which was 8.4 per cent per annum during the eighties declined to five per cent per annum in the last decade. The ninth plan capacity addition target of 70,000 mW as against the *feasible target* of 40,245 mW in the ninth plan working plan paper. With half the time already over the present situation of power projects expected in this Five Year Plan is likely to be near 29,000 mW. According to the ninth plan paper the demand of electricity for the year 2001-02 will increase to 505 bkwh as against 327 bkwh in 1996-97. The generating capacity to meet the above requirement will be 1,31,243 MW as against the capacity of 84912 MW in 1996-97. The demand and supply gap continues to maintain gap which due to associated issues such as population growth, financing and other remains to be bridged. Let us however without going into details of above aspects examine the positive aspects as to what we have been able to achieve without harping the old tune of problems which we leave for the present to planners and experts.

Per Capita Consumption of Electricity in Countries (KWh/Annum)

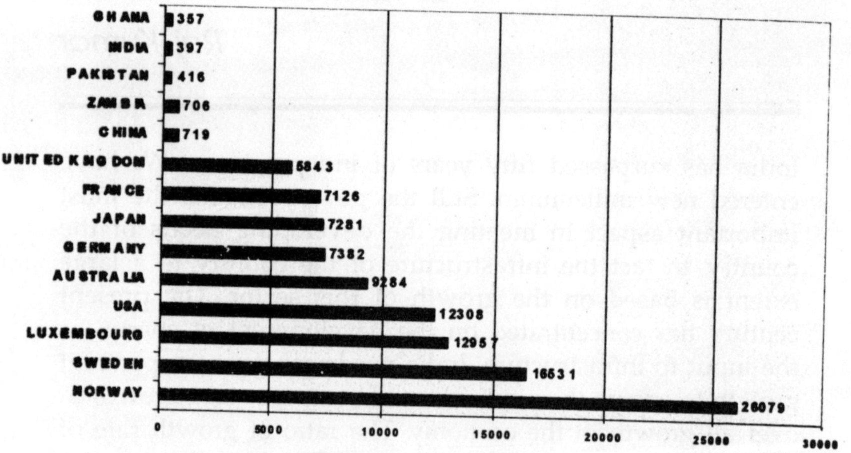

The power position in early fifties was rather pathetic. Technological advancements were yet to begin on account of obvious reasons. The genesis of electricity supply industry in India dates back to the year 1897 when a small two units of 65 kW each (total 130 kW) were installed and commissioned near Darjeeling in West Bengal. The pace of power development in the country was rather tardy with a total installed capacity of 1362 mW. It was immediately after independence that in First Five Year Plan need was felt and many multipurpose projects were taken up primarily for the purpose of irrigation and incidentally for power benefits share of hydro-generation was to the tune of 50.6 per cent in 1963. Our requirements were studied by the then.country planners and Five Year Plans were finalized by the Planning Commission. In the latter plans it was felt by the Government that thermal projects depend largely on coal and have less gestation periods whereas hydro projects are capital-intensive and dependent upon nature and even though problems are encountered due to geological nature of strata the capacity addition would be more fast even at a significant cost would be in the interest of the country. After independence the increase from a paltry 1362 mW we have reached to an impressive 95000 mW. In fact, India ranks eighth in the world after USA, erstwhile Russia, Spain, Germany, France, Canada and China in terms of capacity. Slowly the headway was made in generation, transmission and distribution of power. The industrialists and government both took power sector with keen interest and today we are in a relatively better position and can boast of having complete technology in entire sector.

Growth Profile of Indian Power Sector

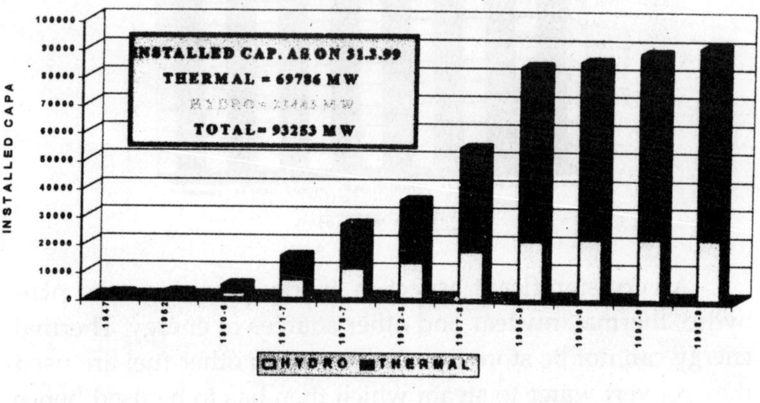

The per capita consumption of power of our country even after fifty years of independence is as low as around one unit of electricity per day whereas developed countries consume almost twenty times or even more. The power position in the country is planned keeping an optimal mix to meet every contingency. In fact the planning is made with Loss of Load Probability (LOLP) of better than one per cent and energy not served (ENS) 0.25 per cent. This would mean that if installation could have been streamlined commensurate with the planned, things would have been much better today. We have very lately realized the need of real strong monitoring, otherwise, in every plan the committed installed capacities have managed to slip. There is a strong need to augment the desired resources otherwise in every plan the committed installed capacities will manage to slip. It is a bitter pill to swallow but even in ninth plan also we are lagging behind the planned capacity addition. Expected target likely to be achieved against planned 70000 mW is in range of 29000.

Hydro/Thermal Ratio

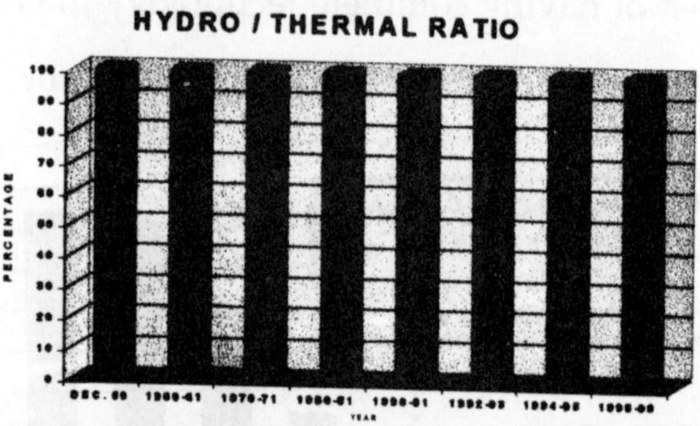

A very significant aspect in energy planning is to plan hydro, thermal, nuclear and other sources of energy. Thermal energy can not be stored and once coal or other fuel are used they convert water to steam which then has to be used hence are suitable for meeting constant demand throughout the day. Hydro units worldwide are known for different types of use and water can be stored. The machines can be kept rolling and whenever need arises, these can start generating. This time is almost one quarter of a minute. Thus, these machines can be successfully employed for meeting pulsating demand. Further to meet above requirements of LOLP a ratio of 60: 40 between thermal to hydro is recommended. It may be seen that this ratio was more or less maintained till early eighties but in last two decades more stress has been given by the planners to thermal generation because of a low gestation period as compared to hydro generation. There are different views on merits and limitations of both type of generations but load shedding in the early morning peak and evening peak can be effectively dealt by hydro stations which essentially should be in higher ratio. Hydro stations once built are of multipurpose in nature and require no investment on fuel and do not pose danger to environment. The power becomes cheaper once the capital cost is recovered.

In the first twenty years after independence the increase in ower generation capacity was rather slow but gradually progress has picked up and has been good in the last couple of years. We have started realizing that power is a basic need for overall growth and accordingly we hear of reforms, private sector participation, special purpose vichle, fast track projects, merger and so on. All India demand and supply gap may be seen figure give on the next page. The energy shortage and the peak shortage has been continuing to the tune of eight per cent and above 11 per cent. In a country like India, there is huge potential of saving electricity and managing demand in all consuming sectors, e.g., agricultural sector has a saving potential of 30-40 per cent, domestic and commercial sector has a saving potential of 20-25 per cent, the industry sector has a potential of 15-20 per cent, public water and sewage works 30-35 per cent shortage.

All India Demand and Supply Gap

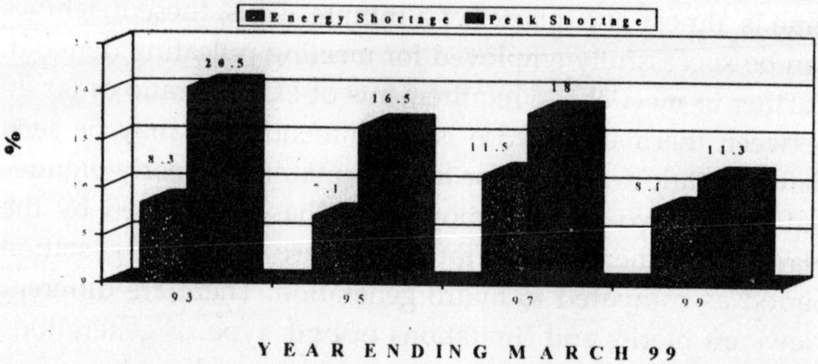

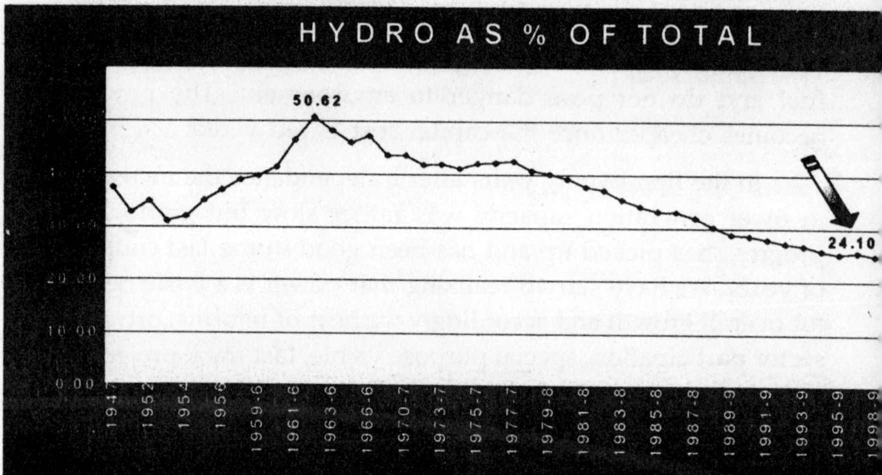

Commensurate with the generation in early 1950s the transmission network was also in infancy. Gradually with the increase of generation, the voltage levels keeping in view the long distance from the load centres were raised to 132 kV, 220 kV, 400 kV and today we are heading towards 765 kV transmission system. The most important aspect which needs to be elaborated here is that to meet this requirement of the country, not only electric utilities but also the support industry have made adequate advances. It is a matter of pride today that with the consistent quality consciousness of the equipment up to 400 kV transmission system are manufactured within the country and in a number of cases India has been identified as a country with export potential for such equipments. The market in Asia has wide acceptability of equipments made by Indian manufacturers. The start of 400 kV system took place with the commissioning of Sultanpur sub-station of Uttar Pradesh in 1977. Since then strong interconnections were planned and built. In fact the concept of National Grid for pooling the regional power was planned based on 400 kV network. This system will be having a latest state of art technic. The construction of lines in difficult terrain have been completed and the systems to ensure power generated at far eastern and northern hydro stations is successfully evacuated/ transmitted to load centres with quality stands available.

Although the long distance transmission needs are being covered by Alternating Current Network but it was felt that pit head stations should be connected to load centres. Accordingly HVDC transmission was conceived in early 1990s. Today underlying HVDC network becomes backbone for transfer of power to the capital. This link between Rihand power complex and Dadri has earned worldwide recognition. India being a big country the power sector is being managed in five different regions. These regions have varied generation and load profiles. This results in variation of system parameters such as voltage and frequency. In order to transfer excess power available in one region and help a region which has deficit in generation of power in hours of need the interconnection is essential. Grid constraints are so much at variance that they do not allow easy interconnections. Besides there is always fear of grid couspse. We have wisely connected the regions with the help of back to back asynchronous links which would be helpful in achieving the above goal.

Similarly, testing facilities have also been developed by nodal agency like Central Power Research Institute with branches throughout the country. Here a significant amount of research and development work is being done for developing material required for the power sector. Even private sector participation has been more than encouraging in the field of testing of items required for transmission and industry. The distribution of power is also increasing with the increase in small-scale industries development. Awareness regarding the new gadgets required, have made reliable distribution networks for transporting power to the consumer. The high voltage cables, switchgear and other associated equipment are being manufactured in the country conforming to international standards. Although systems have been planned and implemented in the right perspective yet there had been some compulsions on account of which supply of power was extended beyond technical acceptance limits. This has been responsible for past losses which are being talked off as Transmission and Distribution (T&D) losses. The T&D losses are in following decreasing order U.P., Maharashtra, A.P., Gujarat, M.P., T.N., Rajasthan, Punjab, Karnataka, W.B., Orissa and Kerala. It is rather unfortunate that our T&D losses are increasing day-by-day owing to increasing theft and partly on account of quality distribution planning.

The topic will remain incomplete if we do not discuss the contribution of State Electricity Boards which in no way can be underestimated. In fact, time has come when the burden they have been sharing on account of free power and subsidised power has to be exposed to cut down negative aspects on their losses. It is after fifty years when structural changes are being considered. The major causes for restructuring are as under:

(i) Large requirements of investments, which are beyond, budget provisions of SEB's and State Governments.

(ii) Awareness to the quality of power and more accountability to the consumers.

(iii) Commercial running of generating units.

(iv) Minimize losses in T&D network.

It may be seen that power sector in the last fifty plus

years has made substantial progress but due to constraints, it has not been possible to match the load requirements. Government of India, therefore, has gone ahead with invitation to private power producing companies to finance and install the power stations in last decade. Enough exercise has been done and a number of changes which are mandatory in IE rules have been processed and other clearances have been streamlined. It is expected that with the dedication of GOI other aspects will also be streamlined and in the next decade we shall be able to reduce gap between generation and load the demand.

7

FINANCIAL SECTOR REFORMS

Dr. Shrawan Kumar Singh

A financial system comprises of financial institutions, markets and instruments which together provide the essential framework for mobilisation and allocation of savings. The primary role of any financial system is to act as a conduit for the transfer of financial resources from net savers to borrowers, i.e., from those who spend less than they earn to those who earn less than they spend.

There has been a controversy over the issue whether the financial development precedes and, therefore, plays an active role in economic development or whether it merely adjusts to the growth of the real sector. Sometimes these alternate hypotheses are termed as "supply-leading" and "demand-following" phenomena. Under the "demand-following" phenomenon, as trade and industry expand the financial services needed by them are provided by the financial system, a case of demand creating its own supply. In this case, financial development is supposed to possessively accommodate to the growth of the real economy. On the other hand, the "supply-leading" phenomenon is the situation in which financial development occurs first and by providing the necessary financial services acts as a stimulant to economic growth and development. However, the cause-and-effect relationship between financial and real sector development is difficult to disentangle. Suffice it to say that financial development and real economic growth are closely intertwined and they interact in any economy over a period of time in a mutually reinforcing manner.

The central economic function of the financial sector is financial intermediation, that is the mobilisation of financial resources and the allocation of these financial resources. The financial intermediaries, essentially provide three "transformation" services:

(i) liability-asset and size transformation (i.e., mobilisation of funds and their allocation, provision of large loans on the basis of numerous small deposits);

(ii) maturity transformation (i.e., offering savers a short-term liquidity deposit they prefer and providing borrowers long-term loans which are better matched to the cash flows generated by their investment); and

(iii) risk transformation, (i.e., transforming and distributing risk through diversification so that risks associated with investors are reduced for savers).

Analysts talk of operational efficiency and allocation efficiency. While the former relates to transaction costs, the latter deals with the distribution of mobilised funds among competing demands. functional efficiency must therefore relate to:

(a) the soundness of the appraisals as measured by the level of overdues,

(b) the resource cost of specific operations, and

(c) the quality and speed of delivery of services. Both operational and allocational efficiency are to a large extent influenced by market structure and the regulatory framework.

Efficient financial intermediation also involves minimising the transaction cost of transferring funds from original savers to final investors.

The financial system in any country plays a crucial role in the smooth functioning of the real economy and its transformation. During the greater part of the pre-reform era since Independence, the successive governments in India treated the financial system mainly as an instrument of public finance. The deposit and lending rates of banks were fixed by a complex web of regulations. A substantial part of the credit was channelled to the Government and priority sectors at below market rates. The financial system was dominated by public institutions and there was hardly any competition. Notwithstanding these restrictions, by 1980, India had a relatively 'deep' financial system for its per capita GDP. The 1990s ushered in the first phase of financial sector liberalisation to coincide with the real sector deregulation. It saw the liberalisation of interest rates, lowering of cash reserve ratio (CRR) and the statutory liquidity ratio (SLR), capital market reform and initiation of privatization of the insurance sector.

With the structural reforms initiated in 1991, the need was recognized to orient the financial sector towards market guided signals. The policies of financial sector reform can be broadly classified into three areas:

(i) the issues relating to overall monetary policy including reserve requirements, interest rates, refinance facilities and the activation of internal debt management instruments;

(ii) in-house issues such as strengthening of banks and institutions by way of prescription of prudential norms, greater competitiveness and more flexible entry in the financial sector; and

(iii) the reform of the exchange rate policy and attendant exchange control and the integration of the domestic financial system into the global economy. Rapid reforms in various segments of Indian economy are underway. It is in this context, that the recommendations of the recent report of the Narasimham Committee I and II on the financial system augur well for the liberalisation process.

Liberalisation of the financial sector is one of the important components of the currently pursued new economic policy. Various measures relating to financial liberalisation need to be undertaken.

What does this liberalisation mean? It means:

(a) softening of allocative regulations and hardening of the prudential regulations;

(b) moving away from the regime of administered rates towards market determined rates;

(c) providing better access to money and capital market to higher credit rated industrial calients with an aim of promoting efficiency, and

(d) providing a chance to the Indian financial system to restructure itself. It is not possible to improve the effiectiveness and efficiency of the financial system without a well-integrated institutional and policy framework that can ensure macro-economic stability, competitive functioning of the financial markets, and operational autonomy to the various financial institutions.

Narasimham Committee Recommendations

In this context, it is better to look at some of the major recommendations of the Committee on Financial Sector Reform (1991). They are as under:

(a) Banking Sector

* Structure of the banking sector to be revamped. Three or four large banks to become global in character.
* Eight to ten national banks with a network of branches to be engaged in universal banking.
* Local bank operations to be confined to a specific region.
* Rural banks to operate only in rural areas, functions to be based on profitability considerations.

* Government should remove the disincentives for the more dynamic among the private banks to grow.
* Abolition of branch licensing proposed and opening or closing of branches to be left to the individual banks.
* Policy of allowing foreign banks to open branches. Foreign banks should be subject to the same requirements as applicable to domestic banks.
* Foreign operations of Indian banks to be rationalised.
* Computerisation of bank operations needs to be stepped up.
* No need to set up a banking service commission.
* Asset reconstruction, institution of capital adequacy and establishment of prudential norms.
* SLR requirement of banks to be brought down to 25 per cent in three years. Progressive reduction in CRR.
* Interest rate paid to banks on SLR investments and on CRR in respect of impounded deposits to be increased.
* Review of various guidelines by the government or the RBI on internal administration of the banks proposed.
* Duality of control over the banking system should go. RBI should be responsible for its regulation.
* Appointment of other executives of the banks and boards should be depoliticised.

(b) Development Financial Institutions (DFIs)

* IDBI should retain only its apex and refinancing role.
* Privileged access of DFIs to concessional finance should be phased out in three years.

(c) Capital Markets

* Substantial liberalisation of capital markets suggested with no need for any prior approval for new issues.

* SEBI to formulate a new set of guidelines designed to protect investors.
* Capital markets to be opened up to foreign portfolio investment gradually.
* New legislation suggested for mutual funds for providing appropriate level framework.

Narasimham Committee's approach to the subject of financial sector reforms was based on three broad and interrelated premises:

(i) the perception that the spirit of competitive efficiency should cover both real and financial sector of the economy;

(ii) to be able to perform this task effectively in a phenomenon of competitive efficiency, the financial system itself should be healthy and profitables; and

(iii) for the financial sector to operate on an efficient basis which would need to have a measure of operational flexibility and autonomy in decision-making and that credit and investment decisions should be based on professionalism and free from any type of extraneous pressure.

The recommendations cover policy aspects, organisational issues, accounting practices and operational procedures but underlying them all, is the central point of qualitative improvement of the portfolio and attention to enhancing the inherent strength of the institutions.

While sequencing of these measures have their own significance, an important pre-condition to be met before implementation is the establishment of an environment of macro stability. Financial reform calls for more nuances than simply "letting the market work". It would be wise to move gradually and improve the fundamentals, until certain basic conditions are met. Reforming the financial system should be thought of as a process, not an event, both because government enact reforms in stages and since institutions take substantial time to adjust. Financial system development is usually accompanied by changes in regulatory climate. Regulatory intervention can be justified in terms of perceived externalities, market failures and impediments to transact. But restrictive regulation can help vested interests to preserve entry barriers and to suppress competition. Hence intervention must be discriminating.

Reform of the Financial Sector: Follow-up Action

The ongoing financial sector reforms are designed to make the financial sector more viable and more efficient. The major policy thrust is to improve its operational and allocative efficiency. India's financial sector reform programmes primarily focuses on the banking industry and aims broadly at four issues (C. Rangarajan, 1994).

(i) To correct and improve the macro-economic policy setting within which banks operate. This mainly involves rationalisation of interest rates, redesigning directed credit programmes, and bringing down the levels of resource pre-emptions.

(ii) To improve the financial health and condition of banks, by recapitalising banks, restructuring the weaker ones and improving the incentives under which banks function.

(iii) To build financial institutions and infrastructure relating to supervision, audit technology and legal framework.

(iv) To improve the level of managerial competence and the quality of human resources by reviewing the policies relating to recruitment, training, placement, etc.

Underlying this process has been the prescription of prudential norms and regulations, directed to ensure the safety and soundness of the financial system, bring about greater transparency and accountability in operations and restoring the credibility of and confidence in the Indian financial system. Most significantly, however, prudential norms and ratios are aimed at (a) bringing out the true position of a bank's loan portfolio; and (b) help arrest its deterioration. These ratios are designed to classify credit according to risk, define delinquent loans and to provide against them. Financial sector reform thus has many dimensions. What should be the set of priorities for financial sector reform? "The reform measures cannot be put through without pain or without waging relentless struggle against the interests affected". The process of financial liberalisation is going to be more long-drawn out than what most people imagine and that it will, of necessity, be a somewhat untidy and oscillating affair (I.G. Patel, 1993).

While the major emphasis of the financial sector reforms has been on the banking system, it must not remain confined to it in its coverage. Although the banking system is the major element of India's rapidly growing financial system, it is only one of the elements. Improved functioning of the other segments has to go hand in hand with banking sector reforms. The supervisory control will soon be extended to fully cover non-bank finance companies and financial institutions. Already the norms relating to income recognition, provisioning and capital adequacy have been made applicable to these institutions as well. The form of the capital market which has grown exponentially over the last fifteen years also is an important element of the financial sector reform. The major emphasis in this area is to put in place regulations and surveillance system which protects the interests of the investors and improves the operational functioning of the securities markets so as to ensure efficiency of their resource allocation function. The Securities and Exchange Board of India (SEBI), which is the main supervisory authority of the capital market has been strengthened as a statutory body vested with necessary powers.

Narasimham Committee II (1998) Prescription

The Narasimham Committee II on banking reforms has recommended the merger of strong public sector banks, selective closure of weak banks, separation of the regulatory and supervisory power now vested with the Reserve Bank and an increase in capital adequacy levels. The committee has also recognised the practice of universal banking–erasing the distinction between development finance institutions and commercial banks. Its major recommendation pertain to:

* Encourage bank mergers
* Selectively close weak banks
* Don't merge weak banks into strong banks, focus on rationalising staff strengths and branches
* Create two to three large banks with international structure; eight to ten national banks; and a large number of regional and local banks
* Increase capital adequacy levels
* Integrate NBFCs into the financial system
* Stop harassment of bank staff by vigilance officials
* Separate ownership and management of banks; depoliticise bank appointments
* Separate the RBI's regulatory and supervisory functions
* Step up legal reforms
* Reconsider an Asset Reconstruction Fund to deal with NPA backlog

The Narasimham Committee-II recognised that with greater volatility and higher risks in the environment, legal impediments to loan recoveries and weaknesses in accounting standards, banks' balance sheets need protection. Thus, the committee concluded that the capital to risk assets ratio (CRAR) needs to be set at a higher level than in developed countries. While recognising that a one-size-fits all approach was not appropriate and that market risks need to be assessed, the committee felt that Indian banks were unlikely to be able to put in place their own internal risk management models. It, therefore, recommended an increase in the CRAR from eight per cent to ten per cent in two stages in the years 2000 and 2002. The RBI should further raise the CRAR for individual banks where the risk profile so warrants an increase. The CRAR should be implemented with the same rigour as the cash reserve ratio and there should be penal provisions for banks which do not maintain the prescribed CRAR (S.S. Tarapore, 1998).

With the problem of non-performing assets (NPAs) of banks and financial institutions assuming serious proportions, the role of the Board for Industrial and Financial Reconstruction (BIFR) and Sick Industrial Companies Act (SICA) has come under attack from many experts. At the end of 1998-99, the gross NPAs of the banking sector exceeded Rs. 58,000 crores. Of this, the industrial units including SSIs, accounted for about Rs. 16,000 crores.

According to many experts, the BIFR has become a shelter for unscrupulous entrepreneurs to stop the recovery process by banks, FIs and the tax authorities. Bulk of the NPAs of banks can be traced to fraudulent diversion of funds by the promoters. Since the launch of economic liberalisation and financial sector reforms, banks and financial institutions are under tremendous pressure to bring down their non-performing assets so as to improve their performance and profitability. The NPAs arise basically because of the inability or unwillingness of the borrowers to repay the loans advanced by banks and financial institutions. A rise in NPAs results in higher operational costs and erosion of capital forcing the institutions to keep their lending rates high. To enable the public sector banks to improve their capital-to-risk-assets ratio (CRAR), the Union Government has so far injected Rs. 20,000 crores into them. However, despite some improvement, the NPAs of banks and financial institutions continue to remain unacceptably high. The gross non-performing assets of public sector banks as a ratio of gross advances were as high as 23.2 per cent in 1991-92. Through higher provisioning, etc., this ratio was brought down to 15.9 per cent in 1998-99.

However, according to many experts, even now the real NPAs are much higher than what is shown in the balance sheets. It is time that the Government takes a fresh look at the prevailing weaknesses in the system to tackle this problem. The project appraisal and monitoring departments in banks and financial institutions are in need of a major revamp to ensure that the loans and advances are based purely on the viability and profitability of projects.

Non-performing Assets (NPAs) reflect the true extent of contamination of portfolios. No doubt part of the NPAs may have been a result of bankers ineptitude or bonafide decisions going wrong: but a substantial chunk can perhaps be attributed to political meddling which polluted the repayment ethos. Analytically, the backlog of NPAs are part of the historical baggage which Public Sector Banks (PSBs) are carrying and these need to be treated differently, rather than adopting an omnibus approach. In fact, in terms of incrementals, NPAs during the period 1993-94 to 1996-97 work out to only 3 or 4 per cent. This has important implications for evolving modalities to tackle NPAs. The point is that for evolving any meaningful policy to tackle NPAs, these need to be analysed in a disaggregated manner, instead of crying hoarse over the total dimensions of NPAs (N.A. Majumdar, 1998).

The Narasimham Committee Report II recommends the setting up of Assets Reconstruction Committees (ARCs) to help some of the weak banks to tackle the problem of NPAs. These companies are different from the Assets Reconstruction Fund (ARF) recommended earlier. The ARF was to have been funded by the budget, but the ARCs are expecetd to take over the NPAs of banks at realisable value and swap them with special bonds guaranteed by the government, which will not finance the purchase of NPAs. The underlying idea is that ARC should emerge as a commercially viable institution. The best agency to clean up NPAs is the concerned bank itself and the bank's board should be the final arbitrator in these matters.

In the Indian situation, rural credit is an integral part of the financial system and there can be no meaningful discussion on financial sector reforms without encompassing rural credit institutions, including the co-operative credit system. The committee "recognises the imperative need to maintain adequate flow of credit to these (agriculture and small industrial) sectors". The committee also recognises the need for small and marginal farmers as well as micro-entrepreneurs requiring small loans which has to be met to make them competitive and efficient. There are some eminently sensible recommendations: that the dual control over cooperative credit institutions by the state government and RBI/NABARD be eliminated and all co-operative banking institutions be brought under the Banking Regulations Act under the aegis of RBI/NABARD. The committee also recognises the need for banking policy to facilitate evolution of cost-effective system for banking for the poor, with satisfactory linkages with NGOs. The committee commends a move to universal banking, development banks played a critical role promoting basic and export industries, small industries, and housing. In India both IDBI and NABARD have a good track record and hence there is merit in commercial banks and development banks confining their operations to their specialised areas—short-term and long-term credit respectively. What is good for developed countries need not be necessarily good for developing countries.

Granting of autonomy to individual banks, distancing the bureaucracy from the management of PSBs, improving the work ethic in banks and motivating the staff—these should form the essential components of the reform package. The somnolent rural credit delivery system needs to be overhauled. The growth ingredient should be reintroduced in the algorithm of utilisation of the banking sector's resources. PSBs should reinvent themselves by dirtying their hands with the business of development, by lending credit support aggressively to the high growth segments of the economy. Addressing these core issues, which have become systemic, alone can ensure the healthy growth of the banking system not privatisation, nor the accountant's approach of raising capital adequacy ratios, or higher provisioning (N.A. Majumdar, 1998).

Conditions for the Success of Financial Sector Reforms

The government, however, must create the conditions, which will at least give the banks a fighting chance to survive. These could be:

(i) rationalisation of directed lending,

(ii) freeing of product pricing,

(iii) freedom to each banks to determine its own personnel policy, including recruitment, and

(iv) put into effect the recommended financial sector reforms.

The immediate task now is to weed out the weak elements and features, consolidate the progress and hasten slowly in the matter of future growth of the financial machinery. India has all the expertise but what is required for this to be achieved is strong political will. The financial sector reform in India is an integral part of the overall programme of economic reforms aimed at improving productivity and efficiency. Financial sector will be successful only if it accompanies by fiscal consolidation, moderate inflation and no sharp appreciation in the real effective interest rate. The Indian financial sector reform has gone hand in hand with fiscal reform, trade reform and exchange rate reform. The three major building blocks of the financial sector reform in India have been :

(i) removing or relaxing the external constraints;

(ii) introduction of prudential norms; and

(iii) institutional strengthening.

The chief merit of the reform process has been the cautious sequencing of reforms and the consistent and the mutually reinforcing character of the various measures taken. Even as the new prudential norms are being introduced, the capital base of the banks has been strengthened and organizational improvements are being put in place.

Improving the profitability and viability is only one aspect of enhancing the performance of banks. The other is how adequately and satisfactorily banks are able to meet the demands of customers. The competitive pressures are on the rise and banks must be able to meet these challenges. In trying to bring about changes in the banking system, care has also been taken to ensure that the social content of lending is not reduced. Banks and term lending institutions are legitimate instruments of social and economic change. What is necessary is to ensure that social responsibility is balanced with the needs to ensure the viability of the institutions. The stipulation relating to priority sector credit and the prescription of two concessional rates for small borrowers are intended to ensure that the needs of certain sectors are adequately met. Through these reform measures, we are laying the foundation for an efficient and a well-functioning banking system. A renewed and a reinvigorated banking system can play an important role in accelerating economic growth. Banking is on the threshold of a second revolution. It has, however, miles to go (C. Rangarajan, 1994).

India's financial system faces six interrelated challenges and concerns in its second phase of financial reforms:

(i) reducing the fiscal deficit,

(ii) improving banks' credit and risk management,

(iii) improving systems for identifying and dealing with banks,

(iv) developing capital markets further,

(v) improving financial services, and

(vi) managing links to external capital markets.

Improving financial services in banking and capital markets, as well as insurance, would yield substantial benefits for Indian firms and households and meet the challenges of the on-going globalisation of financial services. As regards the issues in banking reforms, bringing prudential norms up to international standards is only one part of the reform agenda. The more difficult part is to change the way banks function in practice so that their performance comes up to the more demanding requirements of the new regulatory environment. A more open economy also implies greater volatility in exchange rates and interest rates and banks will have to allow for the direct impact of these uncertainties on their balance sheets because of their own exposure and also the indirect effect via the impact on their client. As such, Dr. Montek Singh Ahluwalia favours moving towards privatisation of public sector banks accompanied by improved regulation and supervision because Government ownership leads to politicisation and bureaucratisation of banking.

S.S. Tarapore makes out a strong case for a further drastic reduction in CRR and says: "A high CRR is a heavy tax on the banking system and distorts the cost of funds as well as deployment". The problem of non-performing assets of the banking sector is perhaps the most worrisome aspect in the second stage of the reform. He emphasises the need for a real qualitative improvement with larger proportion of recoveries rather than write-offs of bad debts. For the problem of weak banks, Tarapore argues in favour of the concept of narrow banking as suggested by the Committee on Capital Account Convertibility headed by him. The concept of a narrow bank implies that depending on the degree of weakness there should be control on the growth of risk assets. In this context, Tarapore also favours a break up of the monolithic structure of public sector banks and the discontinuation of uniform norms for personnel policies, including recruitment and wage policies, upgradation of technology, risk management, and branch network.

It is rightly pointed out that the changes introduced so far have not translated into strong, sustained performance. Also, the improvements have been limited to a few large public sector banks, with endemically weak banks continuing to under-perform. Structural impediments such as overmanning, trade-unionism and lack of administrative autonomy, continue to hinder the efficient functioning of public sector banks. According to S. Venkitaramanan, one should elaborate on regulation and supervision issues relating to banks and non-banks. According to him there is a need to develop a framework, which involves more autonomy with greater accountability. The system of specialised institutions providing specialised services to particular categories of borrowers/industry segments has been disappearing. During the post-liberalisation period there has been a gradual convergence of activities of banks and financial institutions. However, a move towards universal banking is expected to take some time.

Financial Reform and the Union Budget-2000-01

The budget has announced that the minimum government holding in nationalised banks would be reduced from 51 per cent to 33 per cent. This would be brought about without changing the public sector character of banks and fresh issues of shares would be widely held by the public. There has been legitimate criticism that in the absence of induction of strategic partners, the banks would not be able to raise fresh capital at large premia. The shares of such banks and financial institutions as have gone to the market are languishing at well below the issue price and investors are not likely to be enthused. The budget has also accepted the Narasimham Committee recommendation on autonomy of boards of banks, but banks have to earn autonomy and take it and not expect it to be given (S.S. Tarapore, 2000).

On the weak banks, it is not clear how a modified bank-wise Financial Restructuring Authority (FRA) would work. The government constitutes the boards of banks and as such could reconstitute the boards; hence the need for supersession is not clear. There is no provision in the budget for recapitalisation of weak banks and any recapitalisation should be undertaken in a transparent manner with conscious and specific parliamentary approval and not surreptitiously smuggled through as a fait accompli towards the end of the financial year as has been done in the past. Recapitalisation of banks is a drain on the fisc and money poured in by government into the weak banks is sheer money down a bottomless pit (S.S. Tarapore, 2000).

The demand for autonomy, which is a central component of financial reform, assumes that once relieved of the task of financing the government's deficit, the RBI would be 'free' to use monetary policy as a device to control inflation, manage the balance of payments, and influence growth. The two inter-related means to realising these objectives are seen as controlling liquidity and influencing interest rates. Needless to say, there are strong grounds for scepticism regarding the efficacy of this policy. The limited success of the Central Bank in its effort at bringing down interest rates and trigger growth, is a case in point. Despite easing liquidity conditions through a variety of means, including periodic reductions in the cash reserve ratio, and despite reducing the bank rate or the interest rate charged on bank borrowing from the RBI, interest rates in India have proved quite sticky. This has forced the Government to reduce the interest rate on small savings and provident funds, in order to induce individual savers to move towards lower interest fixed deposits and the stock market. It is the Government, rather than the Central Bank, which is at the forefront of the drive to reduce interest rates.

But that is not all. The financial reform has hardly increased the autonomy of the Central Bank, since it not merely involves curbing the government's borrowing from the RBI, but also liberalising regulation of capital flows into and out of the country. Since such flows are extremely volatile, the Central Bank is constantly forced to adjust to these 'autonomous' capital movements. Since an increase in the Central Bank's foreign assets increases high-powered money and therefore the supply of money, monetary policy remains solely concerned with neutralising the effects of foreign capital inflows. Relieved of the dominance of fiscal over monetary policy, the RBI now finds itself straitjacketed by international finance. These are symptoms of the fact that the overall interests of international finance have come to dominate economic policy-making in India. And it is that dominance which has put the Government in a state of paralysis with respect to triggering growth and reducing poverty. (C.P. Chandrasekhar and Jayati Ghosh, 2000).

Conclusion

Academicians have now rediscovered the virtues of finance. They recognise that the quality of investment decisions improves when financial intermediaries disseminate information to economic agents. Risks of investment can be lowered by a diversified portfolio. Costs of capital can be lowered if the financial system provides a wide range of options for spreading risks. The stability of a financial system can be a source of confidence in an economy.

There has been a considerable expansion of the financial system in the last five decades. The Indian financial system has widened and deepened greatly and has demonstrated considerable ability for mobilising savings and meeting the needs of agriculture, industry and trade all over the country. A distinct feature of the Indian financial system is the dominance by public sector institutions whether it be in the area of banking or term lending or insurance. Motivated by socio-economic considerations, the system has also been subject to a high degree of regulation.

The growing size of the financial sector, the blurring of distinctions between the activities of banks and non-banks and the development of a continuum from the short end of the market to the long, underline the need for an integrated view of financial developments and for extending the scope of oversight by the Central Bank of the country. Efficient financial intermediation is an important factor contributing both to stabilisation and economic development. The market for financial services has to deepen and strengthen. Successful and sustainable adaption, to reform, will be conditioned by two factors: (i) nature of the financial sector reform policies, and (ii) appropriateness of the strategies pursued by banks and financial institutions. The major policy thrust is to improve the operational and allocative efficiency of the financial system as a whole by correcting many of the exogenous and structural factors affecting the performance of financial institutions. These reforms should help financial institutions to act as autonomous business units, fully responsible for their performance.

Financial reform, in all its diverse forms, is timely because of the widespread distress in the financial sector and because with funds scarce, authorities are concerned about the mobilisation and efficient allocation of resources in what is perceived as an increasingly risky environment. Thus, a gradual, but sustained, reform process appears desirable. But in concluding, one must point out that norms and rules will not do if the political leadership does not eschew a course of populism.

REFERENCES

1. Chandrasekhar, C.P. and Jayati Ghosh (2000), "Financial Reform and Budget", *Business Line,* March 7.
2. D'Souza, Errol (2000), "Prudential Regulation in Indian Banking", *Economic and Political Weekly,* January 29.
3. Ghosh, D.N. (1993), "Priorities for Financial Sector Reform", *Economic and Political Weekly,* February 20-27.
4. Government of India (1991), *Report of the Committee on the Financial System (Narasimham Committee),* Department of Economic Affairs (Banking Division), Ministry of Finance.
5. Government of India (1993), *Public Sector Commercial Banks and Financial Sector Reform: Rebuilding for a Better Future,* Department of Economic Affairs, Ministry of Finance.
6. Government of India (1998), *Report of the Committee on Banking Sector Reforms,* Department of Economic Affairs (Banking Divison), Ministry of Finance.
7. ————: *Economic Survey. Various Issues,* Department of Economic Affairs, Economic Division, Ministry of Finance.
8. Kulkarni, P.B. (1998), Banking Sector Reforms, Journal of *Indian School of Political Economy,* October-December.
9. Mallhotra, R.N. (1989), *Changing Practices of Central Bank Supervision,* Lacture on the occasion of 125 Anniversary of Allahabad Bank, Calcutta, December.
10. Malhotra, R.N. (1994), Reforming the Financial Sector, *11th C.D. Deshmukh Memorial Lecture,* India International Centre, New Delhi, January.
11. Majumdar, N.A. (1998), Banking Sector Reforms: Second Coming, *Economic and Political Weekly,* November 21.

12. Narasimham, M. (1992), Financial Sector Reform, *Sir Purshotamdas Thakurdas Memorial Lecture, 1991*. The Indian Institute of Bankers, Bombay, January 16.

13. Narasimham, M. (1993), *Financial Sector Reforms: The Unfinished Agenda,* The A.D. Shroff Memorial Trust, Bombay.

14. Patel, I.G. (1993), Some Reflections on Financial Liberalisation: *Sir Purshotamdas Thakurdas Memorial Lecture.* The Indian Institute of Bankers, Bombay, December 17.

15. Rangarajan, C. (1994), The Reform of the Financial Sector: Choices and Lessons *(Y.B. Chavan Memorial Lecture,* December 30).

16. Reserve Bank of India (1999), Some Aspects and Issues Relating to NPAs in Commercial Banks, *RBI Bulletin,* July.

17. Tarapore, S.S. (1998), Thank God for Prudential Norms, *Business Standard,* July 24.

18. Tarapore, S.S. (2000), As good as it gets, *Business Standard,* March 3.

8

INDIAN AGRICULTURAL EXPORT PERFORMANCE AND THE EMERGING WORLD TRADING SYSTEM: PROSPECTS AND CHALLENGES

S.A.R. Bilgrami

India's signing of GATT agreements in 1994 and joining of WTO as a founder member has put its agriculture into the framework of global competition. The emerging world trading system aims at opening up of the economy for active participation and free play of world market forces to attain sustainable growth. This refers the end of an era of protectionism and the beginning of an era of competition, maximum freedom and openness and of continuous improvement of efficiency. Many aspects of the rural economy, directly or indirectly, are going to be influenced by the incorporation of various clauses of GATT and WHO agreement. Some important ones are:

(i) agreement on gradual reduction in agricultural input subsidies;

(ii) elimination of export subsidies;

(iii) provision of minimum market access;

(iv) devamping of the public distribution system;

(v) the agreement on trade related intellectual property rights; and

(vi) elimination of tariff and non-tariff barriers to trade to make it more free.

This is a big challenge for the Indian agriculture which is heavily subsidised and has shown the progress under protectionist planning. Openness calls for efficiency-based competition which, in turn, demand for well-knit infrastructural facilities, institutional support and development of research and technology. Where does Indian agriculture stand is a relevant question which should be carefully examined. In this paper an attempt is made to examine the export potentialities of Indian agriculture in relation to expected influences of emerging world trading system. This chapter is divided into four major parts. Section I, presents agricultural export performance during pre- and post-reform period. Section II presents the optimistic side of the globalisation. Section III gives a critical evaluation of the optimistic view and presents a case study of Punjab and Haryana's wheat and rice exports. Section IV offers some concluding remarks.

Section–I

Indian Agricultural Exports Scenario

During Pre-and Post-Reform Period: Agricultural economy in the rest of the world may interact in several ways. Firstly, it participates in international trade by way of exports and imports. Level of production, prices, income, consumption, savings and investment all are affected by the nature, magnitude and direction of the export-import flows of goods and services pertaining to it.

Secondly, the free regime of foreign trade provide ample opportunities to foreign firms to invest in a big way on modern farming activities based on organic practices and also on agro-based industries. Horticulture, floriculture, fruit-pulp industries, frozen vegetables and fast-food industries are some of the most attractive areas. The work-culture and investment pattern of these foreign firms generate a new cuiture which create new conflicts between traditionalist and modernist farmers. Implications of these conflicts in relation to socio-economic and cultural setting need to be analysed. The new culture shown by foreign investors may boost many large domestic private investors to enter into new ventures and hence the rural-urban gap may reduce sharply. The fear of being marginalised is also paramount. The real benefits will be garnered by the foreign investors and the Indian farmer's position will become akin to that of a middle-man.

Thirdly, the new rules and disciplines that are envisaged under WTO have great relevance for the rural economy. Trade Related Investment Measures (TRIMS), Trade Related Intellectual Property Rights (TRIPS) and the agreements on agriculture, sanitary and phytosanitary measures and services, when fully implemented, would bring about radical changes in the national economy. In this process, the rural economy will come across both challenges and opportunities. The second and third part of the chapter concentrate on this aspect with special attention to agricultural trade.

Table 8.1

India's Exports as Percentage of World Exports

1960-61	1.05
1970-71	0.65
1980-81	0.42
1990-91	0.58
1991-92	0.55
1992-93	0.56
1993-94	0.62
1994-95	0.64
1995-96	0.67
2000-01	0.83

Source: Tata Services, Statistical outline of India 1996-97 table 101 p. 95.

The Indian agricultural export performance since the beginning of planning has been very disappointing. It is the reflection of the over all export performance. India's export as the percentage of the world export during 1960-61 to 1995-96 (Table 8.1) has never been one per cent except in the year 1960-61, when it was slightly exceeded to 1.05 per cent. Although in value term, the total exports (Table 8.2) shows a sharp increase from Rs. 284 crores in 1960-61 to Rs. 487 crores in 1970-71, Rs. 2057 crores in 1980-81, Rs. 6317 crores in 1990-97 and Rs. 13712 crores in 1994-95, the percentage share to total exports shows a continuous sharp decline from 44.2 per cent in 1960-61 to 16.6 per cent 1994-95. Table 8.3 provides the detail information. Eleven major agricultural export commodities have been investigated during the pre- and post-reform period covering the years 1970 to 1995. The export of the most of the commodities in absolute term shows a continuous increase upto 1993. During 1993 and 1995 it gives a mixed picture. While the export of cereals and cereal preparations, rice, sugar, tea and meat, tobacco has been decreased, the export of vegetable and fruits, coffee and coffee preparation, fish and fish preparation, leather and textile yarn recorded an increasing trend upto 1994. The year 1995 again presented a declining trend.

Table 8.2
Exports of Agricultural Commodities

(Rs. in Crores)

Total Exports and Productwise breakup	*1960-61*	*1970-71*	*1980-81*	*1990-91*	*1994-95*	*1997-98*
	284 (44.2)	487 (31.7)	2,057 (30.7)	6,317 (19.4)	13,712 (16.6)	23,691 (18.8)
Coffee	7	25	214	252	1053	1622
Tea and Mate	124	148	426	1070	975	1506
Cashew Kernets	19	57	140	447	1247	1384
Spices	17	39	11	239	612	1408
Raw Cotton	12	14	165	846	140	840
Fish and Fish preparations	5	31	217	960	3537	4313
Processed Foods, fruits, vegetable etc.	7	15	116	429	888	1029

Figures in brackets indicate percentage share to total Exports.
Source: Ibid, table 103, p. 97.

The declining trend of India's share of these commodities in the world trade has been quite alarming. Cereals and cereal preparations during 1970 to 1993 improved from 0.1 per cent to 1.0 per cent but dropped to 0.9 per cent level in 1994 and further to 0.6 per cent in 1995. During pre- and post- reform period as a whole it never exceeded one per cent of the world trade. The export of vegetable and fruit is a slight better. Its share in the world trade was 1.2 per cent in 1970, 1.5 per cent in 1975 and then fell to 1.1 per cent in 1980 and recorded a slight increase to 1.4 per cent in 1985. In 1990 it shows a substantial fall from 1.4 per cent to 0.8 per cent and then a continues but slow improvement from 0.9 per cent in 1992, 1.0 per cent in 1993 and 1.7 per cent in 1994. In 1995 it was only 1.0 per cent. Sugar, coffee and coffee preparations, tea and mate tobacco and leather give a very disappointing pictures. Their shares are more or less continuously decreasing. And if any commodity (Textile Yarn) has shown any improvement during the period 1994-95, it has been only nominal. Tea and leather are the glaring examples of a continuous sharp decline. The share of tea in the world export was substantially high (33.4 per cent) in 1970. It fell to 31.3 per cent in 1975, 27.7 per cent in 1980, 26.2 per cent in 1985, 22.1 per cent in 1990, 16.1 per cent in 1992, 13.8 per cent in 1993 and further 13.6 per cent in 1994. It was merely 11.2 per cent in 1995. The position of leather is not different. It fell from 13.4 per cent in 1970 to 0.3 per cent in 1992. During 1993 and 1995 it remained almost constant at some improved level 3.3 per cent in 1994 and further 3.4 per cent in 1995.

The agricultural export performance, as presented above, may never be called satisfactory. In absolute terms, Indian agricultural exports show a substantial increase, but in comparison to world performance, it stands at the bottom of the list. It means that in terms of productivity, efficiency and competitiveness the other nations are far ahead of India. Their rate of growth of exports is fast enough to keep developing economies like India, despite their expansion in exports, on the lowest side of the rate of growth. This is an alarming situation where sincere efforts are needed for the improvement of efficiency, quality and competitiveness. Since the signing of GATT agreements in 1994 and joining of WTO, various studies have been made to examine and analyse the impact of these agreements on Indian agricultural exports performance. The major areas of impacts which have been examined are :

(a) Impacts of reduction in tariff and non-tariff barriers to trade and elimination of subsidies on major agricultural inputs such as fertilisers irrigation water, power, etc. as well as of food distribution will boost or reduce our agricultural exports. These provisions will make the world market freer and more competitive. Who will be benefited most is a question which should be carefully and thoroughly examined.

(b) Trade between the two countries basically depends upon the comparative advantage. In the emerging trading system, the traditional factors of measuring comparative advantages such as wages, labour, raw-material, cost and price are getting reduced. Instead, access to knowledge and uptodate information, continuous upgrading of technology and ability to create new horizons of knowledge are more significant and effective determinants of comparative advantage. In comparison to developed countries where does India stands? This is a question that needs a careful analysis.

(c) With these agreements, capital mobility would become freer than labour mobility. Hence, the MNCs and capital rich countries would have greater scope in the world market than the developing countries with huge man-power resources. This is also an important aspect of the impacts and needs investigation.

(d) The most controversial part is the agreement on Trade Related Intellectual Property Rights (TRIPS),

Basmati rice is a recent example where the Indian rice exports have encountered a serious setback. It has been realised that this agreement, with prevailing outdated patent rights, will certainly adversely effect our established agricultural exports like rice, natural medicines, fruits, etc. Arguments are given in favour and against the agreements. The following two sections present both the sides of the coin.

Section–II

An Optimistic Outlook: It has been observed that India has tremendous inherent export potential in agriculture due to vast diversity of products and varied agro-climatic conditions. The Commerce Ministry which represented the country in prolonged negotiations of the GATT accord feels that it would result in significant expansion in world trade in agricultural commodities. India, according to Commerce Ministry, "should be able to increase its own exports by 1.5 to 2 billion US dollars annually in addition to the normal growth". This estimate is based on the assumption that reduction in export subsidies on agriculture by the developed countries would make Indian agricultural exports more competitive in the world market. Despite strong reservations of improving rice, countries like Japan and South Korea, after-all agreed to allow market access for rice to other exporting countries. Various agricultural commodities including sugar which have been subsidised by many countries would now find a place in the international market.[1]

Indian agricultural exports before GATT accord were confined to only few traditional commodities such as tea and coffee, few selected fruits, dry-fruits, leather and leather products and some species, etc. After GATT accord, this basket has been substantially widened. Indian grapes have found their way to the dinning tables in European homes. There are several other fruits and vegetables such as banana, guava, *chikoo, lychee, ber,* onion, potato, bitter gouard, tomato which India can manage to have an edge over its competitors in the export market. With a conscious efforts towards export-oriented production, improvement in export marketing management, upgrading of technology and more investment in the areas where India has an edge over the other players in the world market, it can easily improve its export performance. The trend of export expansion shows that after the implementation on GATT accord, Indian agricultural exports would enter into the more attractive European Community market besides the countries like Malaysia, Singapore and Japan.[2]

Floriculture is another area where India has shown a tremendous potential for export earnings. Private sector has demonstrated an impressive success. A private sector companies annual report reveals that "the initial response from both Japan as well as European markets has been quite overwhelming. They bag the orders of top Japanese companies who have selected flowers on regular shipment basis".[3] Floriculture is a hi-tech venture which needs high investment with sophisticated technology. Government provides full support in this direction. The impetus for accelerated growth in agricultural exports, as the Economic Survey reveals, "is envisaged through enhanced infrastructural support and by building up a conducive policy environment". These conducive policy environment includes, "lowering of import duties on capital goods particularly for green-house equipment and plant and machinery necessary for food processing industries as well as easier availability of credit exports". Besides, "market determined exchange rate policy" and the removal of "some of the restrictions on agricultural exports" have also helped in boosting the farm exports.[4]

This has been strongly argued by the IMF and some eminent economists[5] that the agricultural subsidies on major inputs such as fertilizers, irrigation water and electricity have added to the budget deficit in a big way and have distorted the choice of technology in agricultural practices. The "protectionist" approach is, therefore, neither helpful in improving production and productivity nor it is helping in maintaining social justice and equity. Subsidies are the burden, a source of inflation and a constraint on efficiency. Hence, they must go. Agriculture, on an average, will be benefited from their removal instead of being harmed incentivewise. This aspect has created various controversies and has been widely criticised. The question of subsidies has been widely criticised. The question of subsidies has been widely investigated and the Aggregate Measures of Support (AMS) for the product and non-product specific subsidies has been examined by the experts. Government's point of view is that we are within comfortable limits and hence there is no adverse effect of reducing or eliminating subsidies. For developing countries "a limit of ten per cent has been stipulated separately for these two kinds of subsidies below which there is no obligation to make any reduction. Those who have aggregate measure of support in excess of ten per cent are required to reduce the present level of domestic support by twenty per cent". Further, "the expenditure on general government services are also excluded from the perview of calculating AMS". The calculation made by the Commerce Ministry reveals that the AMS for non-specific subsidies (fertilizers, credit, electricity and irrigation water) in India works out to be between around three to six per cent. Further the agreement also provide exemption from reduction commitment to input subsidies to low income and resource poor farmer. Hence AMS in the country would come to only around two per cent".[6]

The subsidised volume of exports is to be reduced by 21 per cent while the budgetary support for export subsidies in terms of value is to be cut down by 36 per cent for a period of six years from the date of enforcement of the new provisions. This would make goods of developed countries costlier and hence will improve the cost effectiveness of Indian product. The developed countries would also cut down agricultural subsidies beyond the 10 per cent level and this would further push up their cost of production. India is well within the prescribed limit and hence her cost competitiveness with developed countries will improve.[7]

GATT accord also provide the concessions in relation to internal transport and freight charges on export shipment. Accord says that during implementation period developing countries shall not be required to undertake commitments in respect of internal transport and freight charges on export shipment. It also reveals that provision of subsidies to reduce the cost of marketing exports of agricultural products including the cost of international transport and freight will not apply to the developing countries during this period.[8] These concessions will help to improve the competitiveness.

It has been realised by the critics that due to these accords the market access of capital-rich countries will increase and the developing countries whose market access is weak in comparison to developed countries will face tough competition. GATT reveals that market access can be restricted only for balance of payments consideration and not for protection of domestic agriculture. It means that such restriction on market access must be price-based so that all non-tariff measures including quantitative curbs would have to be converted into their tariff equivalents. In the beginning the minimum access to imports would be three per cent of the domestic consumption but this would be expanded to five per cent over a period of six years. For developing countries, however, the minimum market access would be less, that is, at two-third of others. Hence it would be two per cent in the beginning and it will go upto 3.3 per cent over a longer period of ten years. It has to be stipulated that the actual market access cannot at any stage be less than actual average imports.

Thus, with the reduction in the level of tariff duties, customs and subsidies the market access of agricultural products will increase. This will benefit the agricultural sector in terms of product diversification, income and employment. These provision will make agricultural product more competitive in the international market and will improve the efficiency. According to the world bank agricultural trade liberalisation policies adopted by the developing countries will benefit through improving the terms of trade, increasing trade efficiency and enhancing welfare effects through induced changes in tariffs revenues. The level of gains according to the world bank, depends upon the level of liberalisation.

Section–III

Challenges: This fact cannot be overlooked that the agricultural scenario, especially of agriculturally advanced states, is changing fast since the beginning of the reform era in 1991. Diversification of product, fast commercialisation, expanding food processing activities, agro-business based on frozen vegetable, fruits, pulps, horticulture, floriculture, fast-food etc. are affecting the socio-economic fabric of rural sector. Agro-based trade is, of course, new area which is gaining better markets abroad. Our agricultural exports as has been indicated in Table 8.3, shows a continuous growth in absolute term. But our share in the world market has been either stagnating or declining. There are items and that too in a few recent years which have shown a slight improvement. It means our efficiency and competitiveness have not been improved. These are the relative terms and when they are showing a declining trend despite showing growth in absolute terms it would mean that the rate of growth of other nations is fast moving upwards. Thus, our performance, despite all the favourable and optimistic view and arguments, remained not merely unsatisfactory but even alarming too.

Table 8.3

Agricultural Exports in Relation to Output

Item	*Year*	*Production*	*Exports*	*Exports as Percentage of Output*
Tea	1970-71	423	199.1	47.1
(Mn. kg.)	1980-81	568	229.2	40.4
	1990-91	705	199.1	28.2
	1994-95	777	151.45	19.5
Coffee	1970-71	71	32.2	45.4
(000 T)	1980-81	140	87.3	63.4
	1990-91	129	86.5	67.1
	1994-95	180	128.5	71.4

Item	*Year*	*Production*	*Exports*	*Exports as Percentage of Output*
Sugar	1970-71	3740	473.0	12.6
(000 T)	1980-81	5148	97.0	1.0
	1990-91	12047	191.0	1.6
	1994-95	14600	51.1	0.3
Tobacco	1970-71	362	49.8	13.8
(000 T)	1980-81	481	91.3	19.0
	1990-91	556	87.1	15.7
	1994-95	534	53.7	10.1
Raw Cotton	1970-71	4763	188.8	4.0
(000 Bales of	1980-81	7010	774.1	11.0
170 kg each)	1990-91	9842	2202.4	22.4
	1994-95	11760	415.9	3.5

Source : Ibid, Table 105, p. 99.

A recent study[9] investigated the export competitiveness of wheat and rice output of Punjab and Haryana. On the basis of cost and price it has been estimated that Indian products are not yet competitive. Indian wheat has been compared with the U.S. wheat and rice with the Thailand rice. Indian wheat export competitiveness of Punjab and Haryana has been estimated on the basis of following charges along with the procurement/market price during 1980-81 to 1993-94 :

(i) Market handling, grading, packing, market fee and taxes;

(ii) Local transport and strong charges;

(iii) Inland transport charges from the sales market to international port;

(iv) Storage charges for the product awaiting shipment;

(v) Transhipment charges;

(vi) Overseas transport and insurance cost;

(vii) Trader's margin; and

(viii) Local charges and taxes.

It has been estimated that in case of wheat, out of 13 years (1982-94) only for the year 1992 the ratio of Punjab wheat price to the US wheat was lower than 100, being 96.89 and 100.20 in 1989. For the rest of years this ratio was between 113.56 and 162.06. This means that Punjab wheat during the period under study has been costlier than the US wheat and hence it is less competitive.

In case of rice the competitiveness has been further effected adversely because production is area specific and in comparison to wheat two more processes : (i) transportation of paddy to mill point and drying out for milling purposes, and (ii) processing of the paddy to separate rice from the husk. The ratio of Punjab rice to the Thailand rice remained lower during new years of pre- and post-reform period, that is, in 1982 (96.08), 1988 (92.11), 1989 (85.02), 1990 (98.73), 1991 (76.52) and 1992 (84.22). In remaining years, the ratio was 102.24 to 137.71.

These results reveal that even Punjab and Haryana which show highest production and productivity within the nation lag behind the most of the developed countries. If these two most prosperous, fertile and technologically advanced states are not internationally competitive, the other states would be much less competitive in comparison to the advanced countries of the world. Further, the declaration of making *BASMATI* brand of rice a foreign patent has jolted our export prospects of *Basmati* rice. This brand of rice is our prestigious export item and have a well-established foreign markets abroad. Now this has been captured by a U.S. firm by patenting it in its similar name. This is a reward of openness and globalisation.

Tea is another alarming case. It is also traditionally important export item. Tea crop accounted for over 18 per cent of the total employment in the organised sector of the economy, 14 per cent of the country's export earning and 1.16 per cent of the GNP. The area under tea cultivation is 3.14 lakh hectares and has been a major source of development of backward regions of tea growing states. In 1950, India was the largest producer and exporter of tea in the world. India's exports' share (Table 8.3) in the world has been continuously declining sharply from 50 per cent in 1950 to 33.4 per cent in 1970, 22.1 per cent in 1990, 13.6 per cent in 1994 and again 11.2 per cent in 1995. It is almost one-fourth of 1950. The main reason behind this is that "there has been little effort in India to maintain or conserve good quality tea through replantation as the cost of replantation is relatively high compared to the loss in export revenue due to substituting exports by producing and marketing a lower quality of tea domestically".[10]

There are various important reasons of such poor state of export performance. Firstly, India constitute 17 per cent of the world population and accounts for 12 per cent of the total cereals and pulses production. It means that exportable surplus lies with developed countries and this is also certain that they are not exporting at the cost of domestic demand. Further, almost 30 to 40 per cent of the population in India live below the poverty line and due to acute income poverty they do not demand even the minimum food. Hence, the possibilities of export earning of developing countries are not bright. Secondly, developing countries do not have exportable surplus, specially of food grains, because of low soil fertility and input deficiency. The possibility of expanding area is almost negligible. Yield rate can only be increased by cropping intensity, technological revolution and scientific practices. Huge investment is needed in irrigation, seed, pesticides and mechanisation. Elimination or reduction of subsidies on key agricultural inputs and adoption of Intellectual Property Rights by the foreign firm for the seeds and "brands" of output will make them costly and non-competitive. This will also discourage investment of industries engaged in producing major agricultural inputs. Hence, reduction in subsidies and introduction of IPR both will not only discourage the incentives of the farmers but the incentives of the industrial sector as well.

Thirdly, the crop uncertainties due to vagaries of nature and perishability of most of agricultural commodities make the supply erratic. We have a weak technological backing for the conservation, protection, processing and handling. Few states like Punjab and Haryana have shown some improvement. But for the nation as a whole the technical status still remains backward. Hence, the shortages and the buffer-stocks both, due to bad and good harvest, destabilise the prices and earnings. This, in turn, also made our export earnings instable. The export earning instability leads to domestic instability and reduced efficiency. Further, instability in prices and earnings will bring more hardship to small and marginal farmers whose ratio in the total farming population is two-third.

Fourthly, the block-wise pattern of trade also goes against India. India has a geographical advantage with neighbouring countries, eastern half of African countries and Middle-East countries. The neighbouring countries such as Bangladesh, Sri Lanka, Maldiv and Pakistan and also the African countries are poor and cannot afford the imports of high valued cereal crops. On cost and price basis India is less competitive in comparison to European countries. Japan's trading advantage is attached with the USA and other financially sound Asian countries. European geographical advantage is attached with China, USA, Maxico and the Middle-East. India, has to depend mainly on Western Asia, neighbouring countries and former USSR for agricultural exports. Thus, globalisation and growing interdependency is not very fruitful for the countries like India.

Fifthly, the bulk of commodities marketed in the world are controlled and monitored by less than six multi-commodity traders of Wester-Europe, the USA and Japan. Table 8.4 gives the percentage control of such international traders. They dominate the world trade to the extent of 85 to 90 per cent. The opening up of trade of agriculture will expose the producers from developing countries to the operations of the giant trading companies. Their size of operation, financial clouts and sophisticated and specialised trading and marketing techniques have given them a strategically strong position. The developing countries would have been forced to enter into the deals with these trading companies. This would be a marginalisation of agricultural trade.[11]

Table 8.4

Corporate Control of Global Commodity Trade 1983

Commodity	*World Export ($ Million)*	*Percentae Marketed by 3-6 Largest Translational Traders*
Wheat	17851	85-90
Rice	3613	70
Sugar	10636	60
Tea	1844	80
Coffee	9636	85-90
Cotton	6567	85-90
Tobacco	4239	85-90
Jute	135	85-90
Natural Rubber	3321	70-75
Cocoa Bean	2051	85
Corn	9833	85-90
Bananas	1324	70-75
Pineapples	74	90
Forest Products	47255	90

Source: Frederic F.C. and John H.C., "World Commodities Trade: Changi Role of Giant Trading Companies, E.P.W., October 15, 1988.

Section–IV

Concluding Remarks. India's signing of GATT agreement in 1994 and joining of WTO as a founder member gives more challenges than the gains in agricultural export. The emerging world trading system calls for an opening up of the economy for active participation and free play of market forces to attain faster and sustainable rate of growth. Are the developing countries capable of facing the influx of foreign market forces due to this openness? Or are they able to enter, capture and establish the foreign markets in agricultural commodities? These are the central themes on which indepth discussion is needed.

In absolute terms our agricultural exports show a substantial growth. But when we compare it with the growth rate of other European countries, we note that our status either has remain unchanged or indicated a declining trend. In some cases (tea) it is continuously declining. If any improvement is realised in some commodities in some years that too is very insignificant. A case study of wheat and rice export of Punjab and Haryana also proves that till 1994, these commodities are not internationally competitive. When our most prosperous, fertile and technologically advance states are not competitive, the other states would be even much less competitive as compared to the advanced countries of the world. Our agricultural production, productivity and efficiency is low. Our technical level is low and whatever growth we have achieved that is "protected-growth". Removal of subsidies, the agreement on trade related Intellectual Property Rights, elimination of tariffs and provision of minimum market access opportunities will certainly put giant challenges before our agricultural sector. How a weak sector will face them is a serious question? No doubt, despite various criticisms, these agreements have been signed and proposal accepted. The only effort which is seriously needed at this juncture is to find out the way that could minimise the damages and maximise the gains. This can be done by improving and upgrading of technology and research, effective state intervention in the international trading of agricultural commodities and encouraging the establishment of cooperative of marketing, seeds, pesticides and other inputs so that the holds of multinationals could be kept to the minimum.

REFERENCES

1. Suds, "Gatt Accord and Agricultural Exports," *Yojana*, Independence Day Special, 1994.
2. *Ibid*.
3. See: *Al-Flah Times*, Quarterly Publication of Al-Flah Group, New Delhi, Sept. 1997.
4. GOI, Economic Survey 1996-97, p. 155.
5. See: World Development Reports and Bhagwati J. Srinivasan T.N., *India's Economic Reforms*, 1993, New Delhi.

6. Sud S, "Gatt Accord and Agricultural Exports," *op. cit.*
7. *Ibid.*
8. *Ibid.*
9. Gill S.S., Brar J.S., "Global Market and Competitive- ness of Indian Agriculture, Some Issues" *EPW*, August 19, 1996.
10. See Krishna Kumar T, Ashok Mittal, Trade Reforms for Agricultural Commodities in Developing Countries: Lessons and Experiences" In Azam K.J., *Economic Liberalisation in India* (ed) Delta Publication, Delhi 1997.
11. Gill K.K., Gill S.S., Agricultural Development and Industrialisation in Punjab: Some Issues Related to The Pepsi Model, *E.P.W.*, Nov, 10, 1990.

9

FINANCIAL SECTOR REFORMS IN INDIA AND FUTURE THREATS

Dr. Dev Raj

In the last more than *five decades since* Independence, Banking in India has evolved through four distinct phases, i.e. (1) Foundation phase from 1950s, 1960s and till 1969; (2) Expansion phase Mid 1960s (i.e. 1969 to 1984); (3) Consolidation phase 1985 to 1990; and (4) Reform phase from 1991 onwards. For preserving the soundness of Banking system in India, it was felt necessary in 1990s century that Banks/Financial Institutions should have effective risk management system, adequate capital provision, sound practices of supervision and regulation, transparency of operation, conducive Public Policy intervention, maintenance of macro-economic stability in the economy and so on.

The recent financial market developments reveal that we have come to live in a world of considerable uncertainty, where prudence and foresight get rewarded, while errors, inadequate judgements and bad decisions impose severe costs on the individual financial intermediary as well as on the financial environment, savers, investors and financial intermediaries are widely dispersed, not necessarily confined to domestic boundaries. This had made capital extremely fluid and highly sensitive to policies and performance of the financial system of the recipient countries. Pursuing policies and practices that ensured improved efficiency and continued stability of the Financial System has assumed critical importance in the present context of a more open World Economy.

World-wide experience confirms that countries with well-developed and market-oriented financial systems have grown faster and more steadily as compared to those with weaker and closely regulated systems. The financial sector in general and Banking system in particular in many of the developing countries have been plagued by various problems which necessitated drastic—structural changes as also a re-orientation of approach in order to move towards the development of a more efficient and well functioning financial system. The problems encountered in the way of efficient functioning necessitated the need for financial sector reforms in India.

The main functions of the Financial System are : payments system; pooling of resources and its transfer spatially and in time; risk management; information generation and management of incentives, accommodation of moral hazard, adverse selection and problems of asymmetric information.

The fast expansion and spread of the banking sector in India after 1969 and its subsequent growth have resulted in surfacing of several internal deficiencies in the system. Owing to those deficiencies, customer service was affected badly, work technology remained stagnant and the transaction cost went on increasing over the years. In spite of positive achievements and meeting various socio-economic goals, the banking system in India during 1980s, experienced several problems related mainly to the profitability and viability of banks. The Narasimham Committee-I observed that gross profits before provisions were no more than 1.10 per cent of Working Funds. This is a clear pointer to the low profitability of Indian Banks.

The major factors eroding the profitability of Indian Banks include higher SLR and CRR requirements, sick industrial advances, deterioration in the quality of assets, priority sector advances, export credit, food credit, political and administrative interference, etc. These factors contributed for low income realisation by Public Sector Banks. Similarly, the expenditure by banks kept a higher pace of increase particularly administrative costs, branch expansion of Public Sector Banks into Rural and Semi-urban areas, lack of improvement in operational methods and procedures, slower computerisation of various operation leading to higher transaction costs, etc. contributed to the lower profitability of Public Sector Banks.

Financial Banking Sector Reforms

When a country is liberalising its capital account, it has to face the challenges of strengthening its financial institutions to ensure their capable operation in a more market-oriented system. It has been observed in the past that capital controls have not prevented outflows of capital. When countries eliminate controls, they usually experience stronger inflows, at least initially, as International Investors and Residents who had placed their capital abroad react to the improved investment environment. Capital inflows can improve a country's balance of payments situation, smooth temporary shocks to income and consumption, reduce borrowing costs, and spur economic growth.

Thus, reforms in the Financial Sector are very much essential in the context of opening up of the Indian Economy through globalisation and liberalisation of policies relating to trade, exchange rate, industry, etc. To have a cohesive and strong financial system capable of responding to these changes in the economy, it becomes important to have a dynamic, autonomous and profitable Financial System.

The Committee under the Chairmanship of Mr. M. Narasimham which was set-up in August, 1991 has put forward various proposals relating to the structure, organisation, functions and procedures of the Financial system. Before, the implementation of Narasimham Committee's recommendations, the Public Sector Banks in India were facing the problems of lower profitability of operations, capital adequacy below two per cent and inadequate technology adoption in banks. To cope up with the International Standards the Public Sector Banks in addition to above were to improve in the area of dissemination of information, to adopt new technology, to improve the industrial technology assessment, to improve the appraisal system, to increase specialisation in both domestic and international operations, to improve the mechanisms for foreign postings and to have better interaction between foreign and Indian operations, product development in the context of globalisation of operations, etc. were the need of the Indian Banks.

Main Features of the Banking/Financial Sector Reforms

The main features of the Financial Sector Reforms in India were as under:

(i) Interest rate de-regulation.

(ii) Stimulating competition among financial institutions.

(iii) Fostering capital market.

(iv) Relaxation of foreign exchange controls.

(v) Contraction of informal finance.

vi) Improved supervision and regulation of financial institutions.

Moreover, mere launching of liberalisation and reforms, if not implemented properly and effectively and not supported by overall economic reforms, may not yield the desired results. The forces of competition, globalisation, deregulation of financial markets in several countries during the last one and a half decade, necessitated the Indian Banks to consider and implement the several strategy options, of which, the following are the main:

- Strengthening the capital base.
- Reorganisation and restructuring.
- Streamlining deposit insurance.
- Evolving better accounting practices.
- Improving quality of customer service.
- Pricing and better management of cost/income ratios.
- Managerial development/human resource development.

Capital Adequacy Concept

Until the acceptance of the Basle Accord, the term "Capital" referred to the owned funds of a bank comprising paid-up capital and disclosed free reserves. The Narasimham Committee recommended that by March, 1993 to attain CAR of four per cent and by March, 1994 envisaged for a eight per cent ratio of recognised capital to aggregate risk-weighted credit exposure. Further, it was envisaged that at least half of the recognised capital must be in form "CORE" (Tier I) capital which includes:

1. Disclosed reserves
2. Common stock, and
3. Non-cumulative Preferences Shares

The remainder (Tier 2) capital includes components such as:

1. Undisclosed Reserves
2. General Provisions
3. Asset Revaluation Reserves
4. Hybrid Capital Instruments, and
5. Subordinated Term Debt.

This served mainly two purposes as under:

(a) reflecting the promoters' stake in the enterprise and acting as a disincentive to them to take up higher risk-investments; and

(b) serving as a buffer to absorb adverse effects on a bank, of various risks.

At that time, the cause for concern of Indian Banks was of low capital base. Capital and reserves average about 1.5 per cent of assets in India, compared to four per cent in Korea and Pakistan and four to six per cent in Taiwan, Thailand and Singapore.

Prudential and Capital Adequacy Norms

The prudential norms relate to Income Recognition, Asset Classification, and Capital Adequacy. Fiscal consideration has been one of the main elements of the economic reform process. Prudential and Capital adequacy norms have been prescribed so as to ensure the safety and soundness of the Financial system and to import greater transparency and accountability in operations.

On the basis of recommendations of the Committee on Banking Sector Reforms (Narasimham Committee II), the RBI tightened regulations in the following areas:

1. Risk weight of 2.5 per cent to cover market risk in respect of Government securities and other approved securities by March 31, 2000.
2. Risk weight of 20 per cent for state government guaranteed advances which have been invoked and have remained in default as on 31.3.2000.
3. Application of provisioning norms in respect of advances granted w.e.f. April 1, 2000 against state government guarantee, where the guarantee is invoked and has remained in default for more than two quarters. Further, provisioning to be made in respect of advances guaranteed by State Governments which stood invoked as on March 31, 2000 to March 31, 2003 (minimum 25 per cent each year).
4. One hundred per cent risk weight to foreign exchange/gold open position limit with effect from March 31, 1999.

5. Reduction in the timeframe for treating assets in sub-standard category as doubtful assets from 24 months to 18 months by March 31, 2001.
6. General provision of 0.25 per cent for standard assets from the year ending March 31, 2000.

As a part of Financial Sector Reforms, the Reserve Bank of India (RBI) has introduced the internationally recognised prudential norms for Income Recognition, Asset Classification and Provisioning atleast partially in the beginning in 1992-93. RBI has also gradually reduced the Statutory Lending Requirements (SLR), deregulated the interest rates both on deposits and advances; brought in a regime of reasonable Capital Adequacy Ratio (CAR).

In the 1990s century the financial sector reforms, liberalisation, globalisation, deregulation, prudential accounting norms, capital adequacy and marked to market were introduced in the Banking and Financial sector on a gradual and consistent basis in India.

The moving from old to new business environment has created the demands on Indian Banks as under:

Old Business Environment	*New Business Environment*
- Labour intensive	- It enhanced work flow.
- Everything in house	- Motivation and control of Third Party Vendors with different countries.
- Customers face to face	- Customers remote/customers in control
- Customers response on a case by case basis	- Full access to customer purchasing habits. Profile matching requiring micro-marketing approach.

The new business environment demands a new set of skills as follows:

New Business Environment

1. In enhanced work flow	: It creates demand for literate and specialised workforce.
2. Third Party Vendors	: Distribution Managers Third Party Vendor Managers.
3. Fast Changing Remote	: Rapid Learning and Response.
4. Customer Remote	: Online Screen phone call centre skills.
5. Micro Marketing	: Data Analysis Interpretation skills.

Basic Principles of Reform

The basic principles of reforms cover rules for contents, bankruptcy, disclosure, protection for shareholders in securities, information needs, regulation for ensuring safety and soundness, promoting competition, consumer protection, promoting access to under-served group and incentives for enhancing franchise value in banks.

The Financial Banking Sector Reform in India

The post 1991 reforms - The Narasimham Committee I—internationalised the norms. It brought both prudential norms and the Capital Adequacy generally in line with the rest of the world. A necessary discipline at the time. In assessing the reform of the Indian Financial Sector, one has to take into consideration the inadequacies of the Legal System, the cult of prosecution, the culture of lending, the perverse effect of Capital Adequacy, the impact of procedure and behest lending.

Narasimham Committee II has recently addressed a number of vital issues pertaining to the health and stability of Financial System and the actions that are necessary to strengthen it. With the Narasimham Committee I and II, a considerable ground has been covered putting in place a financial system which can meet the requirements of a more competitive and open-economy. By and large, financial reforms in India have proceeded in the following four major directions:

(i) Helped in removing the operational constraints of the Financial System to some extent. The reform process has tried to lower the share of pre-emptied resources in the total resources of the banking system through gradual liberalisation of CRR and SLR.

(ii) Creating a more competitive environment in financial sector through reform measures such as relaxation of entry and exit norms, reduction in public ownership in banking industry and letting banks access to Capital Market for meeting fund requirements.

(iii) Strengthening the market-institutions and allowing greater freedom to financial intermediaries. These reforms have taken the form of gradual liberalisation of interest rates, development of money, capital and debt markets and giving operational flexibility to banks in the management of their assets and liabilities subject, of course, to prudential guidelines.

(iv) Safety aspects of the financial system. When the reform process was started in 1992, there was a massive problem of cleaning the balance sheets of banks which had deteriorated over the years. Successive reform initiatives in this area have been aimed at prescribing certain prudential standards for the financial system and addressing certain structural weaknesses to minimise their recurrence in future.

The measures such as income recognition norms, asset classification, meeting minimum Capital Adequacy standards through recapitulation and devising a supervisory framework are steps in the direction of ensuring the safety of the financial system.

The following points pressed for the need of the Financial Sector Reforms in India:

(i) Inadequate accounting, auditing and disclosure practices in the Financial/Banking sector weakened the market discipline in India.

(ii) Implicit Government guarantees encourage excessive, unsustainable capital inflows; and

(iii) Inadequate prudential supervision and regulation of domestic financial institutions and markets, which open the way for corruption, connected lending, and gambling for redemption namely the pursuit of high-return but low-probability investments by institutions with low or negative net worth.

Thus, broadly speaking, Banking Sector Reforms have been concerned with improving the following areas:

(a) the policy framework;

(b) the financial health; and

(c) the institutional infrastructure.

The first stage of the Banking Sector Reform is coming to an end and we are implementing to the second stage of the reform. In the years to come, the Indian Financial System will grow not only in size but also in complexity as the forces of competition gain further momentum, as the financial markets acquire greater width and depth.

Regulation arises owing to the four fundamental Public Policy concerns:

(i) Depositor, Consumer and Investor protections;

(ii) Structure and Competitive character of the market;

(iii) Safety and soundness; and

(iv) Systemic stability

It is at the start of the Second Banking Revolution, which besides consolidating the gains of the first revolution ushered in 1969, will make the banking institutions viable and efficient. Reforms in the financial sector are an integral part of the structural reforms that are under way and are aimed at improving the productivity and efficiency of the system as a whole.

The Financial Sector Reforms perform the basic economic function of intermediation essentially through four transformation mechanisms:

1. *Liability Asset Transformation:* i.e. accepting deposits as a liability and converting them into assets such as loans;
2. *Size Transformation:* i.e. providing large loans on the basis of numerous small deposits;
3. *Maturity Transformation:* i.e. offering savers alternative forms of deposits according to their liquidity preferences while providing borrowers with loans of desired maturities; and
4. *Risk Transformation:* i.e. distributing risks through diversification which substantially reduces risks for savers which would prevail while lending directly in the absence of financial intermediation.

The gains to the real sector of the economy, depend on how efficiently, the financial sector performs the above basic function of financial intermediation.

The functional efficiency of a Financial System can be judged in terms of :

(a) the soundness of the appraisals as measured by the level of overdues,

(b) the resource cost of specific operations, and

(c) the quality and speed of delivery of services.

The Narasimham Committee on Financial System (CFS)-I was appointed to examine all aspects relating to Structure, Organisation, Functions and Procedures of the Financial System.

In order to chart the reforms necessary in the years ahead so that India's Banking System can become stronger and better equipped to compete effectively in a fast changing international economic environment. Financial system reforms recommended by the Committee on Financial System (CFS), the Government of India appointed a High Level Committee on Banking Sector Reforms under the Chairmanship of M. Narasimham. The Committee submitted its report in April, 1998 and its major recommendations are:

- Merge strong Banks, close weak unviable ones.
- Two or three banks with international orientation, 8 to 10 national banks and a large number of local banks.
- Strengthen Legal Framework to accelerate credit recovery.
- Increase Capital Adequacy to match enhanced banking risk.
- Budgeting support non-viable for recapitalisation
- No alternative to asset reconstruction fund.
- Rationalise branches and staff, review recruitment and remuneration.
- Depoliticise Bank Boards under RBI supervision.
- Integrate NBFC activities with banks.
- Review major banking laws.

Where do the Indian Banks Stand after Financial Sector Reforms :

- with the Banking Sector Reforms, the competition is growing with the Private/Foreign Banks/Financial Institutions.
- thinning spreads are demanding the Operational Efficiency in each and every operation.
- the New Technology is providing the efficient Customer Service and better Management Information System.
- Public Sector Banks are concentrating to open specialised branches like Hi-Tech Agriculture/SSI/NRI/PBS/IBB/CBB branches.

- more concentration on profit orientation in various business activities.
- further, Banking Sector Reforms have influenced the business process, re-engineering, de-regulation of interest rates, integration of treasury operation, changes in credit delivery systems, etc.
- with the Banking Sector Reforms, quantum of NPAs increased, adverse deposit mix became visible, market share of PSBs shrinked and large number of loss-making branches emerged.
- the financial sector reforms compelled the Public Sector Banks to think in detail about the return on assets/net worth, about high cost of deposit and declining yield on advances.
- with the growing competition from Private/Foreign Banks, the customer started caring about the products, delivery, service quality, etc.
- net profit of the Scheduled Commercial Banks as a percentage of their total assets has been turned around from a negative figure of 1.0 per cent on an average during 1992-93 and 1993-94 to a positive of + 0.5 per cent during 1994-95 to 1998-99. More details may be seen from the Annexures I and II.
- business per employee in case of most Public Sector Banks and profit per employee have shown improvement in the recent years.
- by March, 1997, almost all Public Sector Banks have achieved the minimum capital adequacy norm of 8 per cent.
- the gross and net NPAs of the banking system as percentage of advances have declined to 16 per cent and 8.2 per cent respectively, by March, 1998.
- In terms of percentage of total assets, Gross and Net non-performing Assets have declined to 7 per cent and 3.3 per cent respectively by March, 1998.

The productive sectors need for their successful functioning an efficient operating banking system which, while transferring funds from the surplus units to deficit units, does so at the minimum operating cost. This indeed is the basic premise of financial sector reforms:

1. Interest rate structure has been rationalised;
2. Reserve requirements of banks have been reduced; and
3. Indirect monetary control instruments are being actively used.

Banking Reforms and Operating Costs

There is a need for improving efficiency and stability in the Banking system. The operating costs depend on :

1. Labour Productivity;
2. Technology;
3. Innovation; and
4. Organisational effectiveness of a bank to harness various static and dynamic economic from the production process.

The above factors differentiate the weak from the strong banking system and provide internal strength and stability to the system. Indian Banking System is still perceived as a relatively high Cost Banking. A comparative analysis indicates that the average operating cost of banks as a percentage of assets was about 2.3 per cent in India during 1990-91 to 1995-96, it was low at 1.1 per cent in China, 1.6 per cent in Malaysia, 1.9 per cent in Thailand, 1.0 per cent in Japan and 2.1 per cent in the European Countries.

Banking Scenario in Future

1. *Competition from Global Majors:* In the years to come, the Indian Banking system will be experiencing the following changes, i.e. (i) the power of financial muscle, (ii) competition among equals; and

(iii) mergers and acquisition-route, which provides a quick step forward for increasing the operational efficiency and functioning of Banks in India.

2. Competition from New Banks.
3. Dis-intermediation and competition resulting into pressure on spread. What Banks lose due to reduction in spreads/margins will have to be compensated through higher turnover.
4. Qualitative changes in the Banking Paradigm like:
   (i) Product pricing and management of their profits;
   (ii) Indian banking scenario would become sharper and widespread. The competencies required from a banker would be sharper, information technology based and knowledge centric, Risk-reward paradigm rather than process-based administration so far; and relationships of mutual advantage.
5. Challenges in-built into the structure and size of the Indian economy. Matter is not the high quality but availability of services and what really works here is not the innovativeness or sophistication of the products but the simplicity and low-cost of their delivery.
6. Self-regulation by the Banks: Beyond the millennium, the Indian Commerical Banks will emerge larger in size, technologically better equipped and stronger in Capital base:

- To handle large amounts of papers/instruments with technology and in a competitive manner.
- To handle variety of products in the market.
- To remain in market with improved standards of service.
- To adopt the new skills of competitors, i.e., Technology, sales and marketing expertise.

- To provide Cash Management Services (CMS) as cash is still an important part of the Indian society.
- The amalgamation of Public Sector Banks.
- Banks are to be given further freedom to manage, if they are to compete in the market.
- To learn new skills of technology management, sales and marketing, human resource management and finally delivering to the customer through service management.
- Competition led to improvement in their efficiencies and profit concept being recognised as a test of commercial viability.

Banking Reforms and Profitability of Banks

Improving profitability in general requires efforts in various directions, i.e. cutting in costs, improving productivity, better recovery of loans; and to reduce high level of NPAs. The public sector banks have to build-up the cost-benefit culture in their operations. When there is a thin margin in banking operations, the Public Sector Banks in India are required to have a very large turnover. Previously, Indian Banks were relying on high credit deposit ratio. Now, the Indian Banks have to depend on the volume of high business turnover. The return on assets need improvement.

Further, the Public Sector Banks in India have to compare them with the highly profitable banks with regards to operating expenses. They have to ensure that each and every account is profitable and product should be such, which generate more profit. The first set of reforms have improved the efficiency and transparency in the Indian Banking Sector.

The gradual increasing of the market and disintermediation have been putting pressure on the spreads. While in the short run, this could cause concern to some extent, in the longer run, one has to concede that it is in the best interests of the system. It will force the Indian Banks to increase their operational efficiency, reduce the transaction cost, reduce the cost of service-delivery and garner higher volumes of business for maintaining their competitiveness.

After almost nine years of the Banking sector reforms, the Indian Banking sector is now gearing-up for the second phase of reforms. This phase, would take further two to three years to complete. It constitute mainly of the following:

(i) Structural changes in the Public Sector Banks;

(ii) Improvements in the regulatory environment and processes;

(iii) Changes in the legal framework affecting the work of the Financial Banking Sector in India;

(iv) Further, demolition of borders between the different segments of the Banking Sector; and

(v) Empowerment of banks, particularly those in the regulatory area, in order that the role of banks institutions in managing the system better and protecting it against undue risks is firmly established and performed well.

The profits are needed by the banks for a number of reasons such as: (i) Banks are basically commercial organisations, to sustain themselves, RBI desires to maintain certain level of capital fund in relation to their risk weighted assets i.e. eight per cent upto March, 1999 and nine per cent by March, 2000, for making provisions against the loan assets, in view of the modified rules relating to Income Recognition and for making huge investment of capital nature for mechanisation and computerisation.

High CRR coupled with higher Capital Adequacy Ratio amount to high double taxation on banks, that is, taxing both the sides of bank's balance sheets.

Non-Performing Assets (NPAs)

A non-performing asset in the banking sector may be termed as an asset not contributing to the income of the bank. As a first step towards bringing in uniformity in practice relating to the recognition of the non-performing status of problem loans and advances.

RBI had advised the commercial banks in the year 1986 that in respect of loans which are categorised under Health Codes 5 to 8 (i.e. suit-filed, decreed, bad and doubtful debts) interest should not be booked and carried to profit and loss account, irrespective of the security position or the realisability assessment of the banks unless already realised. However, in case of category 4 (i.e. sick non-viable) accounts were left to the banks to decide the accrual status.

RBI with effect from April, 1992 decided that if the balance sheet is to reflect a bank's actual financial health, a proper system for recognition of income, classification of assets and provisioning for bad debts on a prudential basis is necessary. RBI, however, issued fresh guidelines in respect of recognition of interest as income, effective from the financial year 1992-93.

The loan assets (accounts) are required to be classified into four categories, i.e. standard, sub-standard, doubtful and loss assets in order to assess the general quality of portfolio and also for making required provision. What has been stressed in the process of Banking Sector Reforms, is the operational efficiency, generally indicated in terms of profit and profitability.

The banks will have to strengthen their loans portfolio by manning them with proper staff, equipped with appropriate appraisal and monitoring skills. Not only this, to attract good borrowers in these days of cut-throat competition and low-offtake of advances, they will have to adopt marketing strategies with the sole object of increasing value of good credit.

Management of Non-Performing Loan Assets

Reserve Bank of India's revised guidelines on income

recognition and further tighter norms for provisions on various category of advances have changed the entire outlook and prospects of earning income from advances. While there is no denying the fact that zero level of non-performing loan assets is not possible, but a favourable advances-mix for better yield in terms of performing and NPA accounts, can be done and ensured by adopting the following strategy:

- Expansion of credit in the existing accounts as well as by sanctioning new loans, but taking care that such expansion does not result in increase in NPAs.

- Recovery of existing non-performing loans.

- Preventing existing performing loans to slip to non-performing ones.

- A mix of credit expansion, recovery of non-performing loans and prevention of existing accounts from turning non-performing loans.

Further, the NPAs in India are reported as percentage of loan assets and not as percentage of total assets. If the latter practice has been adopted the percentage must have been much less in as much as the Indian banks hold 50 per cent of the assets in the form of government securities which are zero-risk investments and there could be no NPA in that category.

But the real test will be the ratio of incremental NPA to total loan assets which alone will reflect the true health of the Credit Management in Banks. There is a need to improve the credit appraisal system, the legal framework, culture of lending, identification of critical branches for recovery, fixation of recovery targets, to select proper techniques for solving the problems of each NPA, to expedite compromise proposals, strengthening of Debt Recovery Tribunals (DRTs) in all States, to set up more Debt Recovery Appellate Tribunals (DRATs) and to improve their working more effective expeditious follow-up of suit filed cases, etc.

The recent RBI study has observed that out of all suit-filed cases of Rs. 1 crores and above studied in 15 banks, there was only one case in which the suit filing was taken to the logical end. That is, the decree was executed, recovery made as per the decree and the borrowal account was closed.

The data from 33 Banks (27 Public Sector Banks six Private Sector banks) and the study of files relating to measures taken for recovery by way of Suit Filed by 15 banks have revealed that banks do file suits after exhausting other means of recovery.

The amount involved in Suit filed cases to total NPAs accounts for the last 3 years as under:

Years	*Percentage to Total NPAs*
1996	26.21
1997	33.91
1998	46.38

The recovery made out of the suit filing by these 33 banks during the last 3 years were:

Years	*Recovery Made out of Suit-filed (Percentage)*
1996	7.33
1997	4.74
1998	4.32

From the above figures, it is clear that recovery is decreasing through suit-file route. In view of such measure recovery, the banks before filing a suit, weight the likely recovery prospects out of any accounts that could be recovered, immediately. Suit filing as such is resorted to as the last alternative as per the RBI study.

Further, as advances in sub-standard category due to temporary problems like slow moving stocks, delay in receivable, etc. are not always recoverable and some of them get regularised and upgraded to the "standard" category, the suit filing in such accounts is neither required nor resortable to.

In view of the cost-benefit implications and time factor in suit filing, banks consider to resort to legal measures only when the account is classified at least as "Doubtful". It was noticed that as many as 14,36,739 suit filed cases were pending for disposal as on March 31, 1998. Besides NPAs Management Policy, RBI has also recommended the introduction of pre-disbursement audit and credit audit system for large advances and also system to tackle potential cases for the Board for Industrial and Financial Reconstruction (BIFR).

RBI study further concluded that the working of Debt Recovery Tribunals (DRTs) had fallen short of expectations by failing to develop a fast track system for recovery of the banking and financial sector's dues and other outstanding payments. The study on the status of NPAs assets after the reforms were initiated noted: "Banks are veering around to the view that so far the constitution of the DRTs has not contributed on a substantial measure in the recovery of problem loans or enforcement of securities by the Bank as they are not equipped with proper infrastructure and required flexibility".

RBI has suggested resorting to the Debt Settlement Tribunals (DSTs) that will improve upon the previous system's shortcomings: "As the system provides for the appointment of a recovery officer by the award". The RBI study also criticises the common plea adopted by borrowers of referring themselves to the BIFR. Since no recovery proceedings can be started till such a case has been resolved by the BIFR and the Appellate Authority for Industrial and Financial Reconstruction (AAIFR), "this is exploited by the borrowers to the hilt", according to the RBI report. RBI has also sought amendments in the legal environment as a step towards effective recovery of bad debts.

As on March, 1995 to March, 1999, the Non-Performing Assets range in Public Sector Banks were as under:

NPAs Range in PSBs	*No. of Banks (March end)*				
	1995	*1996*	*1997*	*1998*	*1999*
Upto 10%	2	19	17	17	18
10% to 20%	15	6	9	9	8
Above 20%	10	2	1	1	1
Total	27	27	27	27	27

On an average basis, NPAs of all the Public Sector Banks as on March, 1998 were 8.88 per cent to total advances. To bring down NPAs to 5 per cent level on a loan base of Rs. 2,60,000 crores and if per annum advances grow at 15 per cent during 1998-99 and 1999-2000, the additional provisions required for Public Sector Banks would be Rs. 12,500 crores. To bring down net NPAs further to three per cent additional provisions would be required around Rs. 8,500 crores.

The success of Asset Recovery Corporation (ARC) would depend upon:

1. The initiative a Banks in setting up jointly or singly a Company of the type, and mobilising the necessary capital.
2. The willingness of the State Governments to offer concessions in stamp duty.
3. Tax incentives by treating the funds deployed in ARCON on par with Venture Capital.

The Future Challenges

Simply copying the international models without providing corresponding legal and other infrastructure will not be productive of efficiency. Tolerance of failure and forebearance in the case of enterprising Banks are both necessary. Transport of concepts across borders without matching the operating environments in India can be *disastrous* in Banking.

In India, Public Sector Banks as such cannot be eliminated in the foreseeable future. In fact, the research scholar feel their governance, especially should be strengthened - public sector banks in India have greater credibility than other entities in finance. Human resource development in such banks need to be strengthened. Governance in Public Sector Banks obviously leaves a lot to be desired. To this extent, less interference and more transparency is essential if the financial sector has to be made effective.

Overall Assessment of the Banking Sector Reforms

It is perhaps somewhat early to assess the impact of the reforms, considering that the process was initiated only in 1992 and has been implemented in phases. Yet even at this early stage one can discern some positive developments. One of the significant areas of improvement has been the greater accuracy and transparency in respect of bank's financial statements. The acceptance of the recommendations with regard to bringing Indian accounting standards closer to internationally accepted norms, coupled with requirements of fuller disclosure on sensitive aspects of operations have rendered financial statements of banks more credible and transparent. Further, the refinement of accounting practices and disclosure requirements to bring them in line with the internationally accepted norms in this regard has to be an on-going process.

As on March, 1998, only one Public Sector bank was having capital Adequacy Ratio less than eight per cent. While 7 PSBs were having CAR of eight to ten per cent, 16 banks of ten to fifteen per cent and 3 Public Sector Banks the CAR ratio between fifteen to twenty per cent as on March, 1998. While, all the new private banks as well as foreign banks have fully complied with the minimum CAR as on March, 1998.

The application of prudential norms on income recognition, stricter definition of NPAs and the revised format for classification and related provisioning since 1992-93 have had the result of some banks showing net losses and consequent erosion in their net worth in the earlier years. As on March, 1998 the position has improved to a large extent in this regard. The details may be seen from the *Annexure - II*, i.e., Operating Profit, Provisions and Contingencies and Net Profits for the year 1995-96 to 1998-99.

Further, the *Annexure - I* reflect the trends in the Profitability of the Scheduled Commercial Banks for the year 1995-96 to 1998-99.

Banking/Financial Sector Reforms and Future Threats

The Narasimham Committee I reviewed and found that the Public Sector Banks in India were facing the problems like : lower profitability, inadequate capital adequacy and in adequate technology adoption in banks. To cope up with the International Standards, the Indian Banks were to improve in the area of dissemination of information, to adopt new technology, to improve the appraisal system, to increase specialisation and to improve domestic and international operations.

The main features of the Banking Sector Reforms in India were interest-rate de-regulation, stimulating, competition among financial institutions, fostering capital market, relaxation of foreign exchange controls, contraction of informal finance and improved supervision and regulation of financial institutions. Basic principles of reforms covers the rules relating to contents, bankruptcy, disclosure, protections for shareholders in securities, information needs, regulation for ensuring safety and soundness, promoting competition, consumer protection, promoting access to under-served group and incentives for enhancing franchise value in banks.

With the implementation of the recommendations of the Narasimham Committee - I, the prudential norms and the Capital Adequacy Norms generally came in line with the rest of the World. In assessing, the reform of the Indian Banking/ Financial Sector, one has to take into consideration the inadequacies of the legal system, the cult of prosecution, the culture of lending, the reverse effect of Capital Adequacy, the impact of procedure and behest lending.

The Narasimham Committee II has recently addressed a number of vital issues pertaining to the health and stability of financial system and the actions that are necessary to strengthen it. With the implementation of the recommendation of the Narasimham Committee I and II, the financial reforms in India have proceeded in the four directions namely:

(i) to remove the operational constraints;

(ii) to create more competitive environment;

(iii) to strengthen the market, institutions and allowing greater freedom to financial intermediaries; and

(iv) improving the safety aspects of the financial system.

The profitability, productivity and performance of Public Sector Banks in the past can be attributed mainly by factors such as directed lending, Human Resource Management Policies, frauds and undesirable work culture. For NPAs recovery Banking Company Act should be suitably amended to give more powers to banks in the recovery of loan. Banks need Human Resource Development intervention automotive the employees is the need of the hour.

Thus, FSRs, constitute an integral part of the overall programme of structural reform and are aimed at improving the overall productivity and efficiency of the Indian Banking and Financial System. The Banking and Financial Sector Reforms are necessary for the faster growth of the economy and thereby to achieve distributive justice as well. Moreover, structural reforms can succeed only if resources are redeployed towards more efficient productions. Hence, Financial Sector Reforms play a crucial role in the success of structural reforms.

The FSRs were initiated with the objective of promoting a diversified, efficient and competitive financial system. But there is still a long way to go in creating an efficient financial sector suitable for a sophisticated modern economy.

The FSRs have provided an opportunity for banks to improve their efficiency/productivity and profitability and to face the future challenges with proper strength and better operational efficiency. Privatisation of Public Sector Banks after making the proper cost benefit analysis, is a step to bring about more efficiency and improvement in PSBs.

The 21st century will be more dynamic, mutually dependent and will give priority to real values in the World Economy. It is, therefore of utmost requirement to adopt dynamic approach towards Banking development in India. Greater specialisation by PSBs in different niches of the market such as Retail Lending, Agriculture, Export, SSI and Corporate Sector, greater reliance on non-fund business, advisory and consultancy services is the need of the E-Millennium Era.

Operational restructuring demands that the basic changes are to be made in the mode of operations, resulting in diversification of sources of income and their steady growth. The adopting of latest modern technology in PSBs will improve the operational efficiency to a great extent. There is an utmost need to drastically bring down the cost of operations and transaction costs.

The functional efficiency of Banking System can be judged from: (a) the soundness of the appraisals as measured by the level of overdues; (b) the resource cost of specific operations; and (c) the quality and speed in delivery of services.

Indian Banking system is, to a considerable extent, fragile and any major adverse development, national or international, can create the same types of problems as experienced by the South-East Asian countries three years ago. The M.S. Verma Committee has added seven specific tests for a greater degree of certainty. They fall in the specific areas of: (a) solvency; (b) earning capacity; and (c) profitability.

The problem of overstaffing and over-unionisation in Indian Banking is too well-known to be recounted here. This is one of the major factors behind the near absence of technology in Public Sector Banks in India.

One of the significant areas of improvement in Banking Sector Reforms has been the greater accuracy and transparency in respect of Bank's financial statements. The acceptance of the recommendations with regard to bringing the Indian Accounting Standards closer to internationally accepted norms, coupled with requirements of fuller disclosure on sensitive aspects of operations have rendered financial statements of banks more credible and transparent.

To have a cohesive and strong financial system capable of responding to changes in the economy, it becomes imperative to have a dynamic autonomous and profitable financial system.

There is a very close connection between the bank's real health and its levels of provisionally against loan losses. There is a need to further strengthen the Audit structure to improve the constraints of *Legal Inadequacies*, to improve the Corporate Governance System in Banks, Risk Management, to strengthen banking regulation and supervision, more transparency in operation, fixing accountability and to strengthen the public policies relating to moral hazards in banking sector.

Conclusion

To have a cohesive and strong financial system capable of responding to changes in the economy, it becomes important to have a dynamic, autonomous and profitable financial system. With the Narasimham Committee I's recommendations and implementation of the same by the Government of India, RBI engaged in the task of clarifying its role and working to make a better contribution to the various problems, issues and opportunities, which lie before it. RBI played the role of vigilant guardian of the Economy in India. Narasimham Committee I and II made important contribution towards the complex question of banking reforms. Internal vigilance is the price of liberalisation. The major factors which were critical for the success in the complex scenario were:-

- Commitment to develop strong lasting relationships with customers and to provide quality services:
- Professional, motivated and innovative staff:
- Commitment to earn highest possible profit with consistent prudence and management of risk; and
- Obesssion for growth.

There is a very close connection between the Bank's real health and its levels of provisions against loan losses. Nevertheless, prudent provisioning can reduce the likelihood shock of losses that may threaten insolvency, while also allowing a troubled bank more time in which to rectify its impaired capital position. Unless provisioning practices, on the other hand, reduce market trasparency and make it much more difficult for both practitioners and regulators to monitor the financial condition of individual banks.

Hence, there is a need to further strengthen the Audit structure, to improve he content and nature of regulation, need to remove the constraints of legal inadequacies to improve the Corporate Governance Systems in Banks, Risk management, to strengthen banking regulation and supervision, more transparency in operation, fixing accountability and to strengthen the public policies relating to moral hazards in banking sector.

It is expected that in the coming years, the Indian Banking will be competing with more global players, change in ownership pattern, further deregulation, more stricter supervisory control, more integration of financial and non-financial services, move towards bigger banks by mergers and amalgamation, etc.

Further, Banking Industry will be more technology driven customer friendly, greater autonomy, further integration of capital and forex markets, full capital account convertibility, more global accounting standards and lesser protection from the Government side. There will be fierce competition among major players, margins will be under pressure, greater volatility, out sourcing of some services, more focus towards customer expectations, learner structure and skilled workforce will be the Indian Banking in the E-Millennium. Only those PSBs will be serving/growing which adopt the policy of self regulation, giving leverage to technology, financial gearing ratios, having ability to withstand disasters and are able to increase market share in business by having New Products and with better Risk Management.

Thus, we can conclude that Banking Sector Reforms are shaping the future of Public Sector Banks in the years to come, towards more operational efficiency, effectiveness in operations, more consciousness about the profit and profitability, by having better Return on Assest (ROA), operating profit and with higher capital adequacy ratios. Whatever radical reform measures may be taken by the Public Sector Banks, it may not yield the desired results till management of the Banks is not strengthened and loopholes in the system and procedure of PSBs are tightly plugged-off.

10

ECONOMY OF INDIA FROM NATIONALISATION TO PRIVATISATION

Madan Verma

Indian economy is one of the largest economy of the world. The conditions which prevail here have a great bearing on the other parts of the world especially in Asia and in the third world.

Our economy has undergone enormous changes since independence, i.e., 1947. It has seen the days of shortages then Green Revolution, Industrialisation Self Reliance and finally the Financial Reforms and Surpluses opening up avenues for India to be part of global economy and compete in the international market. Since 1991 the economic environment in India has undergone sea change:

Pre-independence Era

The country that was handed over to us by the British at the time of independence was in ruins, yet under the British rule it achieved a fair degree of industrialisation. India's entrepreneurial class built industries like textile and steel. This was in spite of the fact that colonial rulers did not play the role of a development agency and hence did nothing to provide protection to, or promoting, the infant industry. The country exported significant amount of textile and jute goods while primary goods were available indigenously. However, the economy was predominantly agrarian without any large-scale industrialisation which kept the economy on a low growth trajectile with an average rate of growth being 1.2 per cent between 1900 and 1947. At that time about 70 per cent of the Gross Domestic Product came from the agriculture sector which gave employment to 80 per cent of the workforce. So it was felt that only industrialisation could bring about a high growth rate.

Socialist Economy as Conceived by Pt. Jawahar Lal Nehru

Accelerated economic growth was the basis of the Nehru Mahalanobis Model. Its underlying premise was that the consequent expansion of gainful employment would lead to greater income and higher standards of living and thus become the most effective way of tackling poverty. For inducing a growth momentum, it was felt large doses of investments were required. A labour rich India could embark on the path of industrialisation. It was felt that economic prosperity would be achieved if all the supply side bottlenecks were removed. These were identified as shortage of savings, foreign exchange, skilled manpower and entrepreneurial abilities, all structural factors that needed planned interventions. At that time it was felt that economic development could not be left to market forces as market imperfections would not transmit the required signals in an underdeveloped economy like India's.

The model laid stress on the importance of creation of capital goods sector mainly to save the foreign exchange reserves. The purpose was inward looking development through import substitution with little stress on the export sector and setting up a strong regulatory framework to channel investment to the priority sector, discouraging import of investment goods and regulating foreign investment. The onus for achieving suitable industrial growth was, thus, put on the state, and though the private sector was encouraged, economies of scale were not given due weightage.

Emphasis on heavy industry predominance of the public sector in the process of industrialisation, economic planning and self reliance with a bias against foreign capital were the four pillars of the economic policy pursued in the post-independence period. Emphasis was placed on heavy industries in order to develop the basic industrial base in anticipation of a future demand in the capital goods sector. However, it was felt industry might not absorb the labour force, and hence encouragement was also given to setting up of cottage and small scale sector. The idea was to contain consumption and promote savings and channel them into industries to accelerate growth.

In the light of post Great Depression situation of the 1930s, economies bore the adverse consequence of free market and the importance of public sector were felt both in the developed countries where it could kick-start the economies and also in developing nations where it could create the necessary industrial base. It was also believed that the private sector at that time was unable to take up large and risky investment projects and that the public sector should be created as the major 'entrepreneur'.

The public and the private sector, it was felt, should be complementary and not substitute of one another in the sense that the former should release the constraints on critical infrastructure and that should generate demand for private sector outputs. Also, it was felt that the public sector needed strategic control over the key sectors of the economy and shape overall pattern of investment. The apparent success of the Soviet economy impressed our leaders like Jawaharlal Nehru of the superiority of the Soviet model as it could ensure rapid economic growth with a low inflation and zero unemployment.

The leading role of the public sector was also endorsed by premier industrialist of the country who under the leadership of the Tatas drafted the Bombay Plan in 1942. It emphasised the crucial role of the government in economic development. However, as against central planning, it proposed a partnership between the state and market.

The concept of industrialisation was conceived with self-reliance as the predominant motivation. It meant low dependence on external assistance through import substitution coupled with export pessimism and a bias against foreign capital. During the 1950s and 1960s, several MNCs dominated the economies of Africa and South America and started wielding political power. This led to a bias against foreign capital which was thought to be undesirable for developing economies.

The Tools of Controlled Economy

The industrial licensing was the key instrument in the hand of the planners to create capacities by controlling both the entry into the industry sector and subsequent expansions.

It was mainly done to achieve balanced industrial growth and check concentration of economic power which was later reinforced by the enactment of the Monopolies and Restrictive Trade Practices (MRTP) Act. Industrial dispersal to backward areas by the private sector was encouraged through specific financial and tax concessions and through freight equalisation for major inputs. There was also a complex system of import licensing to provide physical allocation of imports. Excessive dependence on industrialisation led to resources transfer from agricultural based rural regions to the urban centres.

Poor productivity and lack of modern farming techniques caused severe foodgrains shortage in 1956-1966 which necessitated large scale imports. The crisis gave shape to what later came to be known as the green revolution which primarily involved adoption of high yielding variety (HYV) of seeds.

Four Decades of Mixed Economy: Its Gains and Losses

The country achieved a sustained average growth rate of about 3.5 per cent with a low level of inflation over three decades till 1980s. In the 1980s the growth rate accelerated to

5.5 per cent accompanied by a steady rise in domestic savings and investments rages. Among the sectors, industry grew more than agriculture, while manufacturing showed the highest growth rate. The share of capital goods in the index of industrial production rose from 5 per cent in 1956 to 15 per cent in 1980-81 while that of consumer goods dropped from fifty per cent to thirty per cent.

The public sector dominated gross capital information which increased from three per cent in 1950-51 to 11.5 per cent in 1984-85. Public investment accounted for 50 per cent for investment in the economy after if achieved some sort of well balanced industrial growth.

After facing some teething troubles in the mid 1950s, the agricultural sector took off from the late 1960s with the implementation of the green revolution. Food grain production went up four folds and the country achieved self reliance and an adequate buffer stock which virtually eliminated famines. On the other hand, the external sector contributed a mere two per cent to the gross domestic product during this period, mainly due to lack of thrust on exports and avoidance of foreign capital.

Some drawbacks and failures of the command economy were also coming to the surface. The inability to create a competitive market place led in turn to the rise of bunch of rent-seekers who fed on a steady diet of protection and license permits.

All industries setting up indigenous capacities were provided protection at all cost which, coupled with restrictions of capacity expansion, ensured that domestic prices of industrial goods in most cases ruled over international prices. There was no incentive for quality improvement and cost competitiveness. Public investment went down by half between 1960 and 1970 while infrastructure growth came down from seventeen to three per cent during the same period.

Once the pride of the nation, the public sector units turned into dinosaurs that gobbled up resources and gave a dismal return of three per cent on capital invested. This ate up government revenue and worsened fiscal deficit.

After a failed attempt to turbo-charge the economy, the economic crisis of 1990-91 came like a blessing in disguise. It rudely shook the economy off its narrow groove. The economic reform process followed. Its first phase seen over the past seven years included opening up of the economy to competitions both domestic and foreign while the second stage covered structural reform in the financial sectors.

Although it can be said that the reform process was more or less thrust upon us by International Monetary Fund and the World Bank as a precondition for their bailing out after our fiscal crisis, it is now widely believed that it was the only way out from the mess that the economy found itself in.

Under the overall leadership of The Prime Minister Narashima Rao, Finance Minister Manmohan Singh is credited for being the person who gave a physical shape to the reform process. His biggest contribution was his maiden budget that saw the elimination of the archaic system of industrial licensing in most of the sectors. He gradually brought in convertibility and rationalisation of foreign exchange market and did away with the dual exchange rate regime. His other contributions were simplification of and gradual reduction of, indirect tax structures. All of these greating contributed to integrating the domestic economy with that of the world.

The Chelliah Committee made valuable contributions towards tax reform while the Narashimham Committee looked into making the banking sector more efficient while the Rakesh Mohan Committee addressed the need for greater investment flow to the infrastructure sector.

The study of economic survey 1999-2000 per cent revealed that Indian Economy was expected to grow by 5.9 per cent in the Current Year. The Five Years Plans have not shown any significant landmark in the overall development of the Nation. But they were well conceived. The reasons of lower achievements have been wrong fiscal policies of the

Government causing inflationary trends, rise in prices and acceleration in unemployment sector. Every year so many young people pass out and look for the jobs which are hard to find which gives rise to frustration to youth and a feeling that the Government is not doing anything for them.

By and large, the economic policies of the Government have remained on papers and the implementation of the same has been very poor. The Government took steps to nationalise Public Sector Banks, Insurance Companies and other PSUs and this created a mess which could not be properly handled thereafter. The Government in any country should work as a guardian for its people. The primary job of Government is to provide fundamentals, i.e. Food, Shelter, Employment and a dignified living and the most important work of the Government is to maintain law and order:- Unfortunately, the Indian Government could not keep track of implementation of basic fundamental policies and it resulted in total chaos. Frequent charges at the Centre and nonstable Government was another factor for not carrying reforms too far.

The so-called socialist pattern of society which was conceived by our great thinkers of the Nation, it was targetted to provide decentralisation of power in a democratic framework, equal distribution of income and wealth and provide special assistance to weaker sections and ultimately so balanced regional development in the country. The attainment of the above goal in economic and socialist equalities in distribution of income and wealth of the country was jeopardised as the system of implementation of these objectives were based on unrealistic pattern of distribution.

The system of quota/permit/ration/license/ came in vogue to become an integral part of the economy and the real objective of socialism and upliftment of weaker section was forgotten. Then came an Erawhere the Government wanted to do everything itself or through its own designated agencies. Everything was taken over even business like cement, sugar, cloth and steel, etc. were also nationalised. The other major examples of such nationalisation are Insurance, Banking Sector,

Heavy Industrial Products, Power, etc. The nationalisation of these institutions did not lead to any remarkable achievement nor did it fulfil its purpose except for the fact that the people employed in these institutions became a permanent liability on the part of the Government, thus doing a great harm to the exchequer by giving low productivity.

It is important to note here that the Public Sector generates about 26 per cent of the national income and provide jobs opportunities to 184 lacs persons as against 74 lacs persons engaged in the private organised sector. The annual return of Public Sector is less than three per cent which means it does not even cover the rate of interest of the capital borrowed which was invested in establishing the same.

Conclusion

Unfortunately the Government has been unable to put a check on the drain of hard earned financial resources. The step towards privatisation is a welcome step, well conceived and will give a fillip to the economy. The time has come that our people must learn to earn their living rather living on pensions, charity and subsidies. The government should cautiously, not recklessly, as has been done, open the avenues of privatisation and provide infrastructure to the people to get accustomed to new environment of free economy so that the same mistake is not committed again as was done before.

The fiscal deficit in the current Budget is Rs. 100000 crore this year. In percentage terms it is same as a decade before; so we have not made much headway as far as economic progress is concerned, country will thus rank in the lower cadre as far as per capita income is concerned.

Another important concern is small scale sector which needs to be strengthened so that it can survive as it has a major role in employment to the youth of the nation. Therefore, any policy which deters the growth of small scale sector could be very injurious and harmful to the economy.

The Government should devise means, to create jobs, and provide infrastructure for employment to youth, it could even send the younger generation atleast for one year for development of borders, which will not only create infrastructure but will also help reducing unemployment, and in turn will add to, capital formation.

even send the younger generation abroad for one year for development of borders, which will not only create infrastructure but will also help reducing unemployment and in turn will add to capital formation.

11

ECONOMIC REFORMS AND EMPLOYMENT

Dr. B.M. Jauhari
Ms. Monita Mohan

Unemployment, according to the conventional and most commonly used concept, measures involuntary idleness, that is, the time for which individuals are available for and willing to, but are not able to find work. Employment generation and economic growth both are mutually complementary rather than conflicting processes. Employment has, therefore to be generated in the process for the acceleration of economic growth Employment, to be gainful and sustainable, has to be productive in nature which is to be taken into consideration with care. It should be able to yield a reasonable level of income to the worker and also generate surplus for further growth and employment generation. In our country, growth rates of employment has been high in urban areas, but relatively low in rural areas on one hand and deceleration in the rate of employment growth has been particularly sharp in the organised sector on the other. There are also wide variations in the unemployment rates among different states in our country. In the above facets of unemployment, an attempt has been made to gauge the impact of post-economic reforms of 1991 on employment in the country as a whole.

India's reforms programme began in the middle of a macro-economic crisis that erupted in early 1991. The crisis was brought to a head by a steep fall in foreign exchange reserves to about $ 1 billion which was just equal to two weeks' import, a sharp downgrading of India's credit rating and a cut-off of foreign private lending. Its basic underlying features were high inflation (12 per cent and rising), large public and current account deficits (approximately ten and three per cent of GDP respectively) and a heavy and growing burden of domestic and foreign debt.

One can visualise the impact of above severity a nation like India could have to face, had there been no initiatives taken at that time on various measures in most key economic parameters such as balance of payments, output growth, employment and inflation, which are termed as Economic Reforms by the then Government of India. In the absence of suitable remedial measures and reforms in the economic front, the condition of the country could have deteriorated further. The term Economic Reforms no doubt means many things to many people but without going into the lengthy discussion over reforms measures we have been assessing the impact of on employment economic reforms. As we know that any dynamic economic sphere requires reform constantly, how then can we arrive at a conclusion that a country having one billion of population like India being run without reforms in this dynamic global world. Our focus therefore here is only on the effect of economic measures and reforms initiated by the Government of India in the middle of the year 1991.

The economic reforms of the above period can be gauged by the yardstick in terms of the living standards of India's people, in particular of the poor. Despite efforts made over the past few decades, rural poverty in India continues to be stagnant, while the anti-poverty programmes have been strengthened in successive years and while, in percentage terms, poverty levels have reduced from 56.44 per cent of India's population in 1973-74 to 37.27 per cent in 1993-94, the number of rural poor has more or less remained static and is estimated to be about 244 million persons.

The economic reforms gave way to the flow of foreign investment which supplemented domestic investment with a consequential higher rate of growth. This has the potential to expand employment opportunities for the poor. Economic reforms, therefore, contributed to growth through the promotion of competitive efficiency and increased flow of foreign investment. Simultaneously, it had adverse impact on the largely unorganised sector which cannot compete with multinational corporations. The reforms also improved the allocative efficiency by shifting products from non-tradeable to tradeables.

There are numerous available data which support the favourable assessment of the impact of economic reform on employment and living standard. The Planning Commission's estimates of annual increments in economy—wide employment indicate strong growth (Annual employment increase) from a low of three million in crisis-ridden 1991-92 to an average of six million in each of the following two years (6.6 million in the year 1992-93 and 5 million in 1993-94) and then rising further to 7.2 million in 1994-95. The above surge in employment opportunities is definitely associated with favourable trends in living standards and poverty on the basic fact that the labour is the principal asset possessed by the poor. The second available data on trends in real wages for unskilled agricultural labour indicates (Economic Survey 1994-95) that in average real wages fell by 5.3 per cent in the crisis year of 1991-92 and then rose by 5.6 per cent in 1992-93 and by 3.6 per cent in 1993-94 as the economy recovered from this crisis in response to reforms. In 1994-95, the food production rose to a new record of 1992 million tonnes and agricultural value added by 4.8 per cent. Annual survey data on demographic indicators also shows a similar and interesting pattern. It shows that the trend decline in the Crude Death Rate (per thousand) halted and even slightly reversed in 1991 and 1992 before continuing downwards in 1993. Similarly, the trend decline in the Infant Mortality Rate also paused in 1991 and 1992 and then resumed its secular decline in 1993. The Central Plan budgetary allocations for major anti-poverty programmes have been doubled in real terms over two years can be supported by the actual data in this regard. The Central Plan budgetary allocation for the Department of Rural Development (which encompasses the major anti-poverty programmes) increased from Rs. 3,100 crores in 1992-93 to Rs. 7,010 crores in 1994-95, i.e. an increase of 126 per cent over two years during which general inflation averaged below ten percent per year is an indicator that definitely it has some, if not to the extent it should have been with this increase, positive impact on the growth of employment. The Planning Commission's Eighth Five Year Plan (1992-97) clearly outlined the views of the Government on employment generation as mentioned below:

"If we are to reach ultimately the goal of full employment by the turn of the century, we will have to concentrate on creating job opportunities, particularly in the rural areas. The Central plan has substantially stepped up the outlay for Department of Rural Development from Rs. 4900 crores approved in the seventh plan (against which the actual expenditure was about Rs. 10,800 crores) to Rs. 30,000 crores in the Eighth Plan. In this context the rural development programmes will have to be revamped in order to become more effective and more productive.

The employment has to shift from the creation of relief type of employment to the building up of durable productive assets in rural areas. The productive assets which contribute to the overall development of the rural areas, are rural roads, minor irrigation works like percolation tanks, land levelling and prevention of soil erosion/improvement of soil, social forestry, school buildings and buildings for primary health centres, vocational training and production centres, etc. Any additional resources for generation of wage employment should be restricted to the identified backward district".

The budgets of financial years 1999-2000 and 2000-2001 project that at present, a variety of self-employment and wage employment schemes are in operation, but to enhance the effectiveness of these schemes, the government has committed to follow a four-pronged strategy with the common theme of ensuring greater involvement of *Panchayati Raj* Institutions so that income-earning opportunities for the rural poor could be improved. Accordingly, the Ministry of Rural Development, Government of India have launched a "Swarnjayanti Gram Sawarozgar Yojana (SGSY)" w.e.f. 1.4.1999. The SGSY is a holistic programme covering all aspects of self-employment such as organisation of the poor into self help groups, training, credit, technology, infrastructure and marketing. With the SGSY coming into force, the earlier programme, i.e., Integrated Rural Development (IRDP), Training of Rural Youth for Self-Employment (TRYSEM), Development of Women and Children in Rural Areas (DWCRA), Supply of Improved Toolkits to Rural Artisans (SITRA), Ganga Kalyan Yojana (GKY) and Million Wells Scheme (MWS) of the Ministry of Rural Development will no longer be in operation under their separate name labels. The SGSY will be funded by the Centre and the States in the ratio of 75 : 25.

Apart from the above the finance budget of year 1999-2000 also proposes to start another programme called "National Programme for Rural Industrialisation (NPRI) with the mission to set up 100 rural clusters every year to give a boost to rural industrialisation to be implemented by Small Industry Development Organisation (SIDO) and Khadi and Village Industry Commission (KVIC) both of which are under the Ministry of Industry, Government of India. They have already initiated their action on it. The SIDO has also been running another programme called Prime Minister Rozgar Yozana (PMRY) to boost self-employment.

It can thus be said that the post-economic reforms have definitely given a positive support to employment whether urban or rural but as is said elsewhere that the employment policy should meet to ultimate goal of providing and not generating employment temporarily but with durability. This, in no way reflects that the mobility of the masses in different opportunities should be restricted but implies that it should be accelerated to provide better opportunities to the calibre on one hand and to provide employment to the unemployed on the other. It requires the need of more emphasis not only by the masses themselves but also by the various organisations and authorities to check that the various facets of unemployment—be it involuntary, structural, under-employment, open unemployment, cyclical, technological or disguised etc. in such a way as to lead to eliminate the unemployment. Efforts should constantly be made to create more organised employment opportunities with a healthy environment.

REFERENCES

1. Eighth Five Year Plan (1992-97), Vol. I, Government of India, Planning Commission, New Delhi.
2. Joshi Vijay, *India's Economic Reforms, 1991-2001*, Oxford University Press, Delhi, 1996.
3. *Economic Development in India, 1996-97*, Academic Foundation, Series Editors : Raj Kapila and Uma Kapila.
4. Agrawal, A.N., *Indian Economy Problems of Development and Planning*, Wishwa Prakasan.
5. Misra S.K. and Puri V.K., *Economics of Development and Planning (Theory and Practice)*, Himalaya Publishing House.
6. Speech of Mr. Yashwant Sinha, Minister of Finance, Government of India during presentation of Budget 1999 in the Lok Sabha Parliament House, New Delhi.
7. *The Indian Economic Journal*, Vol. 44, April-June 1997, No. 4, Indian Economic Association, Bangalore.

12

FOREIGN DIRECT INVESTMENT IN INDIA– ISSUES AND PROBLEMS

Monita Mohan • Shailesh Nagar • Nitin Nagar

India's economic policy reforms have played a critical role in the performance of the Indian economy since 1991 (Bajpai *et al*, 2000). The reforms have involved opening of the economy, making it more competitive, getting the government out of the huge morass of regulation, empowering the states to take more responsibility for economic management and thereby creating a kind of competition among the states for foreign investors. The GPD growth rate that had collapsed to 0.8 per cent in 1991-92 rebounded to near normal 5.3 per cent in 1992-93 and then accelerated to 6.2 per cent in 1993-94. Subsequently GDP grew at an average rate of 7.5 per cent in the three years 1994-95 to 1996-97, before slowing down to 5.1 per cent in 1997-98 and then recovering marginally to 5.8 per cent in 1998-99 (National Account Statistics, 2000). It is important to note that despite the slow down, the average growth rate in the four years 1994-95 to 1997-98 was 6.9 per cent most of which can be attributed to the growth in the field of information technology and knowledge industries; however, the growth rate fell to 6.0 per cent 1998-99 (National Account Statistics, 2000). The positive trends being seen in most sectors had the capability to neutralize the negative effects of two general elections in two years, the nuclear explosions, the US and other sanctions (see *Annexure 1* for status on sanctions) that followed, the crisis in the East Asia, and the Kargil operations.

Foreign Direct Investment in India

Foreign direct investment norms in India have been significantly simplified as part of its liberalization policy. In view of this and India's economic growth potential, a number of multinational companies have setup subsidiaries or joint ventures in India. Dr. Veena Jha (2000) summarized some of the results from the surveys reflecting the mood and optimism about India's future FDI prospects.

- (i) According to a study conducted by the German Asia Pacific committee in 1996, India was found to compare favourably with other developing countries in terms of legal and cultural factors, costs and personnel skills and effectiveness in carrying out tasks.
- (ii) According to survey of UK based companies, the main attractions of India are its large market size, a familiar legal system, developed and well established banks and capital markets, as well as liberal policies towards FDI's.
- (iii) According to the Export-Import Bank of Japan, India has been ranked as the third most promising developing country over a ten-year investment horizon.
- (iv) India is among the top ten priority markets for a growing number of business executives in Canada.
- (v) Top US executives visiting India on a business mission have expressed the view that they were confident that further economic reforms would be carried out.

A recent survey by Kearney consultants (Dasgupta, 2000) of the United States pointed out that India was considered one of five most attractive destinations for FDI at the global level. However, it was also pointed out that India was not fully exploiting the vacuum created due to the South East Asian financial crisis, which erupted in July 1997 and spread rapidly across other emerging economies through 1998, by implementing economic reforms speedily and by improving its infrastructure rapidly.

Foreign direct investment inflows to India grew rapidly from start of the new industrial policy in 1991 through 1997. From approximately $129 million in 1991-92, FDI inflows to India increased every year, peaking at $3.55 billion in 1997-98. These figures however, tumbled in 1998-99 to $2.4 billion and it is estimated to fall to $2.1 billion in the year 1999-2000 Table 12.1. However, the proportion of actual inflows to approvals has gone up steadily from 17.4 per cent in 1992 to 23.2 per cent in 1994, 28.7 per cent in 1996, 43.3 per cent in 1998 and 59.5 per cent in 1999 (*Business Line*, 2000). During the current year till March, this proportion has risen further to 93.1 per cent. While the increase in actual inflows-to-approvals ratio may partly reflect the fructifying of past FDI proposals, the main causative factor. Thus, the absolute value of FDI approvals have almost halved from $15.3 billions in 1997 to $6.75 billions in 1999 (*Business Line*, 2000).

TABLE 12.1
Foreign Investment Inflows

	1990-91	1991-92	1992-93	1993-94	1994-95	1995-96	1996-97	1997-98	1998-99	1999-2000 (Est.)
Direct Investment	97	129	315	586	1,314	2,144	2,821	3,557	2,462	2,155
Government (SIA/FIPB)	0	66	222	280	701	1,249	1,922	2,754	1,821	1,410
RBI	0	0	42	89	171	169	135	202	179	171
NRI	0	63	51	217	442	715	639	241	62	84
Acquisition of Shares*	0	0	0	0	0	11	125	360	400	490

Figures in US $ million

*Ralates to acquisition of shares of Indian Companies by non-residents under section 29 of FERA. Data on such acquisitions have been included as part of FDI since January 1996.

Source: RBI Bulletin (Table No. 46) published on October 12, 2000.

Despite much optimism shown by various countries regarding India as a favourable investment destination, India still falls well-short of its ambitious target of achieving $10 billion worth of annual direct investment inflows. As discussed earlier, as a result of South East Asian crisis the FDI inflows to developing countries fell by 3.7 per cent and in the South East Asia fell by 12.0 per cent whereas in India the FDI inflows dipped by 32.6 per cent (Bajpai, *et al*, 2000). The crisis led to the fears of widespread credit crunch, and consequently recession in the economy. However, beginning early 1999, most of the economies affected by the crisis had begun to recover but India's investment inflows are still declining Table 2. FDI in South Asia dipped to 13 per cent mainly due to the fall in capital flow to India, to $2.2 billion in 1999 as compared to $2.6 billion in 1998 (*The Economic Times*, October 2000).

Foreign Direct Investments : Issues and Problems

Given that India's policy for FDI provides clear guidelines for entry, freedom of location, choice of technology, production, repatriation of capital and repatriation of dividends, still the country is not able to attract huge amount of investment inflows which will help improve India's infrastructure and finally the economic standing of the country.

Table 12.2

Foreign Direct Investment Flows, Region-Wise

	1985-1995	1996	1997	1998	1999
India					
Inward	0.451	2.426	3.577	2.635	2.168
Outward	0.022	0.239	0.113	0.048	0.167
Memorandum					
Korea					
Inward	0.854	2.308	3.088	5.215	10.340
Outward	1.227	4.249	3.230	3.893	2.548
Singapore					
Inward	4.113	8.984	8.085	5.493	6.984
Outward	1.683	6.935	8.859	–1.525	3.943

	1985-1995	1996	1997	1998	1999
South, East and South-East Asia					
Inward	29.700	88.000	93.500	87.200	96.100
Outward	16.300	49.500	47.700	27.000	35.700
Developing Countries					
Inward	50.100	145.000	178.800	179.500	207.600
Outward	20.500	57.800	64.300	33.000	65.600
World					
Inward	182.600	377.500	473.100	680.100	865.500
Outward	203.100	390.800	471.900	687.100	799.900

Figures in US $ billion

Source: UNCTAD World Investment Report 2000.

We list below some of the major reasons that can be attributed to the declining inflows of foreign direct investment in India.

Tax Structure for Foreign Investors

Mauritius had been India's leading FDI partner for several years, nearly half of India's portfolio investment is routed through the island. Mauritius is known as "tax haven" among investors willing to invest in India, the island got this name as a result of the double taxation treaty which was signed in 1983 between the two countries (Rao, 2000). The treaty allows residents of Mauritius who invest in India to be taxed under Mauritian law rather than Indian law. India has a 30 per cent tax on short-term (less than one year) capital gains and 10 per cent tax on long-term capital gains whereas under Mauritian law investors are not taxed on dividends as well as on capital gains (Rao, 2000).

Recently, there has been a slow down in FDI inflows to India from Mauritius, the inflows from Mauritius peaked to the highest level in July 2000 when $165.4 million flowed in and thereafter it declined to $59.2 million in the following month and slumped to $18 million in September (Edwin, 2000). The decline in inflows from Mauritius was a consequence of the demand of tax by Indian tax officials from five foreign funds based in Mauritius, which sparked off a market collapse and probably the worst standoff between foreign investors and the Indian government (Rao, 2000). Inflows from the US peaked to the highest level in May 2000 when investors brought in $86.3 million, whereas in July the investment inflows slumped to $4 million and then increased marginally in August to $6 million (Edwin, 2000). The inflows from Mauritius are nothing but routed US investments, since Indian and Mauritius government are planning to review the terms on double taxation treaty, this has caused a decline in investment inflows from Mauritius. On the other hand, the investment from US increased by $2 million in the month of August, 2000.

Corporate tax rates in East Asia are generally in the range of 15-30 per cent, compared with a rate of 48 per cent for foreign investors in India (Bajpai, *et al*, 2000). High corporate tax rate is definitely a major disincentive to foreign corporate investment in India. Foreign fund managers argue that India should abolish capital gains tax for all investors so that they don't need to seek tax havens (Rao, 2000).

Restrictive FDI Regime

The FDI regime in India is still restrictive. As a consequence with regard to cross border ventures India ranks 49th in the GCR 2000 (Global Competitiveness Report, 2000), while other emerging economies in the region, such as Malaysia, China, Thailand, and Indonesia rank 25th, 28th, 31st and 44th respectively. Despite the fact that India is the second largest receiver of FDI after China, it ranks among the lowest ranked countries in terms of global competitiveness. Foreign ownership between 51 and 100 per cent equity still has to go through a long procedural tangle of governmental approval (Bajpai, *et al.*, 2000). This rule should be scrapped in favour of hassle free automatic approval for 100 per cent foreign ownership barring on a small list of select sectors that may continue to require government authorization.

Indian Chamber of Commerce brought out a report (Jha, 2000) that showed that FDI in India has to go through 27 clearances after the FIPB (Foreign Investment Promotion

Board) has approved the investment. Among the problems are ambiguities in policy, lack of unanimity between Central and State governments and the inevitable delay in administrative decision making, which persists particularly at the state operating level. The Indian government has to make efforts to bring about greater amount of coordination between the State and Central governments.

Recently, the government proposed to hike foreign investment limit for MNC Asset Management Companies (AMC's). Under the existing policy, MNCs are permitted to hold 51 per cent stake if they bring in $0.5 million and 76 per cent if they bring in $5 million (Iyenger, 2000). The government received an application from GE capital services, which is proposing to bring in $5 million provided it is permitted to hold 90 per cent stake. FIPB is seeking policy change and propose that the 100 per cent equity investments should be permitted by foreign AMC's the government sources have confirmed that the policy was under review and a decision in GE application would be taken only after an opinion has been formed by the group of ministers of foreign direct investments (Iyenger, 2000).

Since the beginning of the economic liberalization in India the food processing industry, the soft drinks and the confectionery sectors have recorded the highest inflow of foreign investment, followed by the fruits and vegetable products, grain based products, meat and poultry, and milk food sectors (International Market Insight Reports, 2000). India's food industry constitutes a relatively small portion of the economy, although India is the world's second largest producer of food products. The Government of India (GOI) must consider permitting 100 per cent foreign direct investment (FDI) in the food processing sector through the automatic approval route.

Inadequate Infrastructure

There are serious deficits in India's infrastructure that may be a significant deterrent of foreign direct investment. A number of international investors are willing to move their funds to India, as they now see India as a safe bet for their investment but they are put off due to the lack of adequate infrastructural facilities such as uninterrupted power, good roads, adequate port and sound telecommunication facilities. Continuing fiscal difficulties that are often linked to the chronic infrastructure difficulties remain a major challenge for India. Consequently the government budgets are inadequate to cover these infrastructural deficits. The Government of India has formulated specific policy initiatives to render the infrastructure sector an attractive destination for FDI. The main highlights (Jha, 2000) of these policy initiatives include the following (see *Annexure II*).

(i) Establishing a framework for the integration of public and private sector initiatives,

(ii) Market driven pricing for infrastructural services making investment in this sector particularly profitable,

(iii) Packages of fiscal incentives for investment in this sector including reduced import tariffs, tax holidays of five years, income tax exemptions, and cuts in capital gains tax,

(iv) Streamlining procedures for foreign investment,

(v) Encouraging and providing special facilities for financing of such investments.

Stringent Labour Laws

Labour-intensive manufacturing exports require competitive and flexible enterprises that can vary their employment according to changes in market demand and changes in technology. However Indian labour laws prohibit large companies to retrench or layoff any worker or close down the unit without the permission of the state government (Bajpai, *et al.*, 2000). This law was enacted to prevent unfair retrenchment or layoffs, but the employees now exploit the law as a provision for job security. Therefore, India remains an unattractive base among such production units and investor groups.

Lack of Expatriate Interests

In India, efforts to attract expatriate investment have been significantly less systematized. In China and South-East Asian countries, expatriates have played an important role in bringing about economic revival (Dasgupta, 2000). Indian expatriates, in contrast, have been unenthusiastic about bringing funds into the country, partly because of the complicated procedures involved. One chief executive indicated that currently his company does not have even a single expatriate in India, in contrast it has 40 expatriates in China including people deputed from their Indian company (Bajpai, *et al.*, 2000). But greater liberalization in the past year resulted in a 46 per cent surge of flows (amounting to $1.171 billion) into non-resident Indian bank accounts between April and October, 1999. The proposal to allow automatic repatriation of dividend income is also encouraging. India's industry minister Murasoli Maran suggested that if repatriation is allowed through the automatic route, there will be 'India fever' among foreign banks might be allowed to handle and monitor the repatriation, which will make the inward flow of funds more liquid.

No Liberalization in Exist Barriers

The major deterrent to the flow of large volumes of FDI to India is the stringent exit barriers. An exit policy needs to be formulated such that the firms can enter and exit the Indian market pretty easily. As seen above one of the reasons that makes exit for a firm difficult are stringent labour laws. The other drawback is that the current regulatory framework does not give enough room to these foreign funded firms to undertake restructuring.

Political Risk

India suffered political instability for a few years owing to the failure of any party to win an absolute majority in Parliament. Political stability has returned since the previous general elections in 1999. Even, however, political instability did not change India's economic course though it delayed the decision making process relating to the economy. The economic liberalization in India is accepted as a necessity by all parties including the Communist Party of India (Marxist). Moreover, no policy framed by the past government has been reversed by any successive government. Thus, political instability in India, in practical terms, posed no risk to foreign direct investors.

Conclusion

It is no doubt that India has started to focus on second round of reforms and is now concentrating on its strengths and policy measures to attract foreign direct investments. The government has laid out 42 measures that will accelerate the growth of FDI in India. At 33rd annual general meeting (Press Information Bureau, 2000) of Asian Development Bank held at Chiang Mai, Thailand, India's finance minister Yashwant Sinha invited institutional investors, financiers and policy makers for a mutually beneficial relationship adding that India offers substantial potential in IT and communications, knowledge based industries, infrastructure and the energy sector.

The patterns of direct investment in fiscal years 1999-2000 and 2000-2001 will provide strong indications as to whether the recent drop in FDI inflows was an anomaly or the beginning of an unfortunate trend. If an anomaly, then India can start to build up on past successes. If it is the start of a trend of falling investment inflows, then further liberal policy measures will be required. Either way, there are steps India can and should take to increase its inward direct investment. Research and experience indicate that (Bajpai, *et al.*, 2000):

(i) Costs are crucial to attracting export-oriented investment. Labour flexibility, low tax rates, export processing zones, and simpler entry procedures can help.

(ii) Market size is crucial to domestic market-oriented investment, but so are entry procedures and the ability to remit earnings. In addition, such investment is not to be feared, though affected interest groups may require astute political management.

(iii) Infrastructure investment demands transparency in establishing the contract, a commitment to abide by the agreement, and a mechanism for handling unforeseen disagreements efficiently.

All three forms can bring large benefits to India. Ultimately, the deciding factor for each investor will be the ability to generate profits. All investment facilitation measures should aim to enhance that goal. India offers a highly lucrative market to these foreign investors, but the current Indian environment does not offer safe and secure landing place for these investors. The Government of India should be friendlier towards the businesses, and must consider privatization of its infrastructural units, such as telecommunication, highways, electricity, etc. however, privatization can be seen as a threat to unemployment. In contrast, we perceive privatization as the end of slacking by the government employees while performing their duties, end to corruption, end to the heavy leakage of funds allocated to projects. In other words make the entire system inefficient. In addition, privatization can also lead to a rise in employment because of the industrial boom that will trigger off as a result of efficient infrastructure, most importantly communication and transportation which are the backbone of any business.

Another area where India needs to improve and concentrate is the proper implementation and evaluation of the policies framed by the government. It entirely depends upon the current policymakers where they want to place India in the coming years. This is the time to react and make good use of the opportunity of the boom created as a result of information explosion.

Section–II

Polity, Constitution and The Parliamentary Democracy

13

THE CRISIS OF THE NATION STATE IN INDIA

Prof. H.M. Jain

During the British rule it was a widely prevalent view that India was a mere geographical expression and not a nation. The nationalist opinion which prided on unity in diversity in India attributed that view to Imperalist prejudices. The leaders of the freedom movement notably Gandhi and Nehru strove to enlist all sections of people, the Muslims and the outcastes in particular in the national cause and refused to accept the two nation theory of Jinnah and his demand for a separate independent homeland for the Muslims wherein they may feel free of the fear of Hindu majority rule. The nationalists did not accept that the Muslims constituted a separate nation but were forced by events to accept a separate homeland for them. The partition of India in 1947 was carried out in response to this urge of the Muslims led by the Muslim League. Pakistan, the outcome of this partition, was founded on the theory that the Muslims constituted a separate nation and were therefore entitled to a separate state. The basis of the partition was thus religion. Pakistan naturally declared itself to be an Islamic state.

The nationalist leaders who reluctantly accepted partition and formation of a separate sovereign state comprising the Muslim majority areas, refused to accept the two nation theory and therefore opted for a secular polity where religion will be irrelevant to politics and public life. They believed that religion and language were mere forms of cultural expression and what was needed was not recognition of communalism but guarantee of fundamental individual rights and freedom by the Constitution. This approach found expression in the constitutional guarantees of Freedom and Equality in Articles 14-22 of the Indian Constitution.

But the Founding Fathers did not stop with these provisions. They also gave due recognition to the religious and cultural and educational rights of the minorities, thus separating the letter from the mainstream. If the purpose was to protect the minorities from discrimination in public life, in state services, in educational institutions, that purpose was fully served by the guarantees of equality and freedom. The constitutional recognition of minorities and their distinct, separate rights and interests, fractured the concept of a single nation, the conception of the Indian nation, the concept of the nation state, *ab initio*. It was fractured by the Founding Fathers themselves.

Independent India therefore did not start with a nation state; it was not a composite nation either as a section of politicians misled people to believe. It is not surprising that the foremost problem faced by the infant Indian republic, was of national integration. That problem has assumed alarming proportions, so much so that today we are talking of the crisis of the nation state.

The Indian leaders, to begin with, thought that the way to national integration would be a policy of secularism, but secularism needed to ignore the religious factor in the shaping of public policy. The Indian state was precluded from disregarding religion altogether owing to the constitutional guarantees of cultural and educational rights to the minorities. The Constitution itself admits that these minorities may be linguistic or religious. Primarily and predominantly they were religious minorities whose rights were made the subject of special provision in the Constitution.

The result was that while professing secularism as a principle of state policy, the Indian state was following a policy of treating the Muslims as a separate entity, entitled to special *madarsas*, their personal law, to the University at Aligarh, and the like. So much so that where it hurt the Muslim sentiment, the Government is not prepared to redress blatant and patent historic wrongs done to the Hindus by the Muslim rulers in the past.

This was anything but secularism. A section of the nationalist opinion condemned it as minorityism, or pseudo-secularism. The underlying purpose of such an approach was not national integration but political partisan exploitation of the minorities.

This gap between the profession and practice in secularism and national integration has grown and widened over the years, leading to the Ayodhya imbroglio and to a state of continuous tension as between the two principal communities ever since. The crisis of the nation state in India should primarily be understood as one which is rooted in the two nation theory, a theory which is irrefutable in its content and logic alike. Pakistan which was the outcome of this theory has formed one homogenous religious community and though the country was divided on the linguistic basis to form a separate state of Bangladesh in 1971, there never were any communal riots in pre-1971 Pakistan.

India which accepted partition but not the two nation theory has continued to be rocked by communal riots and perpetual tensions and social heterogeneity and hiatus continues to rise, not decline.

Scheduled Castes and Scheduled Tribes and Other Backward Classes

Added to this social hiatus between the Hindus and the Muslims, there has been an additional factor of social disintegration by a policy of identifying and isolating sections of people on the basis of their caste and community. First, for nearly forty years after Independence it was the Scheduled

Castes and Scheduled Tribes who were identified for special treatment, for reservations in services and educational institutions, setting them apart from the national mainstream, with no efforts made at de-scheduling castes and scheduled tribes or even their so-called "creamy layer". Contrary to promoting national integration and nation-building the policy of reservations tended only to consolidate casteism as a permanent factor in Indian politices, making the goal of national integration a distant dream.

In 1990, the National Front government headed by V.P. Singh was driven by inner party strife to announce its decision to implement the Mandal Commission recommendations, in abeyance for a long time, on reservation for 'Other Backward Classes' (OBCs) to the extent of 27 per cent of seats and posts. Coupled with 15.0 per cent reservation for Scheduled Castes and Scheduled Tribes 7.5 per cent, reservation quota in educational institutions and government services would total up to 49.5 per cent.

However, this was not the end of the reservation race. In many states in the south reservation ceilings have been raised much higher, in gross violation of the juridically determined limit. In Tamilnadu it is 69 per cent. Karnataka fixed it at 80 per cent under a G.O. issued on 25 July, 1994. In Andhra Pradesh the reservation net is being expanded to cover more and more communities. In Kerala the whole of Muslims population has been declared backward, though Kerala is the first state to have achieved 100 per cent literacy.

The reservation drive and the politics underlying it have caused deep fissures in the Indian society and the creamy layer of the society comprising the upper castes feels discriminated. It is a case of reverse discrimination and not just of affirmative action. The youth among the upper castes are particularly a frustrated lot today. They are denied equality and equal protection of the laws, the basic assurances of any democratic polity, only because they must recompense for the injustices of their forefathers. Merit has been subordinated to reservation, and reservation is related to caste and not material needs. There is no regard for efficiency in service or maintenance of a minimum level of excellence in performance.

The reservation policy has resulted in an apparent social disharmony in society and sadly enough, divisions are based on caste and communal lines. Even among the OBCs there are innumerable divisions and sub-divisions and there is a strong feeling that reservations must be confined to the deserving ones only, leaving out the creamy layer among them. This forecastes inner strife among the backwards themselves.

These divisions and subdivisions are leading to a state of social disintegration and if social solidarity is one of the prerequisites of nation building, the crisis of the nation state in India can be easily understood and related to this phenomenon of social disintegration caused by a reckless reservation policy.

Factors Contributing to the Crisis of the Nation State

The phenomenon of social disintegration is bound to tell upon political life and institutions which have come to be singularly caste based and caste dominated.

Caste politics has even subordinated the rule of law and led to erosion in moral values from public life. Corruption is now accepted as inevitable and its scale is rising from one scandal to another. In the last few years so many cases of corruption in high places have been uncovered that people and politicians alike have become insensitive to any fresh disclosure. It all began with the Howitzer gun deal with A.F. Bofors of Sweden, followed by or parallel with submarine deal with West Germany. Soon after the country was rocked by the sugar scandal in which several Union Ministers and top bureaucrats were directly involved and were indicated by a Joint Parliamentary Committee which was appointed to probe into the matter. The rumblings of the public criticism were continuing when they were drowned by an explosion in the stock market. There was unearthed the securities scam involving Harshad Mehta who publicly disclosed that he had passed huge sums of money to the Prime Minister himself in a suitcase. Close upon the heels of the securities scam some of the public activists forced upon the CBI investigation in the hawala scam involving a number of union ministers, opposition leaders and the Prime Minister himself.

The Rs. 900 crore Dhabol power project contracted with Enron of USA will reveal several skeletons in the cupboard and these may include the misdeeds and misappropriation of the Maharashtra Government's of Sharad Pawar with the connivance or collusion of the Union Government. Open allegations of corruption and abuse of power were levelled against Chief Minister Sharad Pawar by two top level bureaucrats of the state, one of them swearing in an affidavit in the state High Court. The Bombay blasts case investigations, though in early stages as yet, have made available sufficient evidence so as to implicate the high ups in the government and bureaucracy in this barbaric act wanton discretion of life and property in Mumbai.

Corruption has corroded public probity of politicians and bureaucracy at all levels. It has taken innumerable forms. Firstly, there are cuts or payoffs or kickbacks in the international contracts. The Enronpower company used a new term for this, namely, "educating" the Indians for which it admitted to have spent some 62 crores of rupees. It was ready to reduce contracted price of the project by some 900 crores whereas the Maharashtra Government was insisting on a concession of 1500 crores on a total cost project of 9,000 crores. Secondly, there are deliberate efforts to create scarcity of essential commodities like sugar and thereby extract thousands of crores of rupees as cut of the profits of the trade. Thirdly, there are payoffs from havala transactions, and fourthly, from artificial boosting of the equity prices in the stock market.

These are some of the recent and more sophisticated forms of corruption. They do not take account of the traditional greasing of the palm of the governmental functionary from the highest to the lowest rung for sundry favours from the moving of the file to the taking of decision and the delivery of the orders. Nor do they take into account the gross inefficiency, carelessness, negligence, incompetence, lethargy, unpunctuality, that characterise our administrative machinery.

In fact corruption is so omnipresent, omnipotent and omniscient that it is hard to describe or define it but its impact on the nation state can easily be guaged. It has, in the first place, led to a total decline of public morality. The concept of public morality has simply vanished. Secondly, work culture and work efficiency are immediate casualties. Thirdly, there is a large scale public discontent and encouragement to dubious means and methods to get things done, as it were. Fourthly, the net result is subversion of rule of law and its substitution by what may be called a consensual process in which the rule is you are okay, I am okay, everyone is okay. Since public treasury is nobody's property its mutual loot is quite legitimate so long as there is reciprocity in action and reaction.

The nation state is thereby reduced to an aggregate of self-seeking self-perpetuating individuals, natural and corporate, who monopolise the state power and its resources for their own selfish ends, exploit it and corrupt it even to the point of jeopardising national security and her territorial integrity and political independence.

If there is any single factor which can be held responsible for the crisis of the nation state in India today, it is the corruption of public life, erosion of morality from politics complete divorce between ethics and politics, to reverse the Gandhian equation.

It is this factor which has eroded rule of law and shaken public confidence in the political process, encouraged terrorism and militancy, created the nexus between crime and politics, between political power and the mafia, eroded educational institutions of higher learning and research, subverted public services like health, transport, sanitation, power supply, water supply, and given rise to frequent breakdown of law and order, putting at great risk the life and property of citizens.

The sad part of the nation building process is that corruption has come to be accepted passively. Even the late Jawaharlal Nehru acknowledged that it was inevitable, more so in a growing and expanding democracy. The modern day Marxists or to be more true, apologists of Marxism, dismiss it as an essential component of the bourgeoisie liberal state and as such incorrigible. There is either helplessness or complacency about the role of corruption in the present day public and political life in India. Intellectuals and politicians alike are given to much hypocrisy on this issue which it seems, is having the effect of nipping the emerging Indian nation-state in the bud.

One inevitable outcome of large scale breakdown of public morals and failure of Rule of Law has been the emergence and growth of regional movements for regional autonomy such as Uttranchal, Jharkhand, Chhattisgarh, Vidarbha, etc. or even for secession as in Bodoland, Kashmir, Punjab. The discontent often germinates from developmental imbalance, which ethnic and cultural chauvanists are quick to politicise. In some cases encouragement and aid from abroad (as in case of Punjab) or from across the border (Punjab and Kashmir) may lend militancy to these local regional movements which may, as in Punjab and Kashmir, take to terrorism as a strategy and weapon.

In the fifties there were secessionist forces in the southern states but the Indian state was able to overcome these forces successfully and the factors contributing to their success can teach a lot to those who are engaged in curbing insurgency in Kashmir. In the first place, they had a clear vision in their mind as to what was permissible and what was not. There was a unanimity among ruling elite that secession would not at any cost be tolerated and unity and integrity of the country would at all cost be preserved. To this end they brought in the 15th constitutional amendment and exhibited firm determination in implementing it. The result was that the secessionist movement sponsored by the D.M.K. vanished in thin air. The noise of secession in the south was heard no more. This was not merely a success of appropriate constitutional legal measures. These measures in themselves were the reflection of firmness of mind, of sincerity of purpose, and clarity of vision.

On the contrary, in regard to Kashmir the policy of the Indian state has been quite equivocal, even vague and confusing. One instance which would be enough to illustrate this point is the response of the Indian state to the abduction of the five foreign tourists by the militants belonging to *Harkat-ul-Islam*, the portage like other similar outfits, of Pakistan. The Indian Government had ruled out any option other than negotiations and persuasions to secure the release of these innocent foreigners, one of whom had already been beheaded by the abductors. Simultaneously the Indian Government had been affirming that it had documentary evidence to prove the connivance and even collusion of Pakistan in this heinous act. Were the means of persuasion and negotiation commensurate with the requirements of the situation? And if they were not, they show that the government had no resolve or strategy to secure the release of the hostages. There were a number of other alternatives which the government could have employed to send the right signals to the militants and their patron state, and these included all means and measures short of war, notably, severance of diplomatic relations, confiscation of Pakistani property, both private and public, in India, expulsion of Pakistanis from India, bombardment of militant and terrorist training camps in occupied Kashmir and even in Pakistan, even bombardment of the nuclear installation in Khauta (Pakistan) after or even without annulment of the agreement concluded by Rajiv Gandhi in this regard.

These steps, even one or more of them would have impressed upon the militants and terrorists, upon Pakistan and upon the whole world the sincerity and seriousness of the Indian state regarding its position that Kashmir was an integral part of India, that it would root out militancy from the state, annihilate the terrorists and secure and safeguard each and every life and property.

These steps, require the strength of character and courage of conviction and these come from honesty of purpose and firmness of will. These qualities cannot flourish in an environment of all round corruption in which nearly all politicians are competing with the top bureaucracy together the booty.

The success of the constitutional measures adopted in the early sixties to contain the secessionist movement in the south was due in no small measure to the overall developmental thrust (social and economic) of the Union Government and leadership in a planned manner. Planning and planned development began to wane after the death of Nehru and have been limping ever since until the economy was totally swept away by the wave of privatisation, free markets, globalisation resulting in heavy disinvestment of public sector and leading to free entry of foreign capital.

These changes in the economic field have made political life value free. The only focus of politics now is power, and the struggle for acquiring power is the only occupation of political leaders and parties.

Such leaders and such parties are hardly fit to safeguard the territorial integrity or political independence of the country. They are simply unequal to the task. They have neither the character nor the capability for it. This is where lies the crisis of the nation state in India today.

14

POLITY, CONSTITUTION AND PARLIAMENTARY DEMOCRACY

Dr. M.K. Jain

Democracy means popular government and it broadly has two forms; parliamentary and presidential. These two forms refer to the differences in the distribution of political resources and in the sharing and exercising of power. As Robert Dahl puts it, "In all countries, decisions of the government seemed to be reached as a result of some combination of direct or indirect participation by citizens, activists and elites......". This balance may vary leading to the institution of democracy taking either of the a two forms. Since India has opted for the parlimentary model, the present discussion is limited to that model.

A synonym for a democratic government is a representative government. The term is best defined by John Stuart Mill in his classic, *Consideration on Representative Government*. It is a government wherein:

> The whole people or some numerous portion of them exercise through deputies periodically elected by themselves the ultimate controlling power which in very constitution must reside somewhere... this ultimate power, they must possess in all its completeness.

In simpler terms, parliamentary democracy stands for a form of government in which the people rule through their representatives sitting in the Parliament, chosen by adult suffrage through free and fair elections; the existence of two or more political parties is an essential postulate; fundamental rights are guaranteed; there is communication between the government and the masses and a high degree of coordination between the legislature (the Parliament) and the executive, viz., the Priesident, the Prime Minister and his cabinet.

A basic feature that characterises the parliamentary model is the presence of double executive. The President of India is the constitutional, though titular, head of the state whereas the Prime Minister and his cabinet are the real executive. The PM and his cabinet are chosen from the majority party in the Parliament and are responsible to it for their policies and actions. They remain in office as long as they enjoy the confidence of the legislature. The cabinet works as a team under the leadership of the PM. For the successful implementation of policies, each member of the cabinet is individually responsible. The cabinet is also collectively responsible to the Legislature. The cabinet members have to present a common front and work as a composite whole. All this operates within a system of checks and balances whereby all the three organs of the government exercise a fair measure of control over each other to check tendencies towards absolutism.

The reason why we chose this form of government was the inheritance of the past bearing down heavily on the present. It has been best summed up by Pt. Nehru:

> We chose this system of parlimentary democracy deliberately; we chose it not only because, to some extent we had always thought on those lines previously but because we thought it was in keeping with our old traditions, not as they were, but adjusted to the new conditions and new surroundings. We chose it, also, let us give credit where credit to due, because we approved

of its functioning in other countries more especially in United Kingdom.

The Constitutional Arrangements

Our founding fathers made arrangements for the working of parliamentary democracy vide elaborate articles in the Constitution. Articles 79 to 123 deal with provisions relating to the Parliament. These articles describe the composition of the Parliament, the tenure of the two Houses, their roles in their respective chambers, the conduct of business in the two chambers, the qualifications of members of the Parliament, the legislative and financial procedures and parliamentary privileges. The system of checks and balances on and by the Parliament is not specifically described but the intentions of the Constituent Assembly are quite clear, that the Parliament should be checked from becoming an irresponsible tyrant. Take for instance Article 86, which gives to the President the right to address the houses of Parliament and Article 123 which gives him the right to issue ordinances when Parliament is not in session.

The hallmark of a democratic polity is its ability to provide fundamental rights to its citizens. The Indian Constitution gives an exhaustive list of rights vide articles 12 to 35. These include the right to freedom, quality, cultural and educational rights, right to religion, rights to constitutional remedies and against exploitation—a reference to these has been made in this chapter. While freedom in all forms is welcome and desirable, in a parliamentary democracy, the freedom of speech and press assumes special significance.

Role of Parliament

A few significant aspects of the role of the parliament and discussed below:

As Agency to Control Executive

The words "controlling the executive" do not imply that the Parliament is merely a watchdog over the executive. What is meant is that certain parliamentary procedures have been evolved in the course of time which make the executive accountable, responsive and responsible to the Parliament. Such methods therefore not only control but sustain the government as well, as an uncontrolled government would be an unhealthy government. Some instruments of parliamentary control are questions, adjournment motions, no-confidence motions, calling attention notices, half-an-hour discussions, budget discussions and control through parliamentary committees. All these are effective instruments for securing redress from administrative errors, discussing maters of urgent public importance. The no-confidence motion, could result in even the fall of the government.

As a Legislative Assembly

The major chunk of the Parliament's time is spent in enacting legislation. It legislates on all subjects in the Union List, the Concurrent List and, in special circumstances, on the subjects mentioned in the State List. In addition, mention has been made in the Constitution about the residuary powers of the Union Government in respect of any matter not enumerated in any of the three lists. Though, in the light of the increasing importance of delegated legislation, the bulk of the work relating to legislation is done by civil servants, the contribution of the Parliament can not be neglected. It has an impressive record of legislation on a wide array of social, political and economic matters.

As a Representative Assembly

Every Member of the Parliament represents the segment of the population comprising his constituency. Therefore, each M.P., in his individual capacity and the Parliament as a whole, facilitate ventilation of people's grievances, spread of popular education, and most importantly, the integration of conflicting interests. The last mentioned function is closely associated with the norms of representative behaviour. It demands that a legislator should keep the interest of the nation above that of the masses. Mahatma Gandhi had remarked in this context that "in matters of vital importance, leaders must act contrary to the mass opinion if it does not command itself to their reason". Edmund Burke, too while talking of the role of a parliamentarian, had averred that, while giving his constituency complete attention, "his unbiased opinion his mature judgement, his enlightened conscience, he ought not to sacrifice to you, to any man or to any set of men living...".

As a Public Forum

Speech is the essence of parliamentary activity. It is here that the grievances of the public are ventilated. A very wide range of views find expression here and the parliamentarians shape the emerging legislations, act as social investigators and keep the public educated about the activities of the government.

The proceedings in the Parliament are heard, read and seen by the people and it is for this reason that Bagehot calls it the expressive or 'teaching' function of the Parliament. The right to speech in the Parliament however, ought to be exercised with restraint. "Not the bedlam of a multitude of voices but the balanced and ordered procedure of speech and reply of argument and a debate...".

Parliament and Foreign Affairs

The Indian Parliament has played a very inhibited, rather than an innovative role in relation to the conduct of foreign affairs. The reasons given by S. Nihal Singh, though given in the context of the 1970s, holds good even today. He remarked that the role of the Parliament in questioning defence estimates and appropriations is minimal because:

> Most members lack the expertise that is necessary to question defence assumptions in a complex field. Besides, most political parties are inclined to believe that to suggest reductions in defence expenditure would be to lay themselves open to the charge of being unpatriotic.

Parliament and Social Change

Although the Indian Parliament cannot as yet be labelled as the harbinger of a new social order, it upholds ideals which can bring about a more egalitarian social. Balram Jhakar says, "it is a significant fact of the Indian political scene that our Parliament which has been a converging centre of influence in the polity all along has shown remarkable dynamism as a positive mediating agent of change".

Examples to support the claim are also not lacking. It raises a powerful voice when a *Harijan* is ill-treated, is uncompromising in its oppostion whenever human freedom or rights are threatened and pays special attention to weaker sections during the formulation of socio-economic policies and programmes. There is an impressive list of legislations to curb social evils like child marriage and dowry, laws relating to the welfare of women, labourers and Scheduled Castes and Scheduled Tribes. The Parliament makes genuine efforts to change the society but ironically, the tradition-bound society refuses, on most occasions, to respond to the changing times.

REFERENCES

1. Ashwani K.Ray, "Indian Violent Democracy", *Illustrated Weekly of India.*
2. Balram Jhakar, *People, Parliament and Administration* (New Delhi, Metroplitan).
3. Carl. J. Friedrich, *Constitutional Government and Democracy.*
4. Friedrich, *Constitutional Government and Democracy.*
5. Robert. A Dahl, *Modern Political Analysis* (New Delhi: Prentice Hall, 1999).
6. Ramesh K. Arora and Rajni Goyal, *Indian Public Administration.*
7. Subhash Kashyap, *Jawaharlal Nehru, the Constitiution, the Parliament* (New Delhi, Metropolitan).
8. S. Nihal Singh, "Parliaments Role in Policy Making", in S.L. Shakdhar ed., *the Constitution and Parliament in India* (Delhi, National).

15

JAWAHARLAL NEHRU AND THE CONSTITUTION MAKING IN INDIA

H.M. Jain

The proceedings of the Constituent Assembly do not show Jawahar Lal Nehru playing any dominating, or leading role in its deliberations nor can Nehru's participation in the deliberations of the Assembly be said to be pervasive, limited as it was, to a few though significant subjects, such as the language, right of property, election method of the President, age of retirement for Supreme Court Judges, and above all, to moving and explaining the Objectives Resolution. Nevertheless, Jawahar Lal Nehru was described, along with Sardar Patel, by T.T. Krishnamachari, a member of the Drafting Committee, as the "real architects of the Constitution".[1]

Another member who himself dominated the proceedings of the Assembly, namely, H.V. Kamath described Jawahar Lal Nehru as playing the role of the *Brihaspati in the Kendra* which according to an astrological *sutra* nullifies the effect of the other planets. He said "besides the nine planets and also the tenth *Dasamgrah*, there were two in one which obviated the malefic influence of the other planets and those planets were Pt. Nehru and Sardar Patel."[2]

Seth Govind Das echoed the sentiments of many when he said that it is the PM, Pt. Nehru "who deserves our sincere thanks and gratitude for guiding and leading the Constituent Assembly along the path of constitution making."[3]

As already indicated, Jawahar Lal Nehru's direct role in India's constitution making was nothing extraordinary. He was not a member of the Drafting Committee. His participation in the constituent Assembly debates was limited to a few, though significant, occasions only. His influence on constitution making was however acknowledged by all. This arose from a number of factors.

Firstly, Jawahar Lal Nehru was elected Chairman of two of the most important committees of the Constituent Assembly, namely, the Union Constitution and the Union Powers Committee. As a Chairman of these two committees, Jawahar Lal Nehru had significant and decisive hand in giving shape and content to the framework of the Union Government and its powers and functions. The Constituent Assembly merely gave its stamp of approval to the Principles enunciated in the Reports of these Committees and the Drafting Committee then put them into legal shape. Thus the real, basic policy making and the foundation laying work was carried out by these committees of which Nehru was the chairman. The Assembly, though sovereign and independent had hardly any option but to go by and accept and approve the expert advice in matters fundamental and only in matters of details could it influence the draft. For instance, the Union Constitution Committee had suggested that the tenure of the President be limited to a maximum of two terms of five years each, but the C.A. in adopting these provisions dropped the limit of two terms. Similarly in electing the President it pressed the amendment that only elected members of the Parliament and State Legislature would have the right to vote in the election.

Secondly, Jawahar Lal Nehru held a unique position in the Government, in the ruling Congress Party and among the people. As head of the government, his influence was necessarily great and obvious. As a pre-eminent leader of the national movement, a central figure of the Congress High Command and also as a leader of the Congress Parliamentary Party, his control over the ruling party was unquestioned, and was shared only with another leader, namely Sardar Patel. It could be said that two formed a duumvirate, in complete control of the Congress, and therefore the Constituent Assembly and the country. The nation as well as Constituent Assembly looked to these leaders, as it looked to no one else, for guidance, leadership and command.

Thirdly, added to these were the traits of Nehru's personality and character. He was a philosopher and an intellectual and a writer and his knowledge and understanding of history and command over the English language were second to none. He was inspired by the forces of socialist revolution though he was born and bred in the school of western liberal thought. He was a humanist, deadly opposed to the evils which capltalism brought in its wake, yet he believed in the dignity and freedom of the individual and held high the doctrines of Rules of Law and independence of the judiciary. He was thus influenced by the contradictory forces of liberalism, democracy and socialism. In this phase of India's history, socialism was best suited to give expression to the country's urges and aspirations. He was thus a natural leader of the people, specially of the youth who looked upon him as an ideal and an idol.

Lastly, with the socialist party cpting out of the Constituent Assembly Nehru, who was ardent advocate of the socialist cause within the Congress Party, came to be regarded as the spokeman for the socialist ideology on the Congress benches in the Constituent Assembly to whom other socialist members, few in number (like Shibban Lal Saxena, K.T. Shah, V.D. Tripathi, R.K. Sidhva, Poornima Banerjee, S.C. Banerjee, L.N. Sahu) could look for support and accommodation.

Therefore there was a general sense of satisfaction and assurance when Nehru was chosen to frame and move the Objectives Resolution which was to lay the foundation of the work of the Constiuent Assembly foundation stone of the Constitution laying down, as it were, "the terms of reference" of Constituent Assembly.

In terms of its literary quality and composition, its philosophical depth and ideological synthesis, the Objectives Resolution moved by Pt. Nehru in an inspiring speech, has no parallel. It succeeded in giving expression to the national consensus on high principles which should govern society and government in future, and manifests Nehru's pragmatism and idealism. It is a literary and a political masterpiece and has been very rightly and skilfully adapted to form the Preamble to the Indian Constitution. It is some tribute to its literacy and philosophical merit that Mr. Earnest Barker has reproduced the Preamble of Social and Political Theory. It may be recalled here that the CWC appointed an Expert Committee in July 1946 with Pt. Nehru as its Chairman to prepare a draft of the objectives of Constitution. The other members of the Committee were Asaf Ali, K.M. Munshi, N. Gopalaswami, Ayyangar, K.T. Shah, K. Santhanam, Humayun Kabir and Dr. D.R. Gadgil. As Chairman of this committee Pt. Nehru was largely responsible for the framing of the Objective Resolution which having been approved by the Expert Committee was moved in the Constituent Assembly by Pt. Nehru on 13 Dec. 1946.

Moving it, Pt. Nehru said "it is a Resolution, and yet, it is something much more than just a Resolution. It is a declaration. It is a firm resolve. It is a pledge and an undertaking and it is for all of us, I hope, a dedication. It seeks very feebly to tell the world of what we have thought or dreamt of so long, and what we now hope to achieve in the near future."

He went on to urge upon the House to "consider this resolution in this mighty prospect of our past, of the turmoil of the present and of the great and unborn future that is going to take place soon". The Objectives Resolution laid down the essentials or to use the phrase that become popular after the Supreme Court's decision in the Keshavanand Bharti case, the essential elements of the basic structure of the Constitution. As Pt. Nehru said, it sought to "give some indication to ourselves, to those millions in this country who are looking up to us and to the world at large, as to what we may do, what we seek to achieve, whether we are going."[5]

The Objectives Resolution is significant in setting down the tone and temper as well as the basic framework of the Constituent Assembly delibrations. It steers clear of the dogmatic or doctrinaire approaches and simultaneously proclaims the social and political goals of the future policy.

Pt. Nehru brought the attention of the House to remember that "this is not a moment for us to be technical and legal about small matters when we have big things to face, big things to say and big things to do." The Resolution laid down the fundamentals, which he said, "no group or party and hardly any individual in India can dispute." These essential were :

1. India was to be an independent sovereign Republic.

   Nehru said, "we stand for democracy, the fullest democracy... although in this Resolution we have not used the word "democratic" because we thought it is obvious that the word "Republic" contains that word and we did not want to use unnecessary words and redundant words, but we have done something much more than using the word. We have given the content of democracy in this Resolution."

2. Nehru claimed that we aim in this Resolution not only at Democracy, but more than that, at economic democracy.

   Thus without providing for a socialist state the Resolution aimed at what may be called socialism and democracy. Nehru declared "I stand for socialism and I hope India will stand for socialism and that India will go towards the Constitution of a socialist state and I do believe that the world will have to go that way. What form of socialism again is another matter for consideration, but the main thing is that in such a Resolution, if, in accordance with may own desire, I nad put in that we want a socialist state, we would have put in something which my be agreeable to many and may not be agreeable to some and we wanted this Resolution not to be controversial in regard to such matters". Nehru's approach was that "we have laid down, not theoretical words and formulas, but rather the content of the things we desire."

3. It envisaged a union of the territories comprising of British India and the Indian States with power divided between autonomous units and union.
4. All power and authority are derived from the people.
5. There shall be guaranteed and secured to all the people justice, equality, and freedom.
6. Adequate safeguards shall be provided for minorities, backward and tribal areas and depressed and other backward classes.
7. The integrity of the state and its sovereign rights according to the law of civilized nations shall be maintained.
8. The supreme goal is that this ancient land attains its rightful honoured place in the world and makes its full and willing contribution to the promotion of world peace and the welfare of mankind.[6]

In this memorable speach delivered while moving the Objectives Resolution Nehru underlined the principles governing the approach to the task of Constitution making and this approach was to guide the Constituent Assembly throughout the course of its deliberations. In brief, the principles, he emphasised, were -------

1. We have to bear in mind that we are here not to function for one party or one group, but always to think of India as a whole and always to think of the

welfare of the four hundred millions that comprise India. We are all now, in our respective spheres, partymen, belonging to this or that group and presumably we shall continue to act in our respective party. Nevertheless, the time comes when we have to rise above party and think of the nation, think sometimes of even the world at large of which our nation is great part. We should as far as we are capable of it, rise above our ordinary selves and party disputes and think of the great problem before us in widest and tolerant and most effective manner so that whatever we may produce should be worthy of India as a whole.

2. The Constitution which we frame is not an end by itself; it would be only the basis for further work. The Constitution should lead us to the real freedom that we have clamoured for and that real freedom in turn will bring food to our starving peoples, clothing for them, housing for them and all manner of opportunities of progress.

3. The House should consider that we are on the eve of revolutionary changes because when the spirit of a nation breaks its bonds it functions in peculiar ways. It may be that the constitution this House may frame, may not satisfy that free India. This House can not bind down the next generation, or the people, who will duly succeeded us in this task. Therefore, let us not troubles details will not survive for long, if they are achieved in conflict.

What we achieve by cooperation is likely to survive, what we gain here and there by conflict and by overbearing manners and by threats will not survive for long.

This spirit of conciliation and compromise was to mark the proceedings of the Assembly throughout its course and at the third reading stage many members pointed out and rightly so that the Constitution was the result of and bore the marks of compromise.

Nehru's insistence on economic democracy and his belief that the Constitution is not an end in itself but should be the means to a better future for the common man found the most vocal and definite expression in the constitutional provision on property right. This was Article 24 of the Draft Constitution (Art 31 of the Constitution) and owes its formulation to Nehru who was chosen to move it in the Assembly. It was to determine the whole social and economic philosophy of the new Indian State, and naturally therefore it was one of the most controversial provisions of the Constitution. As Ambedkar disclosed later on, speaking in the Rajya Sabha on March 19,1955:

".... the Congress party at the time when Art 31 was being framed was divided within itself. There were three sections in the Congress Party. One section was led by Sardar Vallabhbhai Patel, who stood for full compensation as enacted in our Land Acquisition Act, namely, market prices plus 15 per cent solatium. That was his point of view. Our PM was against compensation. Our friend Mr. Pant had conceived his *Zamindari* Abolition Bill before the Constitution was being actually framed. He wanted very safe delivery for his baby. So he had his own proposition. There was thus this tripartite struggle and we left the matter to them to decide in any way they liked... Even then we have made that article as elastic as we possibly could in the matter of compensation."[7] Nehru himself admitted, speaking in the Constituent Assembly, that "this draft article... is the result of a great deal of consultation, is the result in fact of the attempt to bring together and compromise various approaches to this question."[8] Giving details of this compromise he analysed the salient features of the draft, he was moving. They were :

1. There is no question of any expropriation without compensation.
2. If property is required for public purposes, the state shall pay compensation.
3. The principles on which and manner in which compensation shall be determined and paid shall be

laid down by law. He made it clear that while for "petty acquisition" it may be; possible to pay the market value as compensation, no such payment may be made "where large schemes of social reform, social engineering are involved." In such cases the state will have different standards of "fair and equitable compensation." For here the future of millions of people may be affected, the whole structure of the state may be shaken to its foundation so that "when we consider the equity if it we have to remember that the equity does not apply to the individual but also to the community." The ultimate balancing authority shall be the sovereign legislature of the country which can keep before it various factors.

4. The final authority is given to Parliament, subject only to the scrutiny of the Courts "in case of some grave error, in case of contravention of the Constitution or the like, and not otherwise."
5. Regarding certain pending measures or measures that have been already enacted, it makes it clear beyond any doubt that there should be no judicial interferences.

In regard to the scope for judicial review of parliamentary determination of compensation for acquisition of private property for public purposes, it is quite evident, Nehru was not sure what the draft provision would actually imply. The "revolutionary" in him pushes forth again and again to exclude Judicial review, but he is aware of the constraints within the party. Following observations made by him in the course of this speach, is evidence of his personal and political dilemma.

1. Naturally the Judiciary comes in to see if there has been a fraud on the Constitution or not. But normally speaking one presumes that any Parliament representing the entire community of the nation will certainly not commit a fraud on its own Constitution and will be very much concerned with doing justice to the individual as well as the community.

2. Within limits no judge and no Supreme Court can make itself a third chamber. No Supreme Court and no Judiciary can stand in judgement over the sovereign will of Parliament representing the will of the entire community.
3. Where the future of the community is concerned, no judiciary can come in. And if it comes in the way, ultimately the whole Constitution is a creature of Parliament.
4. If the question of property is not viewed in its historic, dynamic, moving, changing and revolutionary aspects; the whole thing may be settled in a way which may not have been any process of legislation.

As subsequent events confirmed, this compromise, favoured the advocates of the vested interests, those who demanded fair and equitable and justiciable market value as compensation for public acquisitions of private property, and at best it could be said that they conceded in form only, though not in substance. It is not clear whether Nehru could flatter himself for adhering to his basic principles and upholding his public assurances. There is no doubt that by moving Draft Art. 24 Nehru lent his own authority and prestige to it so that his followers would have no qualms of conscience in voting for it, though, as is evident from third reading observations, many of them realised that it was after all a legal trap.

Another important and vital question that rocked the Constituent Assembly was the question of official language, and in its resolution Nehru had more effective voice and influence. There were more than three hundred amendments to the draft articles dealing with this question. It was so controversial a question that the Drafting Committee was unable to put forward any agreed formulation on this question.

As N. Gopalaswami Ayyangar said, "The problem has been before us for quite a long time. We have discussed it amongst ourselves in small groups, in larger groups in the country, in the press and so on. Opinion has not always been unanimous on this question.[9] Presenting his Draft he said "this draft is the result of a great deal of thought, a great deal of discussion. It is also what has emerged as a compromise between opinions which were not easily reconcilable and therefore when you look at this draft, you have to take it not as a thing which is proposed by an individual member like me or by three members I include my two colleagues whose names are set down here. It is not to be looked upon something which we have put forth. It is the result of a compromise in respect of which great sacrifices of opinion, of very greatly cherished views and interests, these have been sacrificed for the purpose of achieving of this draft in a form that will be acceptable to the full House."[10]

Nehru gave his full support to the amendment of Gopalaswami Ayyangar and the policy lying behind it. He said, "I support that amendment not because I think it is perfect in every way; perhaps if I had my way I would like to change it here and there. But I know that this is the result of continuous effort and endeavour, and thought and consultation, and as a result of all that consultation and thought, some integrated thing took shape.Therefore, although I would have liked, or perhaps if I had chance, to lay greater emphasis on some aspects of that amendment, nevertheless after all that has happened I think that amendment displays not only the largest measure of agreement but also, I think, a thoughtout approach to this difficult problem."[11]

The notable points of Ayyangar's amendment enunciating the language policy to be incorporated in the Constitution were as follows:

1. Hindi should be adopted as the language for all official purposes of the Union and the script should be *Devanagri.*
2. For a period of 15 years English should continue to be used for all official purposes for which it was being used before the commencement of the Constitution.

3. The numerals to be used for all official union purposes should be of the International forms of Indian numerals.
4. Language spoken in the state should be recognised as the official language for that state.
5. The language for the time being authorised for use in the Union for official purposes shall be the official languages for communication between one state and another state or between a state and the Union.
6. Parliament may by law provide for the use of the English language after the said peried of fifteen years for such purposes as may be specified by law.
7. Until Parliament by law provides otherwise, all proceedings in the Supreme Court and authoritative texts of all bills, Acts of Parliament and legislatures, all orders, rules, regulations and by-laws shall be in the English language.

Pt. Nehru concluded with the observation: "We stand on the threshold of a new age. Therefore it is important that we should have the picture of India clearly in our minds. What sort of India do we want ? Do we want a modern India with its roots steeped in the past certainly insofar as it inspires us—do we want a modern India with modern science and all the rest of it, or do we want to live in some ancient age, in some other age which has no relations to the present ? You have to choose between the two. It is a question of approach. You have to choose whether you look forward or backward."[12]

Nehru's approach to the question of language as on other questions was thus determined by the wider goals he envisioned for the future polity. First and foremost in this approach was the consideration of the unity and integrity of India. He believed that while English was great on the basis of foreign language because a for eign language can never be the language of the people. Therefore, however great the English language may be "we have to think in doing our national work, our public and our private work as far as possible, in our own various languages and more particularly in the language that you may choose for all India use." Secondly, the language should be more or less a language of the people not a language of the learned categories.

Thirdly, this language should represent the composite culture of India. It should represent that composite culture which grew up in Northern India and the other parts of India. The word *Hindustani* Nehru thought, represented that composite language which is both the language of the people and the language of various groups. He emphasised that there was no question of our cutting ourselves away from our past but there is such a thing as marching forward and not turning back all the time. He warned in any event, whether you want it or not, world forces and currents will push you forward but if you are looking back you will stumble and fall repeatedly."[13]

Fourthly, there is the culture of a nation and of people which is important for it; there is also the culture of an age, the *Yugdharma* and if you do not align yourself with that culture of the age you are out of step with it. There is a national culture. There is an international culture. There is powerful international culture dominating the world. Call it if you like, a culture emanating from the machine age, from industry and all the developments of science that have taken place. We cannot make much progress merely by repeating old creeds. English is today the nearest approach to international language. Specially in the matter of numerals it would be conducive to rapid progress in the sciences and art to adopt international numerals. If we do not accept international numerals" we would put a tremendous burden on the children's mind and the grown up minds and our work will increase tremendously in our offices and elsewhere, and that work will be cut off from the rest of the world."[14]

Nehru's whole approach was dominated by considerations of the "interests of the development of a powerful nation (Indian) not an exclusive nation, not a nation trying to isolate itself from the rest of the world."[15]

Nehru therefore whole-heartedly lent support to the proposals for doing away with the separatism in Indian polity whether "it took the shape of separate electorate or other shapes" as separatism "has done a tremendous amount of evil to our country and to our people."

He was opposed to communalism and separatism in any form and felt that reservations on communal ground were inherently wrong. In a political democracy, he said, "reservations, instead of helping the party to be safeguarded and aided, is likely actually to turn against it..... where you are up against a full loaded democracy, if you seek to give safeguards to a minority, and a relatively small minority, you in fact isolate it. May be you protect it to some extent, but at what cost? At the cost of isolating it and keeping it away from the main current in which the majority is going."

"The result is that" they may get one anna in the rupee of protection at the cost of the remaining fifteen annas. The only way to proceed about it, whether from the point of view of the minority or from the point of view of majority—is to remove every barrier which separates them in the political domain so that they may develop and we may all work together. Therefore, I think that doing away with the reservation business is not only a good thing in itself but good for all concerned, and more specially for the minorites—but psychologically too it is a very good move for the nation and for the world. It shows that we are really sincere about this business of having secular democracy."

On other question, for instance, appointment of state Governors or election of the President or the Union, Nehru had the same considerations. He felt that from almost every point of view the proposal of a nominated Governor was not only desirable from the practical point of view but from the democratic point of view also. One point in favour of nominated Governor was that an elected Governor would to some extent encourage separatist provincial tendency and there would be far fewer common links with the Centre. He might be some kind of a rival almost in that particular majority group which for the moment controls the government of the province.

Another argument against an elected Governor would be the enormous expense involved and time and energy required and diverting them from the far more worthwhile projects. Nehru said,"I would undoubtedly mean, I think, encouraging that rather narrow provincial way of thinking and functioning in each province. That will make the Governor much more of a provincial figure than the need be. It would be infinitely better if he was not so intimately connected with the local politics of the province, with the factions in the provinces and it would be better to have a more detached figure, obviously a figure that is acceptable to the province and yet not known to be a part of the party machine of that province. On the whole it would be desirable to have people from outside—eminent people, sometimes who have not taken too great a part in politics. He advised that, "we should always view things from this context of preserving the unity, the stability and the security of India and not produce too many actors in our constitutional machinery which will tend to disrupt that unity by frequent recourse to vast elections which disturb people's minds and at the same time divert a great deal of our resources towards electoral machines rather than towards the reconstruction of the country." There was one more advantage in having nominated Governors, Nehru added as a postscript. That was eminent leaders of the minorities, eminent leaders of groups would have a far better chance in the process of nomination than in election.[16]

As chairman of the Union Constitution Committee and the Union Powers Committee Nehru had great influence on shaping the framework of the Union Government, and the method of election of the President is a remarkable example of ingenuity and perfection. The method of election suggested in the draft had many pecularities. It ensured that the President did not entertain any exaggerated notion of his power and authority and remained subordinate to the Government but at the same time "we have made his position one of great authority and dignity."

If the President were elected by adult franchise and did not have any real powers, it might become slightly anomalous and there might be just extraordinary expense of time and energy and money without any result. The method provided was as approximate to popular election as possible and yet did not involve any additional expenditure as in the Parliament and state legislatures there was already an existing electoral college. The method also ensured that there was uniformity in the scale of representation of the legislature of the unit in proportion to the population of the province concerned. Moreover there was also secured by this method a parity between the Union and the States by balancing the votes of the members of the Parliament against votes of the members of the state legislature. In this way Nehru's conception of organic unity of the country could find concrete expression. It would be thus seen that Nehru's approach to constitution making was very broad, secular, democratic, patriotic, flexible, internationalist and was opposed to narrow, rigid, sectarian, autocratic, communal, doctrinaire approach.

He was all the time well aware of the fact that the Constitution was only a means to serving the end of the people and as that end can not be fixed for all times, the Constitution, howsoever permanent one may like to be, must necessarily change with time and circumstances and must not become a prison house for the people from which there may be no escape. It must be a vehicle of life and progress. "A Constitution if it is out of touch with the people's life, aims and aspirations, it becomes rather empty if it falls behind these aims and it drags the people down. It should be something ahead to keep people's eyes and minds up to a certain high mark."

While we want this Constitution to be as solid and as permanent a structure as we can make it, nevertheless there is no permanence in constitutions. There should be a certain amount of flexibility. If you make anything rigid and permanent, you stop a Nation's growth, the growth of a living vital organic people. Therefore, it has to be flexible." Nehru went so far as to suggest that here should be laid down a period of years during which changes to the Constitution could be easily made without any difficult process. "Today.. when the world is in turmoil and we are passing through a very swift period of transition, what we may do today may not be wholly applicable tomorrow. Therefore, while we make a Constitution which is as sound and as basic as we can, it should also be flexible and for a period we should be in a position to change it with relative facility."

Nehru's basic philosophy and approach can be noticed throughout the proceedings of the Constituent Assembly. .. As T.T. Krishnamachari admitted in the closing stage of the Assembly" Nehru has been a source of great strength and help to us. In fact he has followed the Constitution and its various articles right from the beginning, and in many instances we have had his very great abilities as draftsman."[17] and writer. His personality was indelibly impressed on the Constitution.

This overriding influence of Nehru arose from the prominent position he held within the Congress Party and in the country at large. In the formulation of the party ideology and programme, his was a significant share. He was above all an intellectual and a philosopher. This is why he was choosen to draft the Objectives Resolution and as M. Saidulla admitted "The Drafting Committee was not a free agency... We were only asked to dress the baby and the baby was nothing but the Objectives Resolution which the Constituent Assembly passed. We were told that the Constitution must conform and remain within the four corners of the Objectives Resolution."[18]

It is a well-known fact that the Congress party was the dominant party in the Constituent Assembly and as testified by Shibban Lal Saxena "Congress Party meetings became meetings of the real Constituent Assembly and this real Assembly became the mock Assembly where decisions arrived at the Congress party meeting were registered."

Saidulla also admitted that "the Congress Parliamentary Party alone can give the imprimature of adoption in this House" and, therefore, "sometimes we found that they made their own recommendations which had to be put into the proper legal and constitutional shape by the members of the Drafting Committee."[19]

Dr. Ambedkar also acknowledged the importance of the role of Congress party in drafting of constitution. According to him, "It is because of the discipline of the Congress party that this Drafting Committee was able to pilot the Constitution in the Assembly with the sure knowledge as to the fate of each article and each amendment". He gave all the credit for the smooth sailing of the Draft Constitution in the Assembly to the Congress Party. Without the dominating position of the Congress party there would have been nothing but chaos in the Assembly. The Congress party brought into its proceedings a sense of order and discipline". He continued, "The task of the Drafting Committee would have been a very difficult one if this Constitution Assembly had been merely a motely crowd, at tessellated pavement without cement, a black stone here and white stone there in which each member of each group was a law unto itself."[20]

The fact is that the Congress party dominated the Assembly and Nehru together with Patel dominated the Congress Party. The two have therefore been described as the real architects of the Constitution. Nehru's influence is evident in such spheres as the framework of the Union Government, powers of the Union Government, method of the election of the President, decision on membership of the commonwealth, decision on language and in determining the general thrust of the basic social and economic theory of the future polity. Though at the time, the Constitution, essentially a compromise, did not reflect in full measure Nehru's belief and passions, yet future amendments of the Constitutions have brought into full prominence Nehru's ideology and philosophy which can be described as democratic socialism. The Constitution since its inception has slowly but steadily moved on to conform to Nehru's concept of democratic socialism. He, thus, had a hand in the making of the Constitution and also in shaping its future.

He was truly a philosopher, a statesman and and intellectual who had no parallel in modern India.

REFERENCES

1. Constituent Assembly Debates, Vol. XIP. 961.
2. *Ibid.*, p. 690.
3. *Ibid.*, p. 610-11.
4. *Ibid.*, C.A.D. Vol. I, p. 65.
5. *Ibid.*, p. 59.
6. *Ibid.*
7. *Parliamentary Debates* (Rajya Sabha) dated 19 March, 1955.
8. *Ibid.*, p. 1317.
9. *C.A.D.* Vol. IX, p. 1193.
10. *Ibid*, p. 1409.
11. *Ibid.*, p. 1319.
12. *Ibid.*, p. 1416.
13. *Ibid.*, p. 1412.
14. *Ibid.*, p. 1415.
15. *Ibid.*, p. 1411.
16. *C.A.D.* Vol. VIII, pp. 464-66.
17. *C.A.D.* Vol. X, p. 961.
18. *Ibid.*, p. 733.
19. *Ibid.*, p. 733.

Section–III

Social Organisation–Cultural and Moral Values

Section-III

Social Organisation- Cultural and Moral Values

16

CULTURAL AND MORAL VALUES IN INDEPENDENT INDIA

Dr. M.C. Bhartiya
Dr. Ravinder Kumar

A long cherished dream of Indian people was fulfilled on 15th August, 1947 when India saw the dawn of freedom. It was an end to the agony of the Indian people experienced in slavery and tyranny over a period of several centuries. With freedom came hopes of not only the political independence, but also of justice, social welfare, economic balance and an end to poverty.

Before independence, there was an upsurge of the enthusiasm of the Indian people, an upsurge of the spirit of sacrifice for liberty, a firm determination to do or die, an abandonment of the feelings of slavery and a revulsion to self-esteem and self-respect. In persons like Bhagat Singh, Chandra Shekhar Azad, Subhash Chandra Bose and many more, India saw an extreme height of passions for liberty and self-sacrifice. With the dawn of freedom, these passions subsided and hopes took their seat. Let us see how far these hopes were fulfilled, specially in the field of cultural and moral values.

It is more than fifty years since India obtained freedom. Our chequered history of the past fifty years has seen many ups and downs. We have gained and consolidated ourselves in many fields. But we have also lost and degraded ourselves in several fields. Let us first see the positive side. The fields in which India has seen substantive growth are education, industry and agriculture, India has seen a massive growth in the field of education. Literacy has gone up from less than thirty per cent to more than fifty per cent States like Kerala have been declared fully literate. Mass literacy campaign is going on in other states also and many regions have been declared literate. There is a huge growth in the number of schools, colleges and universities. Higher education has become quite popular and has entered into even villages. Our scholars and scientists have spread all over the world and are in important positions in advanced countries like U.S.A. But, though much is achieved, a substantial part of our population still remains uneducated. Education in women is much below the desired standards. A substantive part of children, which should be there in the schools are still working as labourers. Moreover, in the field of higher education, we are yet to achieve the international standards in quality.

India is also rich in industries. Practically everything is manufactured in India now. But what is lacking on this front is quality. India is yet to compete with international standards of quality. With the present liberalization policy of the government, more and more multinational companies are entering the arena and the Indian industry face a great risk in the growing competition with them.

A big achievement in the field of agriculture is that India has become self-sufficient and does not need any import for its own needs. Moreover, there is sufficient grain in stock for the periods of emergency.

Let us now turn to the cultural side. India has inherited a very rich culture perhaps the most advanced culture of the world. Its intellectual and artistic traditions find no parallels. But our culture has seen a dark period of several centuries during the periods of slavery, first that of the Muslims and then of the Britishers. It is, however, to the credit of Indian culture that it has survived the two great onslaughts. But it has gone through substantial changes during these periods. The Muslim impact can be seen in our language which now is full of Arabic and Persian words. The Muslim dresses are also quite popular. The Muslim architecture has influenced the Indian architecture to a great extent. The Muslim poetry, the *ghazal*, is very popular these days. The Britishers have also influenced the Indian culture substantially in its own way. English language is quite popular. All our higher intellectual growth at present is through English language. There was a passionate wave at the time of Independence to bring in Indian languages, specially Hindi, as a substitute of English. But the wave has subsided and there is a growing tendency now in Indian people to get their children educated through English medium. The dominance of English language has both the negative and the positive sides. Its negative side is that it has curbed the growth of Indian languages. India, as a great nation, should have its own national language. Hindi was declared as the national language. But it remained so on paper only. English is still the national language of the intellectual people in practice. An Indian feels pride in speaking English fluently and a person, not able to speak English, suffers with inferiority complex and has often to cut a sorry figure in the intellectual gatherings. If we just look on the state of the national conferences, we find that practically all of them are run through English medium. Even the conferences on our ancient language, Sanskrit, are conducted through English medium. Our own Indian languages now are full of English words. We often take pride in speaking a mixed language: some sentences in our own language and some in English. A mixture of Hindi and English is often called Hinglish. We find this Hinglish spoken very often among the so called educated people. If we just see the popular T.V. programmes, we will find the anchors speaking neither Hindi, nor English, but Hinglish. Our high digniteries, when speaking in India or in foreign countries prefer to speak

English, even if the country they are speaking in, is not English speaking.

What should we make out of this trend? Is it positive or negative? My own feelings are that though knowing a foreign language, specially English, is quite beneficial it is not possible for us to make it our own language. Even after such a dominant role of English language in India, it is only about two per cent people who can understand English, not to say of speaking. Obviously, English is not a language of the masses, it is a language of a few elite people. It is thus responsible for creating a wedge between the ordinary Indians and the so called elite English speaking people. It is responsible for creating a feeling of inferiority in the non-English medium educated people. Moreover, English is responsible for defacing our own language; we perhaps cannot speak a few sentences in our languages without taking recourse to English words and English sentences. From philological point of view, it is not bad for a language to absorb the words of other languages. Even English has grown rich by absorbing the words of other languages including Hindi. What is bad is to lose the identity of our own language. This is often done by losing its own grammatical forms and taking the forms of the other language. Foreign words, when absorbed, should be digested and digestion means to give them our own grammatical forms. Language depicts the very identity of a nation and if we lose this identity, we lose our self-esteem.

There are other fields also of the influence of English culture. It can be seen in our dresses and our ways of living. But such influences cannot be termed negative, because, culture, like other living things, should not be taken as static. The dynamism of the culture depicts its very life. This dynamism is reflected in absorbing the outside influence and adjusting according to the needs of the times. Those who call it the defilement of Indian culture should note that change is the law of nature, and a culture which has no capability of changing with times, is bound to die. Our contact with other countries is fast growing and we have to fit ourselves in an international scenario.

Let us now turn ourselves and see where we stand in our moral values. This perhaps is the field where the situation is most gloomy. We have seen a continuous downfall of moral values since independence. There is rampant corruption in every field. If we go to any office having some public dealing, it will be practically impossible to get some work done without some underhand payment. A good number of Government officers are corrupt. Police department is largely infected with corruption. Even in courts, we find most of the judgements given by judges are influenced by handsome amount of underhand payments. Thus, all enforcing agencies of law are mostly corrupt. In business, we find duplicate goods of practically all items of famous companies. There is adulteration in food items and even in medicines. Crime is rampant. Criminals, even after committing dozens of murders, are moving about freely. Persons having hundreds of criminal cases against them are not only free, they are fighting elections and getting elected. The whole situation is really grim.

What has led to this steep deterioration of moral values? We, in ancient India, had four basic values viz. *dharma,* i.e., duty, *artha,* i.e., money and property, *kama,* i.e., sex and *moksha* i.e. liberation from the cycle of life and death. The last one was to be achieved after this life, but the first three were to be achieved in this life itself. Our philosophy was in favour of a balance of these three in one's life. Not only that, the first, i.e., *dharma* (duty) was regarded as the controlling force of all the values. Manu, our most prominent social philosopher, was in favour of enjoyment of *artha* (money) and *kama* (sex) as controlled by *dharma*, i.e., duty. The stand, after independence has been reversed. *Artha* and *kama* are now dominating *dharma.* But what has led to this reversal of values? The cause perhaps lies in the several centuries of slavery which not only enslaved Indian body but also its psyche and thus made it lose its self-confidence and self-esteem. Though India obtained political freedom, it could not get itself free from the mental slavery. A man with self-esteem does not take resort to corrupt practices; he is always conscious and afraid of the society pointing its finger towards him, but a man who has lost his self-esteem, is not afraid of tarnishing of his image in the society.

After India became independent, though, in the beginning, the power went in to the hands of those who had fought for independence and were high in moral values, but by and by it slipped into the hands of those who were hungry of power and money and had no respect for moral values. Our election system encouraged it. Politics became a business and corrupt people fought elections with the power of money and muscle. The public was not enlightened and could easily be lured through temptations. Where temptation did not work, power of *goondas* did. The corrupt people thus got control of the political power and used it for their own ends. With the corruption at the top, who could stop it in the lower rank? Corruption thus spread all around and it has taken very deep roots now. It has now became a way of life. We have accepted it. The public has stopped despising the corrupts. It seems to have became our destiny. But few people are realising that it is eating our roots. Most of our present problems, viz. proverty, inflation, unemployment etc. stand rooted in corruption. We know there is corruption. We know it is damaging. But we find ourselves helpless. Those who are honest and resist corruption find themselves unfit in the setup.

Can we tackle the corruption? Though it is an uphill task now, even then, I feel, we can tackle it. But first of all, we need a very strong will power at the top level for rooting it out, which is, at present, lacking. Weak coalition governments perhaps cannot help, because they cannot lay that strong hand on it which is badly needed. The first need, therefore, is that of a strong will. For implementing the will, the government, first of all, must purge out the corrupt element from itself. No person of a doubtful integrity should be given an office, whether political or bureaucratic. This tendency is emerging late. The government, forced by the circumstances and the public will, has started taking steps in this direction. But it is yet a weak trend and it has to consolidate itself. Some judges of the top courts are also helping this effort. Let us hope the efforts take a concrete shape.

Another very important step, which is must for rooting out corruption, is overhauling of the election system. The government must see that the money and the muscle powers do not work. Some steps have lately been taken to move in this direction. But more steps are needed. The individual and the party expenditures should be completely banned. The government should itself provide for the facilities of the election campaign. This can be done by publishing in newspapers, the career-records of the candidates fighting the election, publishing the manifestos and programmes of the parties and the candidates, giving time at T.V. and Radio to the parties and the candidates, arranging public meetings where the candidates or their supporters could speak for themselves and more such steps by which the public could become aware of the programmes of the parties and the candidates and the background of the candidates. The government has already started giving time for the political parties to appear at the T.V., but such steps should be more consolidated.

One very important step for rooting out the corruption is the reform in our judiciary. Judiciary should work as a deterrant to the corrupt people by punishing them. This is not being done at present. The criminals and the corrupt people, even if caught, can easily be bailed out and with the blessing of our judicial system, manipulate to get the cases linger on and thus pass their lives out of the jails, terrorizing and looting the common people. The first and the foremost step to be taken for reforming the judiciary is to give a speedy justice. It is the step on which there should be no compromise. For that, steps must be taken to settle the crores of cases already accumulated. Special judges must be appointed to settle them. Services of the retired judges should also be utilised. The system of dragging the cases for long periods must be stopped. A case must be settled within three months. This seems to be somewhat impossible at present, but it is not so provided the will for it is there. More than fifty per cent of the cases in the courts are only those which are taken to the court to prevent a just man from getting justice, because we know that once the case goes to the courts, it will be dormant for years and years. This is equivalent to the denial of justice. Once the system of speedy justice is implemented, such bogus cases will stop coming to the courts and the courts will be substantially relieved of their burden. With speedy justice, the courts will start working as deterrants to the crime and corruption.

On the whole, if we look at the status of the cultural and moral values in Independent India, we find that we have gained less and lost more. We have, of course, gained substantially on the material side, but there is not much to count the gains on the side of the cultural and moral values. There is more deterioration than gains. A very strong will and firm determination is needed to reverse this trend.

Social Organisation: Cultural and Moral Values

Undoubtedly the cultural and moral values represent and mirror the true spectacle of the development of a particular society or a nation. That is to say, how far any society or nation has advanced; has stood sophistically well cultivated, is measured by the relative cultural and moral values of the society or the nation concerned. It is through this media that one can convenietly measure and estimate the personality of its citizens. One can question as to what are actually the cultural and moral values which represent the spectacle of the progress of any society or nation.

In brief, the values which form the basis of any culture, get its recognition and are the cause of its prosperity, are cultural values and which strengthen the morality and make it real are termed as moral values. India is the only fortunate country in the world that its culture has ever remained alive and abiding solely due to its fundamental and unique values as its special characteristics. Morality is its indivisible part. And while remaining ever abiding and invigorating, advancing continuously on the path of progress, ignoring in totality the brutality, division, fundamentalism, bitterness and animosity and above all the violence, the greatest curse, Indian culture has ever taught the lesson of 'live and let live' and has been preaching to the World the gospel and message of "the whole world as a single entity in the form of a family."

Indian culture has treaded the long journey of thousands of years. Even quite prior to the era of 'Indus Valley Civilization', the glimpse of history introduces us to the abiding values of Indian culture. It is natural that there came numerous hurdles in the path of such a long journey. So many difficulties were encountered by Indian culture. Several times, it appeared as if the values of Indian culture have become obliterated; morality has been dwindled. But in reality such a state has never come about. As and when values were struck upon; they were subjected to pressure and suppression, then and there the social organisations not only proved a healing balm to their lacerated soul but also re-established, thereby clearing the outward surface of darkness.

Let us now peep retrospectively to the two thousand five hundred years back history when cultural and moral values were pounced upon and invaded with continuity; humanity was groaning. At such a time, Buddha safeguarded Indian culture; strengthened morality by installing a unique social organisation. Although behind the social organisation installed by Buddha, there was also a religious community-Buddhism but we should remember that Buddhism was initially an effective 'Social Reform Movement' which also influenced a large portion of the world after its propagation in India.

There are numerous instances of medieval period when social organisations not only defended cultural and moral values in reality but also re-established them in the context of prevalent conditions of time and the country. During Sultanate period the organisations like Chistia and Firdausi sprung up against fundamentalism. Not only this, from every corner of the later India this job was done by right thinking and responsible leaders by creating organisations of which there is no parallel till today. The names of Farid Shakarganj and Nanak Dev from Punjab, Chaitanya from Bengal, Namdev from Maharashtra and likewise the names of Kabir and

Sharfuddin Ahmed can be recited with great pride in the chain of great personalities. There is no need of going far off. During British India period, Raja Ram Mohan Roy, Vivekananda, Ishwar Chandra Vidyasagar, Jyotiba Phuley and such illustrious figures consummated glorious deeds through social organisations, set up by them and before all of us the example of Gandhi is quite recent.

India got freedom in 1947. Under the leadership of Gandhi, there was the best team in working, this very team shouldered the leadership of the country. This team represented the Indian cultural and moral values. There is no doubt about it. But one after the other, all the members of the team died. Now, fifty three years of our freedom are going to elapse. If we view at the cultural and moral values of the 53 years period of our freedom, certainly we shall have a feeling of disappointment. A petal of darkness will be discerned overcasting these values.

In different spheres, including science and technology, like the rest of the world, we made marvellous progress. Our standard of living increased beyond expectation. But purity in life was very badly damaged, violence, struggle and tensions, mountingly increased. The entire system was deeply stemmed and drenched in corruption. Not only this, in the public life, alongwith money and muscle power, gangsters and mafias have begun to dominate. This state of affairs is certainly in contradiction to the reality that subsist in cultural and moral values. In such a State how much does the responsibility of social organisations all the more increase; we all understand it. But it is a matter of anxiety that social organisations and people associated with them do not appear to become competent in carrying us from darkness to light. We have a number of social organisations but their role in context of restoration of cultural and moral values is not satisfactory. It is a grave question before us. And how can we solve it?

In my viewpoint, as we all understand, the question is quite intricate, the situation is serious and more or less all are affected by it. Despite knowing all this, being under its effect and impression, it is not that we find it impossible to tackle the problem. It is straightway a fact that when the question is related to us, we are the only competent ones to solve it. It has also happened in the past, the future too has got in store for us. And this is also not possible that the whole of the populace will at once stand up to solve the problem or the question collectively all together. In affirmation, all right thinking, serious and responsible people, ten, fifty or one hundred may come on a single platform, initiate an attempt and march ahead. By and by, the whole of the society will be organised and cultural and moral values will again be revived and re-established. Today it is essential to unite and assemble all right thinking, sincere and responsible people, it is possibly the greatest duty or responsibility of all the social organisations. Certainly, there are the right thinking people in good numbers even today and our society and nation are not at all devoid of them.

17

WATER—A LOOMING CRISIS

Afroz Ahmad

The problems associated with scarcity and pollution of surface water resources are a great global challenge. In India out of 20 river basins, six basins namely; Sabarmati, East flowing rivers between Pennar and Kanniyakumari and West flowing river of Kutch and Saurashtra including Luni, Cauvery and East flowing rivers between Mahanadi and Pennar fall under the water scarcity category ($1000m^3$/capita/annum) and many more are expected to come under this category by the year 2025 and 2050. The eutrophication of most of major Indian rivers and lakes have caused serious problems of drinking water and irrigation water supply. The threat to human health are from sewage, nutrients, toxic metals and the chemicals used in industry and agriculture. The most widespread pollution is undoubtedly the faecal matter present in domestic sewage, which causes high levels of pathogens in water supplies that are not treated before use. Unacceptably high faecal coliforms level were available in more than ninety per cent major Indian rivers and lakes. The deforestation at the rate of 25350 ha. per annum leading to erosion and sedimentation of waterbodies. The excess run-off from agricultural areas containing fertilizers, manure and chemicals pollute rivers and lakes. The destruction of wetlands are taking heavy toll on water quality because it serves as a sink in storing nutrients. The existing state of water (quality and quantity) environment clearly indicate that 'conflicts on water' in future is unavoidable unless the protection and wise management of most valuable of the world's renewable resources are given top priority by all. Water being our common heritage; we all should share the responsibility of protecting it for future generations. Keeping in view the looming crisis of water, a breakthrough for really sustainable water resources development and management is required. The guidelines based on eco-system approach for the integrated management of water resources involving scientific, technical and engineering factors on the one hand and social, economical, environmental and legal factors on the other, have been presented for meeting the looming crisis of Water Resources in India.

The amount of water on Earth is constant and can not be increased or decreased. Of a global total of 1360 million cubic kilometres (m. km^3) of water, which cover about seventy per cent of the Earth's surface, only three per cent (1360 m. km^3) is fresh; of that, some 29 m. km^3 are located in snow and ice, some 8 m. km^3 are in the form of ground water and only about 200,000 km^3 exits for human use in the form of surface waters such as rivers and lakes (UNEP, 1991).

Current annual fresh water consumption is, in round figures, about 4,000 km^3–still less than half the available total. This is the equivalent of 800 m^3 per person per year for a population of 5,000 million. The World Resources Institute in its survey during 1986 found that water availability in 51 out of 100 selected countries was either low or very low Table 17.1. UNDP (1998) pointed out that the situation of safe water and sanitation is alarming in most of the regions of the world Table 17.2.

Table 17.1

Per Capita Water Availability in Selected Countries as Per Survey of the World Resources Institute

Category	*Per capita water availability in selected countries*	
	Per capita availability	*Countries (per cent)*
Very Low	1000 m^3/year or less	14
Low	1000-5000 m^3/year	37
Medium	5000-1000 m^3/year	14
High	10000 m^3/year	35

Source: UNEP, 1991.

Table 17.2

Lack of Access to Safe Water and Basic Sanitation, by Region, 1990-96

Region	*People without access to safe water (per cent)*	*People without access to basic sanitation (per cent)*
Arab States	21	30
Sub-Saharan Africa	48	55
South-East Asia and the Pacific	35	45
Latin America and the Caribbean	23	29
East Asia	32	73
East Asia (excluding China)	13	—
South Asia	18	64
Developing Countries	29	58
Least developed Countries	43	64

Source: UNDP, 1998.

Even so, this available fresh water would seem at first sight to be enough to supply all fundamental human survival needs, if divided by the total population of the Earth. Indeed-although the exact water volume necessary to fulfil human needs is still a matter of debate—it is estimated that theoretically there is sufficient fresh water on the planet to support about twenty billion people. Unfortunately it is not distributed evenly, as the large arid and semi-arid regions testify. And, thanks to seasonal weather pattern, this sometimes not available when most needed, or arrives in excessive amounts, causing floods and loss of human life. To add to this problem, water is polluted when it is used in industry, agriculture and for domestic purposes and thus the amount of water of acceptable quality available for human use is reduced still further. As a result of shortages water for inferior quality is used to meet demand. Conversely, the need for clean water makes heavy demands on total resources. For example it is estimated that some 450 km^3 of water currently enters the world's rivers, some 6000 km^3 water is needed to transport the waste away, and dilute it cleaning the world's wastes thus requires a volume of water equivalent to two-third of total reliable run-off.

The world now have less than half the amount of water available per capita than it was 50 years ago. In 1950, world reserves (after accounting for agriculture, industrial and domestic uses) amounted to 16.8 thousand cubic meters per person. Today, global reserves have dropped to 7.3 thousand cubic metres and are expected to fall to 4.8 thousand cubic metres in next 25 years (Sadeq, 1999).

Water Resources–A Looming Crisis

Global Scenario

By the year 2000 the global population is expected to rise to 6.2 billion people, with highest rate of growth forecast to take place in the developing countries. The problems of safe and sustainable water resource for the need of the growing population has attracted the attention of different classes of the people from all over the world. Boutros Ghali, then Egypt's Minister of State for Foreign Affairs says that "the next war in our region will be over the waters of the Nile, not politics". Likely, Israel's Meir Ben Meir, a former head of the Agriculture Ministry agrees: "If the people of the region are not clever enough to discuss a mutual solution to the problems of water, war is unavoidable. China daily reported in May, 1989 that Beijing's two main reservoirs were diminishing rapidly, water tables beneath the capital drop one to two metres per year, and a third of its wells have gone dry. Some 14 million children under the age of five in developing nations die every year due to lack of safe drinking water, poor sanitation, environmental pollution, common diseases and malnutrition. Keeping in view, the problem of safe drinking water supply, the U.N. has organised special conference on Human Settlements at Vancouver, Canada from 31 May to 11 June, 1976. It was noticed during above meetings that in the less developed countries, nearly two-third of the population do not have reasonable access to safe and ample water supply, and even a greater population lack the means for hygienic waste disposal.

In the Middle East, it is now water, not oil, which is the real threat to regional peace. With Environmental and Political factors dramatically affecting the flow of the Nile, Jordan, Tigris, and Euphrates, the need for water could lead to unexpected and potentially explosive new alliances—between Iraq and Syria, for instance both threatened by Turkey's control of the Tigris–Euphrates. Israel's determination to hold on the West Bank, Golan Height and South Lebanon, for instance, is partly to preserve access to water resources.

Ahmad (1990) reported that the water resources in developing countries of Himalayan region viz. Afganistan, Bangladesh, Bhutan, Burma, China, India, Nepal and Pakistan; of the Andean region of the South America: of the Altas mountain of Moracco and the mountain regions of Ethiopia, Tanzania, Ruanda, and Burundi as well as of the mountain areas of the Pacific Island region are under threat of safe drinking water supply and sanitation. The exhausted river, falling water table, and shrinking lakes, all testify to worldwide human abuse of water resources.

Indian Scenario

India has sufficient water resources on the average in comparison to many other countries in the world. It has been assessed that out of the total precipitation of around 400 million ha. metre (M.ha.m) in the country, the surface water availability is around 185 M.ha.m. in all twenty river basin

(12 major and 8 minor). Out of this only about 69 M.ha.m. can be put to beneficial use because of topographical and other constraints. At present thirteen water surplus basins are available where less than 105 ha of net sown area per million cubic metres of water potential exists. It may be mentioned here that about 45 per cent population of the country lives in the Basin area and a large segment of the Basin's population continues to live below the poverty line on the margin of subsistence.

Agriculture in India is mainly dependent on irrigation. The net sown area in the country has almost stabilised at about 145 million ha. The gross cropped area is about 175 million ha, taking into account areas sown more than once. It is unlikely that net sown area will increase in the future. The only way to increase the gross cropped area is to expand irrigation facilities and to facilitate intensive agriculture, in a sustainable manner. The irrigation potential created in the country at present is about 85 million ha. The present water demand for irrigation is more than 460 km^3. The food grain production which is now about 180 million tons may have to increase to 250 million tons by 2000 and to about 400 million tons by 2025. The demand of water for irrigated agriculture will also go up to 630 km^3 in the year 2000 and 770 km^3 in the year 2025. The scenario of drinking and industrial water are of major concern Table 17.3.

Table 17.3

Water Demand for the Food Security of India

Year	*Population requirements (million tons)*	*Food Grains*	*Water Demand (km³)*			
			Irrigation	*Drinking*	*Industry*	*Total*
1992	860	175	460	25	15	500
2000*	1000	250	630	33	30	693
2025*	1530	400	770	52	120	942

* Projected

Source: CWC, 1991.

The countries having 1000 m^3 water availability per capita and per annum are considered under very low category are scarcity conditions (UNEP, 1991). Based upon this criterion, already six basins viz. Sabarmati, East following rivers between Pennar and Kanniyakumari, Pennar, West flowing rivers of Kutch and Saurashtra including Luni, Cauvery and East flowing rivers between Mahanadi and Pennar fall into this category. More and more basins will become water scarce by 2025 and 2050 as the population increase (IWRS, 1997). The per capita water availability in India which was 5150 m^3/capita/annum during 1947 has now reduced to 2200 m^3/capita annum in 1998. It is predicted that by the year 2017, it will go down upto 1600 m^3/capita/annum which will most likely result in serious water crisis in India, if an appropriate measures are not taken for its management.

Many lakes and other water resources of our country which were main source of water supply for irrigation, drinking purposes, power and tourists attraction are now suffering from serious problems of eutrophication viz. Slow death of Kashmir's Dal lake, Sukna lake in Chandigarh, Wullar lake in Kashmir, Khichipur in Sikkim, Ooty in Tamil Nadu, Bimtal and Nainital in Uttar Pradesh, Ramgarh and Pushkar lake Palance in Rajasthan, Husain Sagar lake in Andhra Pradesh, etc. which are main source of drinking water supply to rural and urban population are now affected from eutrophication due to impact of human activities (Ahmad, 1990).

Deteriorating Water Quality—A Threat to Indian Environment

Water pollution, as known today, is a relatively new phenomenon. Before the year 1800 all rivers in Western Europe were comparatively free from pollution, except in a few restricted stretches. Presently, water pollution is a global problem. The ageing of a body of water by the growth of vegetation, particularly algae their death and decay using up the dissolved oxygen of the water resulting serious impairment of water quality. In lakes, rivers, harbours and estuaries, the accumulation of nutrients is a natural process. These nutrients include carbon, hydrogen, oxygen, sulphur, potassium, calcium, magnesium, nitrogen and phosphorus. Algal 'blooms' thriving on these nutrients, may be blue green, red or brown in colour in small numbers these plants are beneficial as they contribute to the oxygen balance in lakes and streams, and also serve as flood for fish. Industrial and domestic activity may greatly accelerate an otherwise slow ageing process by increasing these amount of nutrients entering the water: effluents from these sources contain phosphorus and nitrogen, in addition, fertilizers containing phosphorus and nitrogen may be carried by rain-water run-off or ground water seepage into lakes or streams.

The monitoring of water quality especially surface water resources like rivers, lakes, wells, ponds, tanks, drains, creeks, canals etc. is being done by a nodal agency of Government of India namely Central Pollution Control Board (CPCB) in collaboration with the State Pollution Control Board (SPCB). Initially the monitoring of water quality started with 17 stations on the Yamuna river during 1997. The monitoring network during the year 1993-94 includes 463 stations covering 392 river stations, 33 lake stations, 21 well stations, 8 canal stations, 2 pond stations, 3 rain stations and 1 tank station Table 17.4.

Table 17.4
River-wise Distribution of Monitoring Station

Name of River	*Location (State)*	*Catchment Area (km²)*	*Number of Monitoring Station (including main stream and tributaries)*
Brahmani	Bihar, Orissa	39,033	16
Baitrani	Bihar, Orissa	12,789	5
Brahmaputra	Arunachal Pradesh, Assam, Meghalaya, Nagaland	1,87,110	12
Cauvery	Karnataka, Kerala, Tamil Nadu	87,900	35

Name of River	Location (State)	Catchment Area (km²)	Number of Monitoring Station (including main stream and tributaries)
Ganga	U.P., Bihar, West Bengal, Haryana, Rajasthan	8,61,404	83
Godavari	Andhra Pradesh, M.P., Maharashtra, Karnataka	3,12,812	23
Indus	J&K, Himachal Pradesh, Orissa, Punjab	3,21,290	41
Krishna	Andhra Pradesh, Maharashtra, Karnataka	2,58,948	41
Mahi	M.P., Rajasthan, Gujarat	34,842	9
Mahanadi	Madhya Pradesh, Orissa	1,41,600	27
Narmada	M.P., Maharashtra, Gujarat	98,756	15
Sabarmati	Rajasthan, Gujarat	21,674	10
Tapi	M.P., Maharashtra, Gujarat	65,145	13
Subarnarekha	Bihar, Orissa, West Bengal	19,300	4
Pennar			4
West flowing medium rivers			10
East flowing medium rivers			12
Minor rivers			40

Source: CPCB, 1996.

More than 25 water variables are monitored, providing information on suitability of water for human consumption, and for agricultural, commercial and industrial uses. These networks have been established under Global Environmental Monitoring Systems (GEMS) and Monitoring of Indian National Aquatic Resources (MINARS). The results of this programme based on Dissolved Oxygen (DO), Biochemical Oxygen Demand (BOD), Total Coliform is presented in Table 17.5

Table 17.5

Water Quality Profiles of some Major Indian Rivers Based on Dissolved Oxygen (DO), pH, Biological Oxygen Demand (BOD), and Total Coliform

Name of River	*Indicators of Pollution*							
River	*pH (Mean)*		*DO (Mean)/mg/l*		*BOD (mean) Mg/l*		*Total Coliforms (means) MPN/100 ml*	
	1993	*1994*	*1993*	*1994*	*1993*	*1994*	*1993*	*1994*
Brahmani	7.6-7.8	7.2-8.2	7.3-10.6	7.3-11.1	2.0-11.9	1.8-8.2	3.0-6.32	2.28-8.44
Brahmaputra	7.5-7.7	7.2-7.9	5.7-8.4	5.4-7.4	1.0-3.8	0.8-2.7	9.0-11.0	8.65-10.60
Cauvery	8.4-8.5	7.2-8.5	5.2-7.9	3.8-13.0	0.5-3.0	4.0-5.0	7.0-11.0	7.38-11.02
Godavri	7.7-9.2	7.5-8.2	6.2-7.2	4.3-7.2	7-12	9-12	4-5	4.31-4.59
Krishna	7.5-8.6	7.4-8.5	5.3-7.2	5.3-8.0	1.0-7.6	1.2-9.2	1.0-7.0	2.49-7.38
Mahi	7.5-8.4	7.5-7.8	5.7-8.8	5.9-8.3	1.5-2.4	1.8-2.7	1.0-7.0	4.91-7.51
Mahanadi	7.0-7.8	8.0-8.1	6.7-10.5	7.0-10.6	1.1-7.7	1.4-5.1	3.0-7.0	3.51-7.93
Narmada	7.3-8.3	7.5-8.2	4.4-8.8	5.9-8.4	1.4-3.3	1.8-3.9	2.0-9.0	3.85-7.38
Sabarmati	5.9-8.1	5.5-8.3	0.5-8.2	3.1-8.7	1.8-104.9	1.7-92.0	10-16	8.68-15.71
Subarnarekha	—	7.0-7.6	—	5.0-7.5	—	0.6-7.6	—	7.89-10.27
Tapi	7.5-7.7	7.5-7.6	6.0-7.1	6.7-7.7	1.3-1.6	1.9-2.2	5.6	5.05-5.12
INDUS								
Satluj	7.3-8.4	7.5-8.2	9.7-243	7.7-9.2	0.1-2.6	0.4-6.1	2.56-4.96	2.13-5.45
Beas	7.3-7.9	7.7-8.1	5.8-85	6.9-9.3	0.6-13.2	0.3-0.7	3.30-5.92	2.41-5.92
GANGA								
Gomti	8.4	7.6-8.3	7.8-8.3	2.6-8.1	2.7-2.8	2.9-8.5	7.0-9.0	7.82-12.04
Yamuna	7.3-8.2	7.8-8.2	1.6-11.1	8.5	5.3-11.3	1.0-4.7	—	2.4-8.19
Chambal	7.4-7.5	7.5-8.1	6.7-7.4	3.4-7.7	3.6-31.8	2.6-19.0	6-7	5.34-7.02
Hindon	7.0-7.7	7.5-7.8	1.9-5.7	2.6-5.6	5.3-142.21	11.7-104.61	7-8	6.89-9.62
Khan	7.5	7.3	1.7	3.3	11.8	47.8	11.0	9.83

Source : CPCB, 1996.

The water quality data were compared with the water quality criteria adopted by the Central Board Table 17.6.

Table 17.6
Primary Water Quality Criteria

Designated best use	*Class of Water*	*Criteria*
Drinking Water Source without conventional treatment but after disinfection.	A	1. Total Coliforms organised MPN/100 ml shall be 50 or less 2. pH between 6.5 and 8.5 3. Dissolved Oxygen 6 mg/l or more 4. Biochemical Oxygen Demand 5 days 20°C 3 mg/l or less
Out door bathing (Organised)	B	1. Total Coliforms organised MPN/100ml shall be 500 or less. 2. pH between 6.5 and 8.5 3. Dissolved Oxygen 6 mg/l or more 4. Biochemical Oxygen Demand 5 days 20°C 3 mg/l or less
Drinking Water Source	C	1. Total Coliforms organised MPN/100ml shall be 5000 or less. 2. pH between 6 to 9 3. Dissolved Oxygen 4 mg/l or more 4. Biochemical Oxygen Demand 5 days 20°C 3 mg/l or less
Propagation of wildlife	D	1. pH between 6.5 and 8.5 fisheries 2. Dissolved Oxygen 4 mg/l or more 3. Free Ammonia (as N) 1.2 mg/l or less
Irrigation, Industrial Cooling, Controlled waste	E	1. pH between 6.5 and 8.5 2. Electrical conductivity at 25°C micro mhos/cm Max 2250 3. Sodium adsorption ratio maximum 26 4. Boron, max 2 mg/l

Table 17.7
Per cent Violations over the Desired Level A, B, C Class of Water in some Indian River

Name of River	*Per cent violations over desired level A, B, C Class of water base year 1994 (meanvalue)*			
	pH	*Dissolved Oxygen*	*Biochemical Oxygen Demand*	*Total Coliforms*
Brahmani	0.0	0.0	53.6-100	12.5-75.0
Brahmaputra	0.0-8.3	10.0	10.0-30.0	20.0-66.7
Cauvery	8.3-41.7	0.0-44.4	0.0-44.4	0.0-100
Godavri	0.0-16.7	10.0-33.3	10.0-91.7	0.0-8.3
Krishna	0.0	8.3-30.0	66.7-83.3	0.0
Mahi	0.0-8.3	0.0-16.7	8.3-62.5	8.3-100
Mahanadi	0.0	0.0	45.5-100	0.0-25.0
Narmada	0.0-11.0	0.0-45.5	0.0-72.7	0.0-100
Sabarmati	0.0-41.7	0.0-91.7	16.7-50.0	91.7-100
Subarnarekha	0.0	0.0-25.0	0.0-45.5	25.0-100
Tapi	0.0-8.3	0.0-33.3	0.0-83.3	0.0-88.9
INDUS				
• Satluj	0.0	0.0-25.0	0.025.0	50.0-75.0
• Beas	0.0-25.0	0.0-25.0	0.0	25.0-100
GANGA				
• Gomti	0.0-16.7	8.3-16.7	0.0-80.0	50.0-100
• Yamuna	0.0-12.5	0.0-100	16.7-100	0.0-100
• Chambal	0.0	0.0-100	0.0-100	0.0-100
	0.0	0.0-90.9	0.0-100	0.0

Source: CPCB, 1996.

The assessment of water quality related to some major rivers based on CPCB monitoring reports is summarised below:

1. Brahmani River. The level of BOD throughout the river stretch is high specifically at Panposh downstream, Rourkela downstream, Talchera upstream and Kanalganga confluence downstream, Dharamshala and Pattamudai. The present violation of BOD and total coliforms over the desired level A, B, C class of water ranges from 53.6-100 and 12.5-75 respectively.

2. ***Brahmaputra River.*** The present violation of pH, DO, BOD and total coliforms over the desired level A, B, C, class of water ranges from 0-8.3, 10, 10-30 and 20-66.7 respectively.

3. ***Cauvery River.*** The level of DO and BOD were always within desired levels in stretches of Karnataka State. In Tamil Nadu, the level of DO, BOD and total coliform were higher than the desired levels at some locations. The present violation of pH, DO, BOD and total coliforms over the desired level A, B, C class of water ranges from 8.3-41.7, 0-44.4 and 0-100 respectively.

4. ***Godavri River.*** The present violation of pH, DO, BOD and total coliforms over the desired level A, B, C class of water ranges from 0-16.7, 10-33.3, 10-91.7 and 0-8.3 respectively.

5. ***Krishna River.*** The present violation of pH, DO, BOD and total coliforms over the desired level A, B, C class of water ranges from 8.3-30 and 66.7-83.3 respectively.

6. ***Mahi River.*** The present violation of pH, DO, BOD and total coliforms over the desired level A, B, C class of water ranges from 0-8.3, 0-16.7, 8.3-62.5, 8.3-100 respectively.

7. ***Mahanadi River.*** The present violation of pH, DO, BOD and total coliforms over the desired level A, B, C class of water ranges from 45.5-100 and 0-25 respectively.

8. ***Narmada River.*** The present violation of pH, Do, BOD and total coliforms over the desired level A, B, C class of water ranges from 0-11, 0-45.5, 0-727 and 0-25 respectively. However at certain locations like Amarkantak, Sethanighat, Hoshangabad upstream and Gurudeshwar the level pH, DO, BOD and total coliforms violates the desired level A, B, C class of water quality. This is mainly due to anthropogenic activities like bathing and discharge of untreated sewage Figure 1.

Fig. 1. **Some Important Locations on River Narmada where Values of pH, DO, BOD and Total Coliform Violate the Desired Level of A, B, C Class of Water**

NARMADA RIVER (per cent violation over the desired level)

HOSHANGABAD UPSTREAM

	Year 1993	Year 1994
pH	25.0	9.1
BOD	58.3	11.1
Total Coliform	75.0	45.5

GURUDESHWAR

	Year 1993	Year 1994
pH	—	10
BOD	10	16.7
Total Coliform	100	91.7

AMARKANTAK

	Year 1993	Year 1994
DO	100	45.5
BOD	91.7	60.0
Total Coliform	77.8	54.5

SETHANIGHAT

	Year 1993	Year 1994
BOD	58.3	44.4
Total Coliform	100	81.8

Sources: CPCB, 1996.

Fig. 2. **Some Important Locations on River Sabarmati where Values of pH, DO, BOD and Total Coliform Violate the Desired Level of A, B, C Class of Water**

SABARMATI RIVER (per cent violation over the desired level)

RAILWAY BRIDGE AHMEDABAD

	Year 1993	Year 1994
pH	9.1	—
DO	16.7	—
BOD	18.2	33.3
Total Coliform	10.0	91.7

KHEROJ BRIDGE

	Year 1993	Year 1994
DO	9.1	—
BOD	36.4	50.0
Total Coliform	100	100

GANDHINAGAR CHILODA BRIDGE

	Year 1993	Year 1994
DO	9.1	—
BOD	36.4	33.3
Total Coliform	81.8	91.7

DHAROIDAM

	Year 1993	Year 1994
DO	—	8.3
BOD	6.0	16.7
Total Coliform	100	100

Source: CPCB, 1996.

9. Sabarmati River. The present violation of pH, DO, BOD and total coliforms over the desired level A, B, C class of water ranges from 0-41.7, 0-91.7, 16.7-50 and 91.7-100 repectively. The situtation of water quality impairment is alarming especially at certain points namely Ahmadabad Railway Bridge, Kharoj Bridge, Gandhinagar Chiloda Bridge and Dhariodam sites where anthropogenic activities are of serious concern Figure. 2.

10. Tapi River. The present violation of pH, DO, BOD and total coliforms over the desired level A, B, C class of water ranges from 0-8.3, 0-33.3, 0-83.3,and 0-88.9 respectively.

11. Indus (Satluj and Beas). The level of DO, BOD and Total Coliform in Satluj river and pH, DO, and total coliforms in Beas river are violating the desired level A, B, C class of water.

12. Ganga River. The levels of BOD and total coliforms violate the desired level of water quality A, B, C. The situation was alarming in places where human activities are more like Rishikesh and Haridwar upstream, Kanpur upstream and downstream, Patna and West Bengal Patal Figure 3.

Fig. 3. Some Important Locations on River Ganga where Values of pH, DO, BOD and Total Coliform Violate the Desired Level of A, B, C Class of Water

GANGA RIVER
(per cent violation over the desired level)

RISHIKESH UPSTREAM

	Year 1993	Year 1994
DO	8.3	—
BOD	8.3	—
Total Coliform	100	66.7

HARIDWAR DOWNSTREAM

	Year 1993	Year 1994
pH	—	8.3
BOD	5.0	30.0
Total Coliform	100	100

KANPUR UPSTREAM

	Year 1994
BOD	22.2
Total Coliform	50.0

KANPUR DOWNSTREAM

	Year 1994
DO	16.7
BOD	77.8
Total Coliform	100

PATNA

	Year 1994
BOD	11.1
Total Coliform	77.8

WEST BENGAL PATEL

	Year 1994
pH	11.1
BOD	11.1
Total Coliform	100

Source: CPCB, 1996.

The GEMS assessment found that Yamuna river, one of the tributary of Ganga river is highly polluted. The finding indicates that water contains 7500 faecal coliforms per 100 ml. water before entering the city and left with 24 million faecal coliforms per 100 ml. The dramatic increase was due to the 200 million litres of raw sewage dumped into the river daily (UNEP, 1991).

Factors Responsible for Pollution of Surface Water Resources

Since the industrial revolution, water pollution problems have become first regional, then continental, and now global. The major factors associated with the accelerated pace of fresh water pollution leading to inadequate safe drinking water supply are:

(i) Urbanization (17.29 per cent in 1951, 23.33 per cent in 1981, 25.72 per cent in 1991 and 33 per cent expected in 2001) and the consequent increase in population.

(ii) Intensification of agriculture and growth in industries leading to freshwater pollution.

(iii) Deforestation (507 km^2 during 1993 and 1995, i.e., 25350 ha/annum) leading to siltation of water bodies and diminishing of perennial water springs.

(iv) Alteration in land use as well as discharge of domestic, industrial and municipal wastes.

(v) Conversion of water bodies into hydroelectric dam without environmental management programme.

(vi) Accidental water pollution (burst pipes and tanks, major leaks, fires and oil spills).

(vii) Destruction of wetlands resulting in loss of capability of storing and degrading many pollutants such as phosphorus and heavy metals.

(viii) Loss of pesticides, fertilizers, and manure from agricultural fields during run-off.

(ix) Encroachment in lake catchment area.

(x) Mining and industrial development.

(xi) Invasion by exotic weeds.

(x) Primary energy consumption leading to increased atmospheric emissions of sulphur and nitrogen oxides, the main cause of acid rain.

These human induced activities have polluted and caused scarcity in supply of hygienically safe drinking water among population and challenges to the scientists and water managers to ensure safe water supply on sustainable basis.

Water Resourses Management—Ecosystem Approach

Global Scenario

The present State of the water environment have attracted attention of all class of people globally. In response to the problems, the Global Environment Monitoring System (Gems) has, since 1977, been working through the World Health Organisation (WHO), UNESCO and the World Meteorological organisation (WMO) to develop a global water quality monitoring network. This network now includes 344 monitoring stations-240 rivers stations, 43 lake stations and 61 ground water stations (UNEP, 1991).

The UNEP has been involved in a number of international water projects, stressing its programme of Environmentally Sound Management of Inland Waters (EMINWA). To date UNEP has cooperated with riparian countries in EMINWA efforts in a variety of regions, including the Zambezi River Basin and Lake Chad Basin of Africa, the Mekong River Basin of Southeast Asia, the Aral Sea Basin of South Central Asia, the San Juan River Basin of Central America, the lake Titicaca Basin of South America, and in the Xinjiang Autonomous Region of north-west China. EMINWA projects are ongoing or planned for the Caspian Sea Basin of Eastern Europe, the Nile River Basin of Africa, and within the Human Autonomous Region of south-west China. The UNESCO is proposing to host the World Water Council's vision management unit which is to determine a global long-term vision for water, life and the environment for the 21st Century. It is also proposed by the UNESCO to establish the world's first international centre for the prevention and management of water related conflicts.

Indian Scenario

The Government of India had played an important role in prevention and control of water pollution. There are a number of policies, acts and plans for the management of precious finite water resources as given below:

- The Water (Prevention and Control of Pollution) Act, 1974.
- Central Pollution Control Board (CPCB)–September, 1974.
- The Water (Prevention and Control of Pollution) Cess Act, 1977.
- The Water Quality Monitoring started in 1977: 17 stations on Yamuna under Global Environmental Monitoring System (GEMS) and Monitoring of Indian Aquatic Resources (MINARS).
- Ganga Action Plan–1985.
- The Environment (Protection) Act, 1986–EIA mandatory.
- National Water Policy, 1987.
- Policy Statement for Abatement of Pollution, 1992.
- National River Conservation Plan, 1995.

The Ministry of Environment and Forests (MOEF), Government of India and its autonomous agency Central Pollution Control Board (CPCB) in collaboration with State Governments are playing an important role in control of the water pollution. It is worth mentioning that 18 Waste Minimization Circles (WMCs) have been established so far in different industrial clusters across the country and effluent and emission standards for fifteen categories of industries were finalised and notified in the Gazette of India during the year 1997. Out of 1551 industries belonging to the 17 categories have already installed pollution control facilities and 112 have been closed down. A National Plastic Waste Management Task Force has been constituted to formulate a strategy and prepare an action plan for management of plastic waste. The Ganga Action Plan phase–I have been launched in 1985 followed series of action plans for the management of water resources especially rivers and lakes. Under National River Conservation Plan, 1995 following major Indian rivers have been taken for rehabilitation:

Brahmani	Wainganga	Godavari
Sabarmati	Satluj	Tapi
Khan Kshipra	Betwa	Narmada
Krishna	Chambal	Cauvery
Subarnarekha	Damodar	
Mahanadi		

India is a signatory to the convention on wetlands of international importance especially as water fowl habitat generally referred to as Ramsar Convention (1971). Under this convention following wetlands are under management.

(i) Chilka (Orissa)	(ii) Keoladeo Ghana National Park (Rajasthan)
(iii) Sambhar (Rajasthan)	(iv) Wullar (J&K)
(v) Loktak (Manipur)	(vi) Harike (Punjab).

The result of conservation and management programme of river Ganga launched by MOEF have shown good result in improving the water quality Table 8. The water quality of river Ganga mainly dissolved oxygen and biochemical oxygen demand at various important locations during the year 1986 (just after implementing Ganga Action Plan) have been compared with the data of 1996 (one decade after Ganga Action Plan) have shown marked improvement in the water quality.

Table 17.8
Summer Average Values for Water Quality on Mainsteam of River Ganga

Station name	*Dissolved Oxygen**		*Biotechnical Oxygen Demand***	
	1986	*1996*	*1986*	*1996*
Rishikesh Upstream	8.1	8.9	1.7	1.0
Kanpur Upstream	7.2	7.8	7.2	2.8
Kanpur Downstream	6.7	6.4	8.6	4.1
Allahabad Upstream	6.4	8.9	11.4	2.5
Allahabad Downstream	6.6	8.5	15.5	2.3
Varanasi Upstream	5.6	8.0	10.3	2.2
Varanasi Downstream	5.9	7.7	10.6	2.3
Patna Upstream	8.4	7.3	2.0	2.0
Patnā Downstream	8.1	7.0	2.2	1.6

* Dissolved Oxygen should be 5 mg/l or more.

** Biotechnical Oxygen Demand should be less than 3 mg/l.

Source: MOEF, 1997.

Recommendations for Water Resources Management

Following recommendations based on eco-system approach deserved due consideration for the management of precious and finite surface water resources:

1. Planning of dam/reservoir should be done on an integrated watershed/river basin basis while considering the multiple objectives of the projects. The planning should encompass environmental, social, cultural economical and institutional sustainability.

2. The catchment area should be designated as water protection area with restriction and prohibitions for the management of water quality. An analysis of catchment area as factors of water quality formation should be carried out at the stage of substantiation of supply systems or individual reservoir. From the

physico-geographics point of view, the study of catchment areas incorporates:

(i) Natural-economic and landscape-geo-chemical zoning-indication of source (both local and areal) of various groups of substances, their capacity and dynamics.

(ii) An analysis of ways of migration of these substances from the source of water bodies and of factors increasing the migration rate (steep slope) or slowing it down (vegetation).

3. Deforestation should be prevented close to river and their tributaries, on reservoir catchments and in other environmentally sensitive areas, so as to check soil erosion. The restoration of critical watershed is crucial for better hygiene and health. Springs should be rejuvenated by launching afforestation programme with broad leaved multipurpose tree species at massive scale through people's participation. Conservation to tillage, buffer strip, strip cropping in watershed should be introduced.

4. The following dimensions of the water protection area should be given due emphasis:

   Catchment zone–I. Any pollution of the bank area and the water in the catchment zone is to be avoided. The catchment zone belongs the waterbody of standing waters and its bank areas, the storage body and take-out construction of reservoirs. Considering terrain exposition and morphological, geological and local conditions, the catchment zone, as a rule, is to determine at 100 to 200m. around the waterbody measured in the projection from the highest storage line.

   Narrow protective zone–II. The narrow protection zone encircles the catchment zone and has to be so dimensioned that the catchment zone is protected against all threats that may result from utilizations or pollution within the broader protective zone. In an inclined terrain it is to be extended to all areas that drain directly into the catchment zone, in a shallow terrain, it can be upto 500 m. wide. All impairing utilizations in this zone that may have negative effect upon the catchment area should be prohibited.

Broader protective zone–III

(i) The measurement of development, e.g., mining, drilling, soils development etc. are to be coordinated with the interest of water management.

(ii) Special places for the storage of residues are to be determined from which no pollution of the water can occur.

(iii) The handling of oil and petroleum products should be carried out scientifically.

(iv) Enterprises, which utilize, store or produce poisons according to the law on poisons have to take special precautions with respect to water treatment and safeguarding against catastrophe.

(v) The waste products of agricultural production and processing plants are to be utilised in agriculture itself.

(vi) Nitrogen, manure and minerals washout should be controlled.

(vii) If colonies get wastewater canalization, the waste water is to be let out of the drinking water catchment area or to be brought to sufficient waste water treatment, considering the necessary nutrient elimination.

(viii) Soil cultivation is principally to be carried out at right angles to the slope.

(ix) A slope with an unfavourable relief, necessary erosion mindering measures are to be implemented.

(x) Slopes with an inclination between 12 to 18 per cent are preferably to be utilized as permanent grass land or forest.

(xi) Slopes with an inclination over 18 per cent are to be utilized by forestry. The plantation has to be carried out to develop special forests with protective function.

5. The objective of the water quality management should involves:

   (i) Protection of water against deterioration;

   (ii) Improvement of water quality as required to meet the standards for it current and planned uses;

   (iii) Guarantee of adequate water quality for planned water bodies (e.g. reservoirs).

6. External Phosphorus Load should be controlled by following strategies:

   Point sources

   (i) Construction of sewage treatment plants including tertiary treatment;

   (ii) Land treatment (grass and soil filtration);

   (iii) High rate algal ponds;

   (iv) Diversion of sewage from the catchment area;

   (v) Introduction of water-saving technologies in industrial enterprises;

   (vi) Controlling storm overflows from sewer systems;

   (vii) Relocation/Sanitation of livestock farms from catchment areas;

   (viii) Restriction of detergents with high quality of phosphorus;

   (ix) Regulation of industrial development to ensure that enterprises producing entrophicating wastes are not sited in this catchment areas. If there are no alternative, necessary measures should be taken to control eutrophication.

Non-point sources

(i) Proclamation of the catchment area of drinking water reservoirs as drinking water protective areas with various protective zones by the water management authorities;

(ii) Appropriate dose and technology of fertilizers application in agricultural areas;

(iii) Soil stabilizing techniques in agriculture;

(iv) P-removal by seepage trenches;

(v) Construction of Pre-dams (Biological P removal)

(vi) Afforestation and Landuse control;

(vii) Pesticides use should focus upon those chemical which are the least persistent in order to reduce accumulation effects in humans and environment;

(viii) Chemical P-removal by flocculation using aluminium and iron salts and filtration of the inflowing water;

(ix) Reed belts (e.g., macrophytes sp);

(x) Human settlements should be within the carrying capacity;

(xii) Retention basins for storm water and overflows from combined sewers.

Strategy for Internal Control

The tropic state of a reservoir or lake does not depend on the external nutrient load alone. There are many factors and mechanisms within a reservoir or lake ecosystem, which can enhance or decrease the trophic state. This means that a given external nutrient load determines the tropic conditions not in a strongly deterministic way but rather with a certain probability. On the other hand, these internal ecological mechanisms (ecotechnology) can be used to control eutrophication within the limits given by the nutrient load.

7. Association of community in planning, implementation, and more particularly in operation and maintenance should be addressed towards answers of the following:
   (i) Why is community participation important?
   (ii) How can community participation be developed?
   (iii) What are the forms of community participation?

8. Safe water supply and hygienic waste disposal should receive priority, with a view to achieving measurable quantitative and quantitative targets serving all the population by a certain date. Due consideration should be given to the following:-
   (i) Promotion of an increased awareness of the problem.
   (ii) Expansion of manpower training at all levels like water users and village level workers dealing with water resources development.
   (iii) Increasing public participation, training and education in relation to domestic hygiene, and involvement in the planning, construction, operation and maintenance of facilities.
   (iv) Rivers, lakes, reservoirs and other water bodies which are main source of drinking water supply suffering from eutrophication should be rehabilitated using ecosystems approach addressing at three ecosystem levels: the whole river/lake basin; individual lake; and major critical ecosystems within the lakes.

9. Aquatic weeds which generally make water unfit for drinking purposes should be controlled through

Integrated approach using chemical (herbicides), mechanical, biological methods with people's participation. Ahmad (1988) reported that aquatic weed can also be controlled by ecological measures including appropriate shading by trees and maintaining weed biomass below 250 gm/m^2 dry weight.

10. The domestic, industrial and municipal wastes, should be utilised in a proper manner rather than its direct discharge into water bodies inducing the problem of eutrophication introducing, pathogens, organic matter and nutrients rendering fresh water unfit for drinking purposes. The household waste generated in rural areas generally free from the toxic elements should be utilised as raw compost for increasing agricultural productivity and maintaining soil fertility. The punishment for breaking rules related to pollution control in water resources should be severe enough to deter offenders.

11. In major cities the sewage management should be carried out keeping in view the reduce, reuse and recycle (collection and treatment) concepts. It should satisfy the criterion like health, reuse, ecological, nuisance, cultural, operational, and cost.

12. The responsibilities for treatment of their wastes, including microtoxins, should be placed on industries and municipalities. Legal liabilities for what they release into the environment should be established. Municipal wastes should be treated and where possible, reused. If reuse is not possible, landfills should be constructed to maximize pollutant containment.

13. Improvement of water resources requires that there is a concern for water quality as well as for water quantity at the earliest possible stages of national programme development. It is not only necessary to provide a certain minimum amount of water

required to sustain life, but the ready availability of good quality water is also essential to limit the transmission of some thirty-five bacterial, viral, protozoal, or helminthes diseases. Therefore, water quality surveillance and control is a component of any national health programme.

14. Special emphasis should be given to water's different parameters viz. aesthetic, major and minor constituents, trace elements and pollutional characteristics and World Health Organization's action levels for different parameters for characterisation of water regarding its use in drinking water supply to the population.
15. Special emphasis should be given to check nitrate content of the water, which can, among other thing leads to methaemoglobinaemias with infants and formation of carcinogenic nitrosoamines.
16. Generally water for drinking purposes is treated by chlorine therefore, water treatment by chlorine deserve due attention because of the chloride product formation in presence of organic substances for reference haloform compound. Chloroform is a haloform compound and its toxic effects are well-known. It is therefore important to learn more about the metabolic products formed during water treatment for checking the formation of toxic compounds.
17. Health education plays significant role in the success of safe drinking water supply programme. Therefore, it should be aimed at teaching of those aspects of man's physical, mental and social well-being that depends on the environment. It embraces the health aspects of biological, physical and chemical pollution of water, food, air and soil. The specific objectives should be developed towards the knowledge and understandings:

(i) of those factors in man's physical environment that have a relationship to health;

(ii) of the role of these environmental factors in causation or transmission of diseases;

(iii) of effective measures of protection, to prevent disease and to promote health and efficiency;

(iv) of the interrelationship between the biological, physical and social environment;

(v) of community health in the area, of health regulations in the community;

(vi) of reliable source of information for environmental health.

18. Safe water supply is the main part of sufficient primary health care. It is available to the whole population when at least the following conditions are realised:

(i) Safe water in the home or within 15 minutes to walk and adequate sanitary facilities in the home or its immediate vicinity;

(ii) Immunisation against diphtheria, whooping cough, tetanus, measles, poliomyelitis, tuberculosis, etc.;

(iii) Local health care;

(iv) Training personnel for attending pregnancy, childbirth and caring for children up to atleast one year of age.

19. Appropriate education and training is necessary for all levels of personnel dealing with water resources development, such as professionals, water users, village level workers etc. Training programme should be implemented to improve data gathering, planning and assessment of water resources. It will also provide water management planners an understanding and appreciation of the various

disciplines involved in water resources development and utilization, to provide professional, technical and skilled manpower in hydrology, hydrogeology, hydraulic, social, biological and health services and to provide managers for water resources system, operations for water distribution and for treatment plant and monitors for water quality installation.

20. Rooting out of trees from the storage basin may be carried thoroughly immediately before storage starts; with drinking water reservoirs without removal of stubs.

21. Generally with the establishment of standing water not only new hydro-geological but also hydro-biological conditions are created. This way, the management of water quality also requires management of water condition, according to a condition balance that has to be set up. The points that deserve due attention are:

    (i) Preventing protection of the stored water against poor condition development.

    (ii) Improvement of water condition in the storage body.

    Among these activities priority should be given to the preventive protection by respective measurement in the catchment area. The points that deserve due attention involves:

    (i) The utilisation of reservoirs for drinking water supply must aim at treatment of the untreated water from the reservoirs into drinking waters.

    (ii) The water should be obigotrophic or mestrophic one.

    The improvement of standing water condition should be carried out by:

    (i) Deep water aeration

    (ii) Upheaval of water body

(iii) Removal of water from certain depths

(iv) Utilizing chemicals (eg. for phosphorus precipitation, change in pH value, reduction of nitrate; oxidation of hydrogen sulfide).

22. The agricultural farms should be divided into four groups by the degree of potential risk for water bodies; non-pollution, weak pollution, medium pollution, and heavy pollution to evolve strategies for better water quality management.

23. The dynamics of introducing minerals and organic fertilizers (nitrogen, phosphorus and potassium) to arable lands within the catchment should be studied for controlling the problem of eutrophication of reservoir which deteriorates the water quality, and restricts its application. Companies which produce fertilizers and pesticides must label their products, indicating those countries which have banned the use of the product. The contamination of the water with genetically altered micro-organisms should be given due emphasis for its reduction and control. The dangerous pesticides DDT and PCBs should be banned.

24. Public awareness should be raised through appropriately couched media efforts and other avenues viz. Involving televisions, radio, and calling on the skills of journalists, science writer and other communications specialists. Such understanding is crucial to popular support of water resources management efforts in the region.

25. Rain water harvesting for households and commercial enterprises should be encouraged for supplementing the supply of the national distribution systems.

26. Improved assessment and management of risk, increased reliability of traditional, technical and new demand-oriented data, improved awareness of water

and enhanced public participation are needed. The action for water management must be participatory, transparent, creative and technically sound.

27. Water related information systems should be integrated with other aspects of water management systems, especially on demand and use, and with information on comprehensive environmental management.
28. Integrated approach to planning for future water requirements is necessary. It must consider the full spectrum of options, for a structural (such as conservation, pricing and bio-engineering).
29. The water resources management should take into account socio-economic, cultural technical and environmental aspects alongwith principles such as 'the pollution pays' and 'user pays principles'.
30. The incentive structure should be changed/modified for promoting better management of water resources. The market friendly policies should be implemented.
31. The environmental management programme should be based more on incentive and less on regulations for efficiency and to reduce damage.
32. Participatory approach should be encouraged in planning and implementing the projects. The planning should be demand-based, from the lowest appropriate level, ensuring stake holders in decision-making and participation of women.
33. The participation of private sector should be encouraged to improve the quality of water management, resources mobilization, efficiency improvement and for the increase of the quality of services for users. Private sector participation will also play an important role in reducing the financial burden on Government budget.

34. Women as important ecosystem managers should be encouraged to be equal partners in development.

35. Detailed Environmental Impact Assessment (EIA) should be carried out before implementing any programmes and projects, which might have negative impacts on water resources and based on EIA report management plans should be evolves for ecologically sustainable development.

36. Rapid population growth has major impact on inter-generational equity which ultimately affected resources use and renewal ratio. Therefore, it has been realised that environmentally sound and sustainable development can only be achieved through inter-generational equity in resources use.

37. International Coordination Committee (ICC) should be established for shared International Water Resources, to ensure effective management and long-term sustainability; patterned after the Helsinki Commission, which covered the protection of the marine environment of the Baltic Sea.

REFERENCES

1. Ahmad, A. 1988: *Environmental Impact Assessment of Water Resources Projects in India.* UNs (UNEP-UNESCO) Ecosystems Management Course Materials, Technical University, Dresdon, Germany, p. 89.
2. Ahmad, A. 1989: "Eutrophication with Special Reference to Himalayas and Strategies for its Rehabilitation in: *Management of Aquatic Ecosystem* (Eds. Agrawal, V.P., Desai, V.N. and Abidi, S.A.H.) Narendra Publishing House, New Delhi, India, pp. 363-99.
3. Ahmad, A. 1990 : Safe Water Supply in Rural Himalayas: Environmental Problems and Strategies. In the Proceedings of the 10th National Conference on Health Problems of the Nineties, Lahore, Pakistan, pp. 28-29.
4. Bulloch, J. and Darwish, A. 1993: *Water Wars-Coming Conflicts in the Middle East.* Victor Gollancz, London, England, p. 213.

5. CPCB, 1996: Water Quality–Status and Statistics (1993 and 1994) Central Pollution Control Board, Ministry of Environment and Forests, Delhi, India, pp. 459.
6. CWC, 1991: Theme Paper on Water Conservation. Central Water Commission, New Delhi, India, p. 1990.
7. IWRS, 1997: Theme paper on River Basin Management-Issues and options. Water Resources Day Volume, Indian Water Resources Society, New Delhi, India, p. 11.
8. MOEF. 1997: Annual Report 1996-97, Ministry of Environment and Forests, Government of India, p. 163.
9. Sadeq, H.T., 1999: A Rare and Precious Resources. UNESCO, the Courier, February Issues, Paris, France, pp. 18-21.
10. UNDP, 1998: Human Development Report, New York, USA.
11. UNEP, 1991: Fresh Water Pollution. UNEP/GEMS Environment Library no. 6, Nairobi, Kenya, p. 35.

18

IMPLICATIONS OF BHAGAVAD GITA FOR SUSTAINABLE HUMAN DEVELOPMENT

Dr. M.M. Goel

Sustainable Human Development (SHD) as defined in Human Development Report by UNDP "is development that not only generates economic growth but distributes its benefits equitably that generates the environment rather than destroying it; that empowers people rather than marginalising them. It is development that gives priority to the poor, enlarging their choice and opportunities and providing for their participation in decisions that effect their lives". Human Development cannot be sustained without introducing Indian Ethos which has implications for SHD. The Indian Ethos primarily taken from the 'Bhagavad Gita' and in general from Vedic literature. It lights the lamp of wisdom in the hearts of human beings and removes cultural, behavioural and management pollution prevailing in the modern society. Our life is full of miseries and we have to struggle for existence. There is something wrong which is eating into the roots of our society. *Bhagavad Gita* can give proper guidance to the modern human-being about the methods of perfecting his/her life. It needs to be understood very clearly that *Bhagavad Gita* can change the hearts of people and free them from sinful activities and purify their lives. The teachings contained therein are meant for one and all and certainly essential for the development of human beings. When our life is confronted with problems and is full of confusion and doubts, *Bhagavad Gita* provides effective advice. It offers philosophy of optimum welfare by doing duty of labour, knowledge and having dedication and commitment. In fact *Bhagavad Gita* is treatise of welfare Economics.

Human beings are born with certain potential capabilities. The purpose of development is to create an environment in which all people can expand their capabilities and opportunities can be enlarged for both present and future generations. The paradigm of SHD values human life for itself. Development must enable all individuals to enlarge their human capabilities to the fullest and to put those capabilities to the best use of all fields. Human development should be seen as a major contribution to sustainability. As there is no tension between human development and sustainable development; both are based on the universalism of life claims. The essence of SHD is that everyone should have equal access to development opportunities now and in the future.

Though SHD is a complex process but here it has been made a simple process. The word 'SIMPLE' consisting of six alphabets also called model of SHD having various human development activities such as:-

S - Spiritual Development

I - Intelligence Development

M - Mental Development

P - Physical Development

L - Love Yourself Attitude Development

E - Emotional Quotient Development

The synergy of these six aspects of human development constitutes a central objective of SHD. These factors are responsible for the all round development of an individual so that he may become quite fit for the society and can express himself freely. The *Bhagavad Gita* has a definite role to play in SHD. It is essential to understand that *Bhagavad Gita* is the only hope for development in the modern context. We have reversed knowingly the sequencing of alphabets for explaining the model. Now, we venture to discuss the components of our model one by one.

I. Emotional Quotient Development

Everyone wants success in life. What determines success then? A recent spate of management thoughts and practices champion the cause of EQ (Emotional Quotient) as that arm, which when added to IQ, define success. How simple is it to test, measure and take steps to increase your IQ: But we ususally run into difficulties even in defining EQ, let alone getting to the bottom of it. A variety of words and phrases have been used to define the factors which govern EQ. 'The ability to get along with people and situations'. 'A positive and proactive attitude towards all aspects of life'. 'The ability to command respect by building relationships'.

EQ focusses on the softer skills of building and maintaining human relationships. This aspect of life assumes a lot of importance since nowhere is a person detached from the human element. Be it the workplace; the home front or the social circle, human interactions are inevitable and our success depends to a large extent on what we make of these interactions and relationships. For this *sloka* number 15 of chapter 17 of *Bhagawad Gita* needs to be adopted.

Anudvegakaraṁ Vākyam Satyṁ Priyahitaṁ Ca Yat

Savā̃dhyā̃ Bhyasanaṁ Caiva Vākmayaṁ Tapa Ucyate

meaning thereby Meditative communion with one's own true self, and uttering words that cause no agitation and that are truthful, pleasant and beneficial are called the authenticity of speech. Persons with high EQ can be great leaders; get promoted and thrive during uncertainty and change.

There are four cornerstones for emotional intelligence. Executing EQ begins with 'emotional literacy' as the first cornerstone which develops self-confidence through emotional honesty, energy, emotional feedback, intuitions, responsibility and connection. The second cornerstone is of 'emotional fitness' which strengthens our authenticity, believability and resilence. The third cornerstone of 'emotional depth' explores ways to align our life and work with unique potential and purpose. The fourth cornerstone advances to 'emotional alchemy' through which we extend our creative instinct and capacity to resolve problems constructively.

There are three major components to EQ—motivating oneself, motivating others and empathiasisng with others; which clearly describe the functional areas which determine the EQ of a person. All these three components of EQ are related to the teachings of *Bhagavad Gita* to a greater extent. We can motivate ourselves by understanding, analysing and adopting the most secret teachings of *Bhagavad Gita* in our life. We can motivate others by directing them to understand, analyse and adopt *Bhagavad Gita* in their life. The increasing acceptance of EQ as an important contributor to SHD helps in taking momentous decision, or even decisions which are not repetitive in nature. EQ takes the participants through the process of improving their positions in life to achieve a win-win situation.

II. Love Yourself Attitude Development

In *Bridharanyak Upnishad.* Yagnavalkya says to his wife Maitri that -"Husband loves his wife not for wife's sake but for the sake of the self and a wife loves her husband not for husband's sake but for own sake; mother loves her child not for child's sake but for own sake and a child love his mother not for mother's sake but for own sake". It means all the activities which we are doing in our ordinary business of life are guided by self-interest, i.e., love for our oneself. It is a love of ownself that urges to take those activities where we get pleasure and discard all these activities where pain is there. So everywhere self-interest or love for oneself is the guiding force.

According to Swami Ram Tirth, there are two types of selves—little self, i.e., our body which is composed of all sense organs and the purest self, i.e. our soul. Now in the first chapter of *Bhagavad Gita* when Arjuna throws away his Gandive and wants to run away from his Dharma, that is, he is not ready to fight for the sake of truth by arguing that there is no use of killing our own relatives, friends, gurus even for the kingdom of three lokas. Now this is the little self which is speaking in Arjuna. He is in the grip of *Moha*. He does not realise that his foes want dominion. This type of *Moha* distracts one from one's *dharma* (duty), and have been oppressors and have heaped inequities on the just and the innocent. Arjuna justifies his dereliction of duty with fancy rationalization.

Bhagavad Gita teaches us self-love of the highest order. So, a person is to develop himself so that he can shun love for little self and act according to the dictates of the purest self, i.e. soul. So it is the realisation of the purest self when a person loves his soul than his actions and he becomes a useful member of the society. Then he has no desire and no object to gratify himself. His *karmas* are automatic as the sun shines. As sun gives light to everybody irrespective of caste, creed and religion, in the same way, he works for the welfare of everybody and he observes the same purest self. In brief, a journey from little self to purest self constitutes SHD.

III. Physical Development

An old and wise saying, 'A sound mind resides in a sound body' makes the justification for physical development. Having a sound body is very essential for the proper development of one's life. If our body is not working properly, it is diseased. We cannot perform our duty well and will be inefficient in our work. The growth and development of one's life depends upon the development of physical powers. Physical development contributes a lot in human life and hence necessary for SHD. Physical development is possible by understanding, analysing and adopting *Bhagavad Gita* in our life.

For the proper maintenance, growth and development of the body, first of all, we must have knowledge about the constituents of our body. In *sloka* 4 of chapter seven of *Bhagavad Gita*. Lord Krishna clearly explains the constituents of body-

bhumir apo nalo vayuh

kham mano budhir eva Ca

Ahankara itiyam me

bhinna prakrtir astadha

(Earth, water, fire, air, mind, intelligence and ego; these constitute My nature eight fold divided)

The body which is transient and ever changing consists of five elements—ether, fire, water, air and earth; within which five sense objects are included. They are manifestations of the physical sound, touch, form, taste and smell. If these senses are active and competent, then we will have a sound body. Air must be devoid of pollution and it is possible through *yagnas* as prescribed in *Bhagavad Gita.* Some of the bodily disease are due to polluted water. Rainy water is considered pure containing many useful elements for the bodily development. In the past, we used to perform *yagnas* for rain which is also the basis of our agricultural development.

To have a healthy body, we must know, what are its need? It needs proteins, vitamins, carbohydrates, minerals and fats for its proper growth and development. It needs a balanced diet. Balanced diet is one that contains all these elements in a right proportion required for proper growth of the body. This balanced diet provides energy to our body which in turn provides us the power for our routine work. The purpose of food is to increase the duration of life, purify the mind and aid bodily strength. In the past, great authorities selected those foods that best aided to health and increased life's duration; such as milk products, ghee, wheat, fruits and vegetables. In *Bhagavad Gita*, (17:8.9.10) food which is agreeable to different man according to their innate nature is of three kinds.

āyuh-sattva-balārogya
sukla-priti-vivardhanāh
rasyāh snigdhāh sthira hrdyā
āhārāh śattvika priyāh

(Food which promotes life's duration, intelligence, vigour, health, happiness and cheerfulness are dear to 'Sattavika' type of man. Such food are juicy, fatty, wholesome and pleasing to the heart)

Katv-amla-lavanāty-usna
tiksna-suksa-vidahinah
āhārā rajasasyestā
duhkh-sokāmaya pradāh

(Food which are bitter acid, salty, over hot, pungent, dry and burning and which cause suffering, grief and sickness are dear to the 'Rajasika' type of man)

Yātā-yamaṁ gata rasaṁ
puti paryusitam ca yat
ucchistam api cāmedhyaṁ
bhojanaṁ tāmasa-priyam

(Food which is half cooked or half ripe, insipid, putrid, polluted and stale is dear to a men of Tamasika disposition)

As already stated, our body needs such balanced diet as contains all the essential components required for bodily growth. So a diet must contain all these; such as cow milk and Ghee. The cow milk contains protein (3.4 per cent), lactose (4.1 per cent), solids (13.7 per cent), fats (4.9 per cent), solids without fats (8.8 per cent), minerals (10.7 per cent). That is why cow milk has been prescribed by Krishna in *Gita* as a food which promote intelligence, vigour and bodily strength. On the other hand, the third type of food liked by tamasika has adverse effect on our body. It increases infection and diseases. Such food stuffs although very palatable to the persons but the conclusion of a systematic medical study shows that it is not an essential diet for human and is unsuitable. It actually has harmful effects on various parts of the body.

Lastly, regulation of diet and sleeping is recommended for healthy body. Too much eating and sleeping, both are injurious to health. In *Bhagavad Gita* (6.16) it has been clearly explained that-

Naty-asnatas tu—yogo'sti
na caikantam anasatam
na cati svapna-silasya
jagrato naiva carjuna

(There is no possibility of one's becoming *yogi*, if one eats too much or eats too little, sleeps too much or does not sleep enough)

Extravagance in the matter of eating, sleeping, defending and mating, which are the demands of the body, can block advancement of physical development. We should be regulated in our eating, sleeping, mating and all other bodily activities for proper growth and development.

IV. Mental Development

Without the mind's help, nothing can succeed. So in the process of development, the co-operation of mind is essential. As a means of growth, external actions and inward attitude of mind, both are needed. Action is must if you want to test your mind. External actions reveal the quality of mind. The surface of the water is clear, but throw a stone into it and at once mud rises up. Our mind is just like that.

Now the question arises—what makes our mind polluted? When we do any work, we are guided by our senses which in turn are guided by our mind and mind ultimately is guided by our discriminating intelligence (*Vivek*). If our mind has a mixture of lust, *Krodha* and illusion, it will not guide us in proper direction so these three can be treated as obstacles in the way of mental development.

The most important thing what a man should cultivate in his life is the need to purify the mind. We have to cleanse the mind of its dirt. To light a lamp, one need not only the oil and the wick, but also a flame. When the lamp is lit, the darkness disappears. Purity of mind is the flame which will dispel darkness in our life. To attain purity of mind, many things are prescribed. Firstly, there is *Yagna* and *dana* (sacrifice and gifts). *Jap* and *Tap* (prayer and penance), *dhyan* and *dharma* (meditation and concentration). These means can be compared with washing soda and soap. But *Bhakti* is water. Without water these other things are useless; but even without these water can cleanse. If in *yagna, yoga, dhyan* and *tap,* the heart does not enter, how can purity of mind result? It is the involvement of heart that is *Bhakti*. *Bhakti* is essential for all kind of effortes. If a trained nurs, attending on a patient, has not the *Bhavna,* the mental attitude of service, how could it be a true service. In work without heart, there is neither strength nor satisfaction. Secondly, the things we practise day and night stick to us. We will have to train the mind right from childhood. Take constant care that good impressions alone come to the mind. By letting the mind go as it pleases, we will defeat ourselves. Then we will never acquire good impressions. Similarly wisdom should be gathered without wasting even a single moment. Noble thoughts should pass though our mind so that good impressions should be created. These should go on constantly. Thirdly, purity of mind can be attained by assuming erect posture. All our activities should be pure. To purify activities, its motive should be transformed. Activities should not be performed for one's individual profit, for satisfying the instinct or for outward object but for the whole world. In *Bhagavad Gita* (17:16),"

Manah prasādah saumyatvam mounam ātmavinigraha

bhāv saṁsudhir ity etet tapo mānasam ucyate

Meaning thereby A calm and contented mental clarity, kindness, silence, self control and purity of character constitute the austerity of the mind.

V. Intelligence Development

As students, how often have we heard the dismissive statement-"if you do not do well in class, you can never be successful." And while in job, how many times we have been told, "your success is not related to your performance in class." It was a very surprising statement by a senior official of the examination board which went on to say the same thing in the light of the recent furore over the Mathematics paper in an examination. Taken together, the two statements send very contradictory messages to those who are striving for success.

What determines success then; if it is not Intelligence Quotient (1.Q.)? By stating otherwise, are we not shifting from an old age paradigm which has premeated the very consciousness of every parent, child and educationist? A recent spate of management thoughts and practices champion the cause of EQ (Emotional Quotient) as that arm which when added to IQ define success.

Where sailing in the life-boat, we have to face many hurdles and obstacles. For a successful journey, one must be aware of all hurdles and obstacles that come in the way of journey of life. Now even to have a very correct and precise picture of all these obstacles, intelligence is required. Intelligence refers to the power to analyse things in their proper perspective. The individual is the passenger in the car of the material body, and intelligence is the driver. Mind is the driving instrument and senses are the horses. The self is thus the enjoyer or sufferer in the association of the mind and senses. Intelligence is supposed to direct the mind, but the mind is so strong and obstinate that it often overcomes the intelligence sometimes, although the mind is supposed to be subservient to the intelligence. The ability is not just to read many books on different subjects but understand them and apply them when necessary, is intelligence.

It is *krodha* that hinders in the way of intelligence development. In *Bhagavada Gita*, 2.63:-

Krod ad bhavati sammohah
sammohat smrti vibharamah
smrti bhramsad buddhi-naso
buddhi-nasat pranasyati

(From anger, complete delusions arise, delusion bewilderment of memory. When memory is bewildered, intelligence is lost and when intelligense is lost, one falls down again into the material pool)

So, to attain sustainable development, it is very important for us to develop intelligence to understand and accept situations, people and the changes happening around us.

VI. Spiritual Development

Spiritual development is essential for the removal of stress and strain as well as social and economic health of the society. Spiritual development must be performed in order to convert human beings into human capital. Besides the development of senses and mind, there is one more thing which is most important—that is spirit, soul or *atma.* We are to realise it which is the spiritual path.

The figure which we see with our eyes, we call it body or image. But even after seeing with our eyes the outer form, we still have to enter into the object and see it from with in. We have to remove the armour, the skin of the fruit and taste the pulp within. Despite the rough and sharp exterior of the coconut, the jack fruit is full of sweet juicy pulp. When we look at ourselves or others, we have to distinguish the inside from outside. The soul can be compared to a driver and the body to a vehicle. It is the spark of life that makes the body appear. The sole prevades the body with consciousness as a lamp fills a room with light. The lamp that gives light to the entire room may be in one corner of the room. Similarly the soul is situated in the region of our heart. The soul is not removed during heart transplantation, as soul is spiritual. For example when stepney or radiator of a car is changed, nothing happens to the driver, In *Bhagavad Gita* (2:23) Krishna tells—

nainam chindanti sastrani

nainam dahati pavakah

na chinam kledayanty apo

no sosavati marutah

(The soul can never be cut to pieces by any weapon, nor burnt by fire, nor moistened by water, nor withered by the wind).

Now Krishna says that we are to realise our soul: once a person realises his soul, then his outlook becomes quite different from that of the worldly people and he becomes the source of inspiration to all. It is the ideal state of spiritual development. So, as long as we do not realise the soul, we remain absorded in ordinary activities. We know nothing beyond eating, drinking, sleeping and mating. For these, we fight, in this way, we are involved in activities relating to the body. Progress begins only later. All this while, soul remains merely watching like a mother watching her child crawling near the well. With some care, the soul watches us. One day the soul wakes up and knowledge dawns upon it that it had been living like an animal. When the soul begins to think like this, the foundations of ethics are laid. It starts exercising the power of discrimination. Discipline takes the place of self indulgence. When the soul thus enters the domains of ethics, the soul does not merely stand aside and watch. Then it expresses approval from within saying -'well done'. In the next stage, a man through doing his duty tries to cleanse his mind and heart. When he feels tired, then the soul begins to pray- 'I have come to the end of my efforts. Give me more strength.' Until a man realises that he cannot achieve success by his own efforts, however hard, he cannot understand the secret of prayer. When a man's own efforts to do a work prove inadequate, he should call on the supreme with a sad and yearing heart as Draupadi did. The stream of Lord's compassion and succour flows continuously. This is the third stage: The supreme now comes very close. He comes running now to help you.

Thus progressively, we should learn to experience the Lord; the Lord comes towards us for our help. After this, we have to give over to the Lord the fruit of action, and make him the enjoyer. And in the end, we should surrender to him the right to resolve and thus fill all our life with him. This must be the ultimate goal of man and it is the ideal stage of spiritual development. In true sense, the SHD is possible through self realization and spiritual development. In true sense, the SHD is possible through self realization and spiritual development, the process of which is simplified in *Kaliyuga* by chanting his name through *Mahamantra* as -

Hare Krisna, Hare Krisna, Krisna Krisna, Hare Hare

Hare Rama, Hare Ram, Rama Rama, Hare Hare

Chanting this *Mahamantra* (sixteen malas of 108 beads) is the basic requirement to become *Krisna conscious*'. Spiritual development in the true sense is self realization and to become '*Krisna conscious*'.

To sum up, 'Simple' model of SHD is a sweet dream and wishful thinking for which *Bhagavad Gita* must be considered as an essential input. *Bhagavad Gita* is like an elevated lamp which throws light on every aspect of human life. It has its significance in emotional quotient development, love yourself attitude development, physical development, mental development, intelligence development and spiritual development. The synergy of these six aspects of human development constitutes a central objective of SHD. These factors are responsible for the alround development of an individual so that he may become quite fit for the society and can express himself freely. In fact. *Bhagavad Gita* has a definite role to play in SHD and it is essential to understand, analyse and adopt *Bhagavad Gita* in our daily life as it is the only and only hope for sustainable development in the modern syntex.

REFERENCES

1. Human Development Report, 1994.
2. A.C. Bhaktivendanta Swami Prabupada, *Bhagavad Gita*— As it is; The Bhaktivedanta Book Trust, Bombay, 1983.
3. Parmhansa Yogananda, *The Bhagavad Gita; Royal Science of God-Realisation*, Vol. 1-2, self Realisation Fellowship, California, 1996.
4. M.M. Goel and Ravinder Mittal, Simple model of Sustainable Human Development: Implications of *Bhagavad Gita* conference Volume of the Indian Economic Association (1998).

Section–IV

Science, Education and Technology–Future Perspective

19

PREVENTIVE ENVIRONMENTAL MANAGEMENT

A.K. Chaturvedi

India is a large economy, which is rapidly growing in terms of industrialisation. Industrialisation would result in a great burden on the environment and the effects will not just be local but will be felt globally. Hence it is important to see what is happening in such a large economy with respect to the environment. The environmental legislation in India is implemented to control pollution. Many specific projects and areas have been identified which need attention from an environmental point of view. The basic problem in the country is that despite some good laws, poor implementation owing to insufficient infrastructure results in an environment, which is getting from bad to worse. The laws themselves are lacking at places to promote Preventive Environmental Managemant (PEM).

Of late, steps are being taken to improve the situation but one wonders if they are sufficient. Many steps are required at the policy level as well as implementation level to improve the condition. If correct action is taken the condition may improve. However the progress is likely to be slow.

Background

India is the second largest country in the world in terms of the population. It is the world's eighth largest economy and also the tenth most industrialised nation. The population is growing at a rate of 1.91 per cent every year and is expected to stabilise by the year 2050, by then it would be the most populated country in the world. The increase in size of the population puts a tremendous pressure on the country's natural resources. The challenge being faced today is of economic development with the need of safeguard the environment.

To ensure that the economic development continues at a steady rate, the country has moved towards economic liberalisation and new investment policies have been formulated to attract foreign investment.

The economic growth and the rapid industrialisation are having adverse effect on the environment. The country is the second fastest growing producer of green house gases. The increase in demand for power is resulting in new power plants being set up which are coal based. This further increases the emission of carbon dioxide, a global problem and also results in the generation of fly ash, which is 45 million tons per year, which is becoming a major concern locally. Similarly the problem of air pollution, water pollution deforestation, waste disposal etc. will become a major concern in the years to come.

To save the environment many environmental laws and rules have been framed and implemented and are being revised as the need arises. This is in line with the Constitution of India, under Part IVA on Fundamental Duties, Article 51A(g) states "It shall be the duty of every citizen of India to protect and improve the natural environment including forests, lakes, rivers and wild life, and to have compassion for living creatures."[3]

A further investigation needs to be done to see the role of PEM and how it can help to improve the environmental situation in the country.

What is Preventive Environmental Management?

United Nations Environment Programme (UNEP) defines cleaner production as "the continuous application of an integrated preventive environmental strategy to processes, products and services to reduce risks to humans and the environment. This UNEP concept is similar to the concept of Pollution Prevention as defined by the United States Environmental Protection Agency (USEPA). The USEPA has defined "pollution prevention as 'source reduction' as that term is explained under the Pollution Prevention Act, as well as protecting natural resources through conservation or increased efficiency in the use of energy, water, or other materials."[5]

The concept of PEM is not different from the above mentioned concepts. It relates to adopting preventive approaches to environmental management systems. It essentially aims at preventing the pollution from taking place or reducing it at source rather than tackling the problem at the end. It encompasses all the aspects related to a good or service, starting for the initial stage to the end. It has been called by a different name merely because environmental management is a well-known concept in India. Thus, the people as compared with Cleaner Production of Pollution Prevention more easily understand the concept of Preventive Environmental Management. Within the context of the EU funded, JEEP project, PEM "represents the constellation of strategies, tools and concepts that aims to reduce/eliminate environmental impacts at source rather than at the end-of-pipe stage. The constellation of strategies covers Cleaner Production (CP), Environmental Management Systems (EMS), Cleaner Technologies (CT), Industrial Symbiosis/Ecology (IE), Life Cycle Assessment/Perspective (LCA) etc."[6]

This can be further elaborated into three main categories, including Management, Process and Product. Within each category, there can be topics such as those shown in the Table 19.1. These topics are those which were identified when the JEEP project was started.

Table 19.1
Three Board Categories of PEM and their Sub-topics

Management	*Process*	*Product*
Environmental Management System (EMS)	Environmental Technology (IE) Assessment	Industrial Ecology
Environmental Performance Evaluation (EPE)	Toxic Use Reduction (TUR)	Extended Produce Responsibility (EPR)
Environmental Audits	Best Operating Practices (BOP)/Environmental Best Practice (EBP)	Eco-Labelling
Environmental Reporting/ Communication	Best Available Technology (BAT)	Design for Environment (DFE)
Total Cost Accounting (TCA)	Waste Minimisation (WM)/Pollution Prevention (PP)	Life Cycle Assessment (LCA)
	Cleaner Production (CP)	Eco-efficiency
	Cleaner Technology (CT)	

In general Cleaner Production or PEM are not in absolute state, but is continually evolving as new knowledge, improved technologies, and changing attitudes are applied in the production and delivery of products and services. These are dynamic concepts and it must be borne in mind that the Table above showing the different categories would not be stagnant and change with time. Topics such as Environmental Economics, Business Ethics, and Governmental Policy could be incorporated into the table for PEM categories, keeping the present situation in mind.

To put it in simple terms PEM is aimed at prevention of pollution rather than control of pollution. The implementation of several concepts of PEM results in increased productivity and contributes to the bottom line of the business. A simple example would be implementation of waste minimisation, which would result in savings.

Thus, in short it may be stated that PEM is a tool which can help us to improve our environmental performance and also generate other benefits to us. So it is important that we learn about PEM. This can be achieved at two different levels (a) at the university level and (b) at the job level. For the first category we need to have courses offered by the universities and institutions to the students to learn about PEM. For the second level we need to have training programmes for "on the job" professionals so that they may directly influence their place of work.

Existing Situation in India

Presently there is a growing awareness about environmental issues in India and to address these issues several environmental courses have been started in the universities. To compliment this there are also some training programmes being conducted to increase the level of awareness related to environmental impacts. To add to these the regulatory authorities are also regularly adding new laws and regulation to control the environmental pollution.

However, a quick look at the courses being offered by the universities shows that these courses, which are offered by the universities, may be categorised into three categories.

(i) *Courses that evolved from Civil Engineering:* These course mainly focus on topics like air pollution, water supply and sewage, industrial waste treatment, etc. These courses are focused on either control technologies or are introduction to various aspects of environmental pollution. These are not sufficient to meet the demand of the industries that seek more from their environmental managers rather than just running the control plants.

(ii) *Courses that specialised into Environmental Science:* These courses are more science based as compared to the previous one, which were engineering based. Here the focus is on subjects like Environmental Chemistry/Microbiology, environmental monitoring and instrumentation, ecology etc. These courses result in playing a supporting role for other

environmental activities but do not result in control or prevention.

(iii) ***Interdisciplinary Courses:*** These courses are technology focussed and relate to process innovation, source reduction, etc. These are courses more in line with the present day demand. They are more than just an ordinary environmental manager who is engaged in controlling the treatment plants but looks beyond towards prevention. However, such courses are scarce and the course curriculum is often not regularly updated.

What we observe from the above is that though these courses exist in the country but they lack the direction of PEM. It shall be further investigated as to the reasons why PEM education is required in the country.

Why PEM Education is Required?

Several reasons, which favour the implemention of PEM education, could be explained in simple terms now. As the title itself suggests, Prevention is better than cure. Prevention of environmental pollution enhances productivity and profitability. This has been demonstrated by several industries that have implemented PEM. When the focus is on pollution control the result is that the pollution is not reduced but the problem is transferred from one media to another. A simple example to illustrate this is the installation of effluent treatment plant in an industry. What is achieved is that the pollutants are transferred from the liquid phase to the solid phase in the form of sludge and then it becomes a problem. PEM however, focuses on elimination the pollution from the process and thereby solving the problem. PEM easily makes the efforts put for environmental management more result oriented and effective in protecting the environment.

Efforts to Promote PEM Education in India

In order to promote PEM education in India, Network for Preventive Environmental Managemant (NetPEM) was set up in India. The International Institute for Industrial Environmental Economics (IIIEE), Lund University, Sweden co-sponsored the NetPEM. NetPEM is founded to promote the implementation of PEM strategies in Asia through better exchange of information, training, research and advisory services.

One of the important projects presently being implemented at NetPEM is the "EU-India Joint Environmental Education Programme" (JEEP). The JEEP project is co-sponsored by the European Commission under its EU- India Economic Cross-Cultural Exchange Programme.The JEEP project is designed to reach mutual enhancement/ interaction of the European Countries with India in the field of Preventive Environmental Management (PEM) by a constructive dialogue and exchange of knowledge. A network of four university institutions, two each from Europe and India, and a nodal information centre,"Centre for Preventive Environmental Management" C-PEM, is implementing the JEEP project.

The C-PEM, is hosted at NetPEM, Nagpur, India. Its key objective is to facilitate implementation of PEM- Education within Indian academic institutions. The main activities of this project are:

(i) PEM curricula development and adaptation;

(ii) Educating the educators for PEM education;

(iii) Pilot testing curricula at IIT Bombay (integrating key elements of PEM in the existing engineering courses) and at University of Hyderabad (specialisation in PEM being offered for management graduates); and

(iv) Enlarging the network for promoting PEM education to 25-30 Indian and 10-20 EU universities.

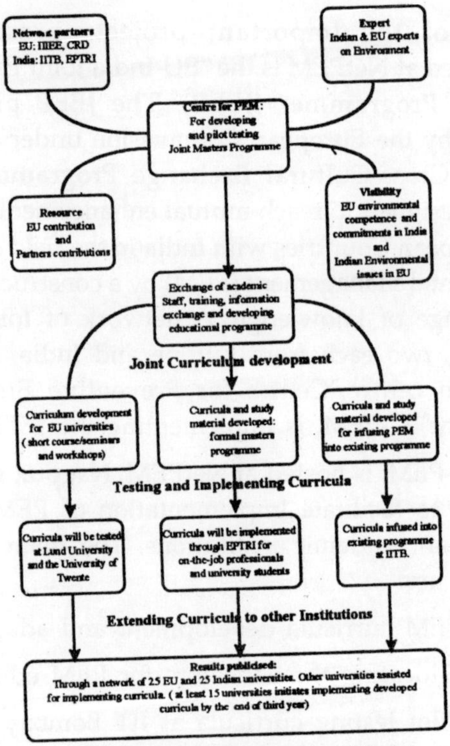

Figure 1: The JEEP Project Model

Barriers to PEM Education in India

The initial findings of the JEEP revealed that there are several courses being offered by the Indian Universities and other institutions but they are lacking in their focus to preventive strategies. These courses are mainly focussed at control technologies or other related issues like monitoring and measurement. There are several training programmes being conducted on environmental issues but the focus of these programmes is either on environmental systems, environmental audits etc. but once again lack the focus on prevention. The technical skills in the country are however, reasonably good but the implementation of preventive approach is usually missing. Even from the regulatory side there are no incentives for promotion of preventive strategies. The industry is required to ensure compliance but there is no incentive to beyond the compliance level. In contrast the countries in the West have economic incentives for the industry to go even beyond compliance. The barriers to PEM can be categorised into three simple categories, which are described below:

I. Political Barriers

Sixty per cent of the barriers are contributed to by this category which includes the following reasons:

(i) Bureaucratic resistance,

(ii) Human conservatism,

(iii) Uncoordinated legislation,

(iv) Media sensationalism,

(v) Public ignorance/misinformation.

II. Financial Barriers

Though people in practice indicate these as the main barriers but in implementing PEM the reality is that these barriers contribute only thirty per cent and are as follows:

(i) Disposal subsidy,

(ii) Scarce money,

(iii) Entrenched disposal industry.

III. Technical Barriers

This category is often stated as the main category by the developing countries wherein the belief is that appropriate technology is not available with them. However for implementing PEM this category contributes only ten per cent. The two barriers that exist are as under:

(i) Lack of reliable information,

(ii) Lack of assistance in applying waste minimisation to industrial needs.

IV. Barriers for PEM Courses in India

Going more specifically to the barriers for PEM courses in India the following are the once, which were identified:

(i) There is no link between university programmes and other agencies like the industry or the potential employers of the PEM professionals. This leads to a gap in the requirement of the employer and the qualification possessed by the professional who has undergone the course.

(ii) The Postgraduate programmes, which are available, are not regularly evaluated to respond to the needs of the changing environment. This again leads to the courses being obsolete in terms of the market requirements.

(iii) Another significant barrier for PEM courses is that the potential employers themselves do not know about PEM and so there is no demand from their side for such professionals.

(iv) Another mistake that often takes place is that sometimes even if the courses are available they are simply taken for some other country or university there and implemented in India. The courses need local adaptation for them to be more practical and useful. Learning only about foreign experiences is not enough and it is important that we learn how to work in our country where the situation is very different.

V. Efforts to Overcome Barriers to PEM Education

As earlier mentioned the JEEP is one strong step in the direction of promoting PEM education in India. The approach to enhance PEM education in India can be shown as follows in Figure 2.

Fig. 2. Approach to Enhance PEM Education in India

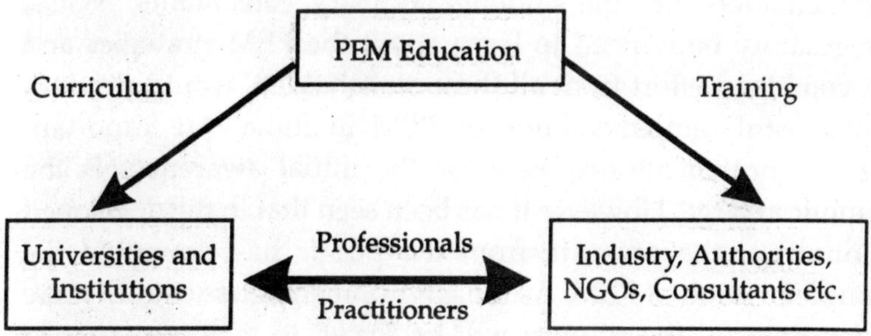

The figure illustrates the efforts being done at two levels to promote PEM education. The first is by helping universities and institutions with the course curricula for PEM education. The second is by providing PEM training to the industry, authorities etc. to make them aware of the advantages of implementing PEM. This would result in two-way interaction of professionals and practitioners of PEM. Thus, on one side there would be demand for PEM professionals and on the other side the universities and institutions would be producing such professionals.

As a result of the above efforts one MBA course has already been started in Hyderabad University. Some elective courses have been finalised for IIT, Bombay that will be offered to the students in the coming semesters. Some of the other efforts to promote PEM education are promotion of Global Environmental Youth Convention in Asia region by NetPEM. Here the target audience is the teenage students.

Conclusions

There is definitely a need for PEM education in India at both levels; University courses and for professional working in the environmental field. The initial problem is about the awareness of PEM strategies and their benefit. In the author's opinion, once the awareness is established then there would be a demand for PEM education in the country. All the stakeholders, i.e., the students, industry, consultants, NGOs, regulatory body need to learn about the PEM strategies and a combined effort from all these stakeholders would result in successful implementation of PEM in India. An important group not mentioned here for the initial awareness is the public at large. However it has been seen that in the developed countries, the pressure from the public has promoted the implemention of PEM. As the environmental issues gain more importance, the country will be forced to take measures to improve its environmental performance and it would be difficult to achieve the results with our existing approach of controlling pollution. Sooner or later the preventive approach will have to be adopted and PEM would then be established in the country.

REFERENCES

1. Chaturvedi, A.K.: *Environmental Business Opportunities in India.* New Delhi, CII, 1995.
2. *Cleaner Production: A Training Resource Package.* (Paris UNEP IE, 1996), ISBN 92-807-1605-0.
3. Codner, Gray; Donald Huisingh and Michael S. Jorgensen: "Environmental Education for Engineers," *Industry and Environment* 16 (1993): 4, 23.
4. Filcak, Richard: *Approaches to Develop a Curriculum for a Formal Educational Programme. The Case of Master's in Preventive Environmental Management in India. Lund: IIIEE, 1999. Industry Environmental Compliance: Training Manual.* (Paris: UNEP IE, 1996), 0-5. ISBN 92-807-1565 8.
5. Jain, Deepak: *Analysis and Adaptation of a Training Module for Preventive Environmental Management: The Case of a Short-Term Training Module for India.* Lund: IIIEE, 1999.

6. Kumra Shisher and Pullela, Ratna P.: *Proceedings of "The First Workshop to Design Curriculum for PEM"* held at EPTRI, Hyderabad, India, NetPEM, 1999.
7. Marshall, M.E. and D.W.Mayer: "Environmental Training: It's Good Business." *Business Horizons* 35 (1992):2,54.
8. Palmer, Joy A.: *Environmental Education in the 21st Century: Theory, Practice, Progress and Promise*. London: Routledge, 1998.
9. Venselaar, Jan. "Environmental Training; Industrial Needs." Journal of Cleaner Production 3 (1995) 3, 9-12.

Internet Sources

10. Environmental change in the First Fifty Years, http://www.teriin.org/green-india/sum.htm, 29.3.99.
11. Fundamental Duties, http://164.100.24.8/const/p4a51a.html, 28-3-99.
12. India Programme http://www.lu.se/IIIEE/research/india/india_program/pem_def.html. (20 Aug., 1999).
13. USEPA. *Pollution Prevention*-Policy. http;//www.epa.gov/opptintr/p2home/p2policy.htm. (19 Aug.,1999).
14. Jha, V. (1999, January). Investment Liberalization and Environmental protection. Conflicts and Compatibilities in the Case of India. [on-line]. Available HTTP://http:www.cbs.dk/departments/ikl/cbem/paper2.doc
15. Naik, G. and Supekar, D. (2000, June). Investment Boom Attracts Expats. *International Tax Review*; London. v11 i6 p. 33(3).
16. National Account Statistics. (2000 November 23). National Informatics Centre. *Government of India*. [on-line]. Available HTTP://http://www.nic.in/stat/t1.htm.
17. Nicoll, A. (1994, November 8). Fast Start, Still Trailing. *The Financial Times*. n32518 pFTS3(1).
18. Press Information Bureau, Government of India. (2000, May 6). India has Emerged as an Attractive Destination for FDI-Sinha. [on-line]. Available HTTP://http://finmin.nic.in/press/press061.htm
19. Press Trust of India (2000, October 4). FDI in S Asia Hinges on Reforms, stability: UNCTAD. *The Economic Times*. Available at HTTP:http://www.economictimes.com/today/04fina08.htm
20. Rao, K. (2000, May). Tax Issues Raise Heat and Dust. *Euromoney*; London.p16(3).

21. Special Report. (2000, July 16). The Great FDI Rush. *The Economic Times*. Available HTTP://http://www.economictimes.comm/today/16repo03.htm

22. Status on Sanctions. (November 27, 2000). *Ministry of External Affairs, Government of India*. Available HTTP://indiabudget.nic.in/es99 2000/chap69.pdf

23. UNCTAD, World Investment Report 2000 (November 27, 2000). [on-line]. Available http://www.unctad.org/wir/wir2000/docs/country/ps4wir00 fs IN.en.pdf.

20

SCIENCE, TECHNOLOGY AND EDUCATION: PERSPECTIVES AND PATH AHEAD

Monika Jauhari • Anurag Saxena

New millennium has just begun. We have to believe that much more has happened in the past decade than in the past fifty years and similarly, much has happened in the past fifty years than in the past century. And more happened in this century than during the last millennium. It's high time that we look back at the significant moments, technological breakthroughs and measures, which made the world of today. It's also the time to deduce and fix our eyes on what's in store and more prominently what could be planned for future. Newer technologies will keep substituting the existing ones and no wonder, the one who would not adapt itself to the pace of the wave, will not be able to swim (meaning that he will sink). We are about to talk about the future. The bizarre (or future) becomes normal (present) when fantasy meets fact. The investment of time and effort in looking ahead and planning for the future can be a very important one for academia. We may also need to revisit past issues, as they may remain and present themselves in new and different frameworks in the future. Science and Technology and especially their impact on education continue, in many respects to be an everlasting frontier. Reassessment of context (especially sociological) in which science, technology and education progresses would be desirable in rearticulating policy, particularly considering the enormous impact of them on our society and the critical ability of science and technology to make up for our acts.

Science and Technology

The world has seen a major revolution in science in the past fifty years. The progress at the Indian front is comparatively slow but one positive thing has definitely happened, i.e., this revolution has outstripped our capacity to cope, made our laws obsolete, reshuffled our economy, reordered our priorities, redefined our workplaces and shifted our concept of reality (Sale, 1995). We have seen some great developments in Nuclear power, industries, animal and human experiments, medicine, level of life, food and agriculture and communications etc. These developments have given really good benefits like speed, ease, power and wealth. Science and Technology should become the prototype for all human common action and use of scientific approaches and methodology needs encouragement to be widely accepted. It is of intrinsic importance in advancing our understanding of the natural world. We should view Science and Technology from the angle of intellectual challenges rising over our sphere in the next half a century, of the biggest problems facing our nation and our planet in the future, in overcoming them with the help of Science and Technology and about the changes we would have to make (Vernon Ehlers). Not only in India but also in the part of the world where advancements were more vigorous, during the last fifty years, the strongest efforts in pure science have been concentrated in highly impenetrable fields remote from contact with everyday problems. Such efforts are unlikely to do harm, or to do well, either to the rich or to the poor. At the same time, the strongest efforts in applied science have been concentrated upon market-driven projects, that is to say, projects that are expected to lead quickly to products that can profitably be sold. Since the rich can be expected to pay more than the poor for new products, market-driven applied research will usually result in the invention of toys for the rich. The failure of science to produce benefits for the poor in recent decades is due to two factors working in combination, the pure scientists becoming more detached from the mundane needs of humanity, the applied scientists becoming more attached to immediate profitability (Freeman Dyson).

Say about a decade ago, the slogan was "what you see is what you get". By the end of the decade, science and technology has transformed it to "what you need is what you get". At present "we are getting only some" so the only and only action required for the future would be to try and get the entire "some". The progress at the international front has been fabulous. We need to incorporate the same zeal in our fraternity. The Table 20.1 given below shows the milestones in the area of communications:

Table 20.1
Milestones in the Area of Communications

Years	*Milestone*
1791	Claude Chappe, a French engineer, developed a system of *Optical Telegraphy*
1837	Wheathouse , Cooke of England developed a *working telegraph*
1843	Morse invented the *telegraph code,* Public use inaugurated in USA
1866	First *submarine telegraph cable* laid between USA and France
1876	Bell invented the *Telephone*
1878	*First commercial telephone exchange* was setup in USA
1896	Marconi sent a *telegram by radio* over 3 km
1925	Scientists at Bell labs, USA *invented fax*
1934	*Radar Technology* evolved from British research
1945	Clarke propounded the concept of *Satellites*
1947	Bell scientists invented *transistor*
1951	It became possible to contact a *paging subscriber through PSTN*
1961	Bell labs built the *First electronic exchange*

Years	Milestone
1971	First *E-Mail* was sent over
1977	Bell Telephone initiated a developmental *Cellular Service*
1990	Lee and Cailliau submitted proposal for *World-Wide-Web*
1995	*Wavelength division multiplexing*
1998	*Mobile Satellite services*

It can be easily seen that communication industry is being shaped by the several factors: a rapid growth falling tariffs, competition as well as liberalization. The above example is just mindbogling. Unfortunately, we didn't find any Indian contribution there. But the things have changed. Just to give a glimpse of the present - "Silicon Valley and the Bay area in the US have more than 1,30,000 skilled Indian professionals". So what is required is a science education and popularization policy, overcoming of difficulties and frustrations faced by scientists in the current system of conducting science. To help provide for the enduring continuation of robust scientific research in this country, we need to ensure a healthy social, political, and economic environment for the conduct of science. We should try to address who, what, when, how and where sort of questions, e.g., what should be the role for science and technology? What types of scientific knowledge should we as a society seek out?, How should we decide what types of scientific knowledge should be pursued with funding?, By whom should such choices be made? What input should scientists have? Who should direct and manage research? What should their guidelines be? What mechanisms should we use to apply new scientific knowledge? Etc.

World-wide-web

Internet is widening the web on the world. Never before in such a short span of time a new technology has gained such a global acceptance. The Internet threatens to challenge the commercial and societal norms as never before. In this millennium if there is one force that is transforming the lives of people, and promises to deliver turbulent impact as a constant in the future, it is the Internet. The highlight of the future net will be convergence of technologies like the television, computer and the telephone. And believe it or not it will open new ways of thinking, communicating, learning and working. It has made information easier to grab, store and disseminate, simply because of its digitized form. In India also, though the technology has just taken off, we are finding newer and newer ventures into the e-commerce. Various academic disciplines have already started research on how to use Internet effectively and purposefully to their advantage. Internet 2 is the beginning of such effort. Internet 2 is a collaborative effort to develop advanced Internet technology and applications that are vital to the research and education mission of higher education. Over 160 US universities are working together with industry and public sector to provide applications like, telemedicine, digital libraries, virtual universities and virtual laboratories. It is an effort to bring together institutions and resources to develop new technologies and capabilities, which can be used globally in the future. Internet has really changed the role of a general desktop computer to a commoner.

Education "Anew"

Education today is hit by many changes due to technological advances in information and communication technologies. It has to accommodate new designs of teaching, learning and evaluation. There is a change in attitude towards education. People are inclined towards "Lifelong Learning" "Education" seems to be bending towards "mass education". There is also a change in "need" for education, i.e., there is need for "specialized professional education". Education today is striving to provide a "deus" system. The literal meaning of "DEUS" is "the creator" and the creator always try to make the system Dynamic, Efficient, Unbiased and Sufficient i.e. DEUS. IGNOU in particular has taken concrete steps to provide an innovative system to cater to higher 'education anew'. It has tried to provide flexibility with respect to the tools and the timing of learning, flexibility with respect to the course-combinations, flexibility with respect to the openness for entry, flexibility with respect to the age-restrictions and flexibility with respect to the methodology of assessment.

Education today is thinking of self-paced evaluation i.e. 'On-Demand Examination'. Formulation of newer models for the next millenium is on cards. In a nutshell, providers are consciously and continuously working on the following themes:

(i) How to make the process of learning and certification simpler for the learners,

(ii) How to make learners progress according to their own pace,

(iii) How to upgrade the system with respect to the technogical advances, educational advances of the societal issues including the challenge of Growing Numbers.

Educationists in USA have already started to use Latent Semantic Analysis (LSA) based computational models and other models for evaluating essay-type questions through computer. These models are capable of providing feedback to the students, which is a must for reinforcement. Use of new technologies to automate the processes and procedures is also on cards.

Institutions are thus working on walk-in admissions, providing efficient computer-based models of evaluation to obtain the consistency and reliability, providing an efficient information system to strengthen student support. In this stupendous effort, IGNOU is also trying to redefine the teaching-learning paradigm. IGNOU is convinced that their approach should be to create a technology-rich environment. High-cost, high technology is not the only model. In the last five years, IGNOU has established that electronic media can enhance the learning environment at an affordable cost, and that mass media does not necessarily dilute serious academic engagements. Besides the nation-wide telecast of curriculum-based videotapes, and the live tele-conferencing for academic counseling, IGNOU has, in the last year introduced interactive phone-in-radio counseling facilities, which can be accessed from 21 different locations. With the support of Government and ISRO, IGNOU has now the privilege of being the nodal agency for Gyan Darshan, the Educational Channel of Doordarshan which in effect is a cooperative venture involving a host of institutions and organizations. It is hoped that this initiative will be a big step forward in enriching a learning environment in our country with the applications of modern technologies (A.W. Khan, 2000).

The Future

What would be the future of Science, Technology and Education in the new age (Net Age) could be found from the Table 20.2 given below:

Table 20.2

Technology	*Present*	*Future*
Microprocessors	550 MHz	1.5 GHz
The TV-PC	Pentium-III can barely decode a single NTSC signal	New media ready chips will handle high definition TV resolution.
Hand-held appliances	Wireless connectivity is scarce	People will talk to their hand-heads
Home Networking	Absent	All household works would be done sitting miles away.
Database Systems	RDBMS	Object Oriented DMS
Floppy Disks	3.5 inches with 1.44 MB Space	Zip drives with upto 200 MB
Hard Disks	4 to 10 GB	Spin-valve heads 60 to 80 GB
Connecting Peripherals	Conflicts, struggle to properly install drivers.	Digital videos, still cameras, digital VCR, modems, satellite interfaces, LAN and video Conferencing
Operating Systems	Microsoft Windows	64-bit UNIX or JAVA based
Internet Connectivity	33.6 Kbps	Upto 10 Mbps
Wireless Communication	Not available	Only wireless would prevail

The developments show that the entire atmosphere is going to change as we would be talking about tele-living, tele-medicine, tele-administration, tele-governance, virtual laboratories, virtual universities, web-tutoring and a consortium of collaborative projects. In closing, we can only hope that we would be able to implement them in our system so as to enchance the capability of the system and for advancement of the bliss we live in.

REFERENCES

1. Vernon J Ehlers: "The Future of U.S. Science Policy," editorial in *Science, On the World Wide Web.*
2. Freeman Dyson: "Daedalus after Seventy Years," in Haldane's *Daedalus Revisited*, ed. Krishna R. Dronamraju, pp. 57, 62 (Oxford, Oxford University Press, 1995).
3. Kirkpatrick Sale: "Setting limits on Technology" adapted from "Rebels against the Future: The Luddites and their war on the industrial revolution: Lessons for the Machine Age" (Addison-Wesley, 1995).
4. IGNOU Profile 2000, "Message from the Vice-Chancellor", pp. 5, 6, IGNOU.
5. *Best of Needs Assessment*, Alexandria, VA: ASTD Publishing, 1995.

21

TECHNICAL EDUCATION IN INDIA: GROWTH AND FUTURE CONCERNS

Dr. S.P. Singh

During the last several decades, the world has become more integrated through trade and technology. Financial and economic boarders are collapsing and world is on the way to become a 'Global Village'. Intra-net and Internet technologies have opened new vistas of opportunity to world business community. Today, it is the velocity of information processing and dissemination that is determining the speed of trade and commerce. However, under the tower tutelage of technology. pattern and volume of employment are changing. In the years gone by public sector was the biggest source of employment to manpower, in the years to come, it may be the private and corporate sectors that are going to play the leading role in providing employment. As things stand today, employment opportunity may shrink for those who are the 'rolling stones', but may increase for those who keep pace with the twists and turns of technology (Singh and Agarwal, 1999: 919).

With the opening up of economy to outside world, Indian industries have become more competitive and quality conscious. This changing environment calls for a highly diversified human resource capable of acquiring, utilising, adapting and improving technologies that ensure low cost but high quality products. The responsibility of making this resource available lies on institutions of higher education in general and technical institutions in particular. Technical education needs to be oriented to meet the growing demand of Indian as well as foreign companies. It must be able to address the cross border and global problems from interdisciplinary perspective and be able to mould the students to work with people of multicultural and multi-lingual background. This chapter examines the growth of technical education in India and also addresses its major future concerns.

Growth of Technical Education

Technical education in India has emerged over the years as a three-tier technical education system imparting training at three distinct levels, namely, certificate (ITI), diploma (Polytechnic) and degree (graduate and postgraduate engineering colleges/universities). At present, there are over 2500 ITIs with an annual intake of over 3,00,000 students. About 1900 institutions conduct vocational courses at higher secondary level with an annual intake of 95,000 students. There are over 1000 polytechnics with an annual intake of about 1,86,000 students and over 420 degree level institutions for training engineers with an annual intake of over 1,10,000 students. The focus of this paper is only on degree level technical institutions.

We started our economic development through planning. First Five Year Plan stressed mainly on agricultural development. From Second Plan onward which and was based on Nehru-Mahalanobis Growth Model through establishing key and basic industries in public sector. With the development onward, more emphasis was given on industrial development of industrial sector, demand for technical manpower also increased. Planning Commission in 1955 estimated that by 1960-61, there would be shortages of engineers and diploma holders to the extent of 1800 and 8000 respectively (Mishra and Tiwari, 1995:16). Therefore, starting from Third Plan, Government of India made more investment in establishing new institutions and enhancing the capacity of existing ones. Private agencies and organisations were also encouraged to open new colleges of technical education. In 1951, there were only 33 technical institutions offering education at degree level and above with the total enrollment capacity of 13000. In 1961, facility of technical education extended to 111 institutions with total enrollment of 48,000 students.

Table 21.1

Growth of Technical Education in India

Years	*1951*	*1961*	*1971*	*1981*	*1986*	*1991*	*1996*	*1997*
No. of Institutions (degree and above)	33	111	134	171	248	351	422	422
No. of students (in thousands)	13	48	93	130	197	241	317	328

Source : Human Resource Profile India, IAMR, New Delhi, 1999.

Regional Imbalances

To understand the disparity in the distribution of technical education across states, seven parameters, namely, number of seats per million of population' number of seats per district' number of seats per hundred high/higher secondary schools; number of seats per ten thousand enrolment in XII std; number of seats per hundred thousand enterprises; and number of seats per Rs. thousand crores of Net Domestic Product, are taken for consideration (Shrivastava and Khare, 1998).

Table 21.2
Intake Capacity Per Unit of Parameters

States	*Seats per Million Population*	*Seats per district*	*Seats per hundred high/ higher Sec. School*	*Seats per thousand enrolment in XII Std.*	*Seats per hundred/ thousand enterprises*	*Seats per thousand crore of net domestic produce*
Madhya Pradesh	47	69	61	121	160	81
Orissa	43	45	24	119	120	86
Assam	29	29	17	73	130	56
West Bengal	32	130	33	97	80	53
Uttar Pradesh	24	51	50	72	130	48
Bihar	27	48	57	69	190	81
Haryana	95	98	59	157	340	87
Himachal Pradesh	40	18	20	57	110	75
Punjab	98	142	67	216	330	75
Rajasthan	37	53	36	118	140	70
Andhra Pradesh	130	376	95	363	350	191
Tamil Nadu	345	838	340	708	910	399
Karnataka	432	973	268	1216	1150	591
Kerala	155	322	165	496	370	230
Gujarat	84	183	62	154	230	108
Maharashtra	313	797	189	536	940	271
Others	84	25	41	194	410	17
India	120	202	110	292	410	165
Per cent contribution	10	15	9	22	31	13

Source : Shrivastava and Khare, 1998, p. 35.

The data given in Table 21.2 evince that intake of students per unit of these seven parameters are unevenly spread among the states. It is evident from the Table that four states-

Karnataka, Maharashtra, Tamil Nadu and Andhra Pradesh, have relatively higher number of seats available to students according to these parameters, while Uttar Pradesh, Assam, Orissa, Bihar, Rajasthan and Himachal Pradesh have relatively lesser number of seats. Upto 1990, more than sixty per cent of degree level institutions were concentrated in these four states and most of these institutions were under private ownership. However, in recent times, state governments, initiative to establish engineering colleges in private sector and liberal attitude of AICTE in according approval to them, the number of engineering colleges in several states such as Uttar Pradesh, Rajasthan, Madhya Pradesh, etc., are growing very fast. It is hoped that in years to come, disparity in the distribution of technical education across states will gradually be alleviated.

Discipline-wise Growth of Engineers

Discipline-wise stock of engineering degree holders in the working age group is presented in Table 21.3. The Table reveals that the stock of engineers has been increasing very fast. The total number increased from 4,92,180 in 1990 to 70,45,450 in 1996, recording a 43 per cent increase. However, during this period the percentage share of some basic disciplines in total stock of engineers has seen a steady decline. Civil, mechanical, electrical, metallurgy etc., are the branches whose share has declined over time. Contrary to this, percentages of electronic and communication, agricultural engineering, instrumentation, and others have gone up. The share of electronic and communication, increased from 8.52 per cent in 1990 to 12.53 per cent in 1996. Similarly, the share of others (mainly computer engineering) has increased from 6.59 per cent to 9.24 per cent during the same period. The changing share of different disciplines indicates that the policy of liberalization, globalization and privatization initiated in 1991 has augmented the demand for some disciplines such as electronic and communication and computer science and undermined the role of others such as civil engineering.

Table 21.3
Estimated Stock of Engineering Degree Holders in the Working Age Group by Selected Disciplines in India

Discipline	*1990*	*1991*	*1992*	*1993*	*1994**	*1995**	*1996**
Civil	119940 (24.37)	126980 (24.43)	133330 (24.11)	139220 (23.70)	145000 (23.26)	151130 (22.79)	157560 (22.36)
Mech.	131200 (26.66)	138030 (26.56)	144940 (26.21)	152350 (25.94)	158840 (25.48)	166800 (25.15)	174960 (24.83)
Elect.	87030 (17.68)	90180 (17.35)	94180 (17.03)	97880 (16.67)	101530 (16.29)	105430 (15.90)	109500 (15.54)
Chem.	27510 (5.59)	28300 (5.45)	29520 (5.34)	31280 (5.33)	32500 (5.21)	33770 (5.05)	35150 (4.99)
Elx. and Comm.	41830 (8.50)	45970 (8.85)	52350 (9.47)	59390 (10.11)	68390 (10.97)	78050 (11.77)	88290 (12.53)
Met.	13120 (2.67)	13440 (2.59)	13710 (2.48)	13940 (2.37)	14170 (2.27)	14420 (2.17)	14699 (2.09)
Mining	4490 (0.91)	4730 (0.91)	4950 (0.90)	5100 (0.87)	5380 (0.86)	5640 (0.85)	5840 (0.83)
Automobile	1140 (0.23)	1350 (0.26)	1450 (0.26)	1550 (0.26)	1680 (0.27)	1780 (0.27)	1870 ((0.27)
Aeronautical	1530 (0.31)	1570 (0.30)	1600 (0.29)	1620 (0.28)	1680 (0.27)	1670 (0.25)	1710 (0.24)
Agriculture	3060 (0.62)	3170 (0.61)	3280 (0.59)	3330 (0.57)	3450 (0.55)	3570 (0.54)	3700 (0.53)
Production	4860 (0.99)	5270 (1.01)	6220 (1.12)	7110 (1.21)	8400 (1.35)	9730 (1.47)	11110 (1.58)
Sugar	1250 (0.25)	1240 (0.23)	1230 (0.22)	1280 (0.22)	1290 (0.21)	1290 (0.19)	1290 (0.18)
Oil	560 (0.11)	610 (0.12)	630 (0.11)	640 (0.11)	670 (0.11)	700 (0.11)	730 (0.10)
Textile	7930 (1.61)	8220 (1.58)	8430 (1.52)	8530 (1.45)	8680 (1.39)	8860 (1.34)	9060 (1.29)
Arch.	9590 (1.95)	1016 (1.96)	10800 (1.95)	11330 (1.93)	12110 (1.94)	12910 (1.95)	13750 (1.95)
Food	850 (0.17)	890 (0.17)	900 (0.16)	920 (0.16)	940 (0.15)	970 (0.15)	1000 (0.14)
Inst.	2680 (0.54)	3080 (0.59)	3888 (0.61)	4620 (0.79)	5440 (0.87)	6260 (0.94)	7410 (1.05)
Ceramic	560 (0.11)	620 (0.12)	670 (0.12)	888 (0.15)	920 (0.15)	960 (0.14)	1010 (0.14)

Discipline	*1990*	*1991*	*1992*	*1993*	*1994**	*1995**	*1996**
Leather	610 (0.12)	650 (0.13)	680 (0.12)	710 (0.12)	740 (0.12)	770 (0.12)	800 (0.11)
Others	32440 (6.59)	35160 (6.77)	40200 (7.27)	45610 (7.77)	51590 (8.28)	58470 (8.28)	65110 (9.24)
Total	492180 (100)	519640 (100)	553000 (100)	587340 (100)	623370 (100)	663210 (100)	704540 (100)

Source : Human Resource Profile India, IAMR, New Delhi 1999.

Projected

Stock at the beginning of the year.

Figures in parentheses are percentages to the total.

Another fact, which seems to be accountable, is the rising unemployment prevailing among engineers of these disciplines. It is evident from the Table 21.4 that out of total 14,879 unemployed engineers in 1995, 85 per cent belonged to only three disciplines civil, mechanical and electrical. As is obvious from the table, the percentage of unemployment among the out turn engineering graduates was highest in civil (73 per cent) followed by metallurgy (40 per cent), electrical (35 per cent) and mechanical (33 per cent). However, there are few branches where shortages of qualified engineers are felt, for instance, computer engineering. Therefore, to remove the mismatch in demand and supply of different types of engineering manpower, efforts will have to be made to adopt the effective manpower planning.

Table 21.4

Discipline-wise Unemployed Engineers, Out Turn of Engg. Graduates and their Percentage Ratio for 1995

Branch	*Civil*	*Mech.*	*Elect.*	*Elx.*	*Chem.*	*Met.*	*Total*
1. No of un-employed Engineers	5960	4182	2518	1739	286	194	14879
2. Out Turn of Graduates	8127	12457	7108	11405	3213	489	59853
3. Ratio of (1) (2) (per cent)	73	33	35	15	9	40	25

Source: Shrivastava and Khare, 1998, p. 37.

Future Concerns

Globalisation of Indian economy has made producers as well as customers more quality conscious. Adoption of newer technologies will constitute a key strategy in the emerging global competitive environment. In this changing scenario, technical education in India requires to be reöriented and restructured to face the challenges of 21st century. Following are the major future concerns in technical education in India.

Globalisation

Development in information and communication technology and opening up of the economy for MNCs and NRIs has facilitated the process of globalisation of technical education in India. Foreign Universities and institutes are opening their offices in the country and attracting bright students for overseas admission. Moreover, these institutions with the collaboration of some private institutions are providing degrees to Indian students through distance mode. Indian technical institutions will have to gear themselves up to face these challenges. The ultimate product in technical education is outgoing students and the quality of this end product depends on the standard of components (students, teachers, well-equipped laboratories, etc.) used. For better quality of our product, it is essential that our institutions should identify the potential customers and their needs; measure satisfaction of their needs; and improve constantly the level of satisfaction of the customers. For this purpose, we have to introduce Total Quality Management (TQM) in our institution. As a general TQM situation, the quality of technical education system is the effectiveness of offering services to satisfy the explicit and implicit needs of customers (Natarajan and Subbiah, 1998:17).

Another issue before technical education is whether these institutes should cater the need of Indian customers or should develop their products for global economy? Government of India spends crores of rupees every year on institutions of excellence such as IITs, ISC, IIMs, university of Roorkee etc., but most of the products of these institutes migrate every year to advance countries in search of better opportunities. According to Ramanujam (1999:39):

> All professional institutions like IITs, IIMs, engineering colleges, medical colleges are centres of excellence. They are supported by public money. Even before the last examination results are announced, ten per cent of the students from all these centres of excellence leave the country preferably for USA. Once the results are announced another ten per cent leave. Eventually, within another 2-3 years, 50 per cent leave. Why should the public money be spent on these centres of excellence? From one platform we are saying we should stop and arrest the brain drain. And from another door we are encouraging our younger generation to leave the country. The question is excellence versus alienation.

Regarding brain drain several questions emerge: Should a poor country like India subsidise high quality technical education without expecting more socially relevant returns? Is it possible for us to reorient the attitudes of students and create conditions with a view to reducing the incidence of brain drain? Is the brain drain from India a problem or an opportunity? Should we train students in our technical institutions that are able to address cross-boarder and global problems? As is evident from the present trend in world economy, globalisation has led more international practices and approaches to technical education. The growing global competition, and subsequently restructuring of industries, explosion of information and development in information technology, all have necessitated to put greater emphasis on development of technical institutions in international setting. Brain drain in future should not be regarded as a problem but an opportunity. Remitting money to their families and donating funds to their *alma mater*, engineers and professional working abrad are significantly contributing to foreign exchange earnings of our country. Moreover, most of the professionals miggrated abroad are successful industrialists. They are now looking for an opportunity to invest in India.

NRI investment in India has been picking up. The financial and technical collaborations made by these people are contributing a lot to the economy. Now the term 'Brain Trust' is being used in place of 'Brain Drain'. Mr. K.S. Rekhi, who is trying to raise $ 1 billion for siX IITs, said, "We are credibleX successful people. Many of us more worth of hundreds of millions of dollars. We are available to the Indian Government and we provide a bridge to United States" (*The Times of India*, March 2, 2000:17). Therefore, instead of thinking of drainage of manpower, we should impart training and education to our students in a multi-cultural, multi-lingual and multi-disciplinary environment so that they may acquire the ability to work in a team; exposure to commercial disciplines; creativity and innovation; integrated skills; international outlook; and adaptability and flexibility.

Holistic Approach to Technical Education

Delors' Commission on International Education considers four pillars of learning—'learning to know', 'learning to do', 'learning to live together,' and 'learning to be'. For holistic education, integration of these four pillars is essential. Learning to know emphasises on skills of learning to learn. The stress here is not so much on what you have learnt but whether, you have developed the ability to learn or not. Technologies are changing very fast. Wherever you look, there are astounding developments taking place. Lots of information is available in books, CDROM, and on Internet. A student today has access to almost unlimited information. The age of information super highway has been brought in by the spectacular developments in satellite and terrestrial communication technology (Singh, 1999:17). One should, therefore, learn the skill of retrieving the relevant information form these sources and ability of analysing and interpreting these information.

The second pillar of learning—learning to do emphasises on the material side of education. One of the important goals of education is to develop the skill among human resources to increase production and productivity in the economy.

Education should be job productive. Third pillar—learning to live together is very important for maintaining national and international harmony and peace. Educational institutions should inculcate the social values, values of cooperation and harmony, democratic values and environmental values among the students. Learning to be is the fourth pillar of learning. It involves developing of the multi-dimensions of human personality. According to Joshi (1999: 14), "To be is to unfold what you are. You are a product of nature. There are certain inherent qualities in each of us. To be is to enlighten them, to give them full potential to develop." To impart technical education in a holistic manner, we have to integrate these four pillars of learning. The first two pillars of learning are properly taken care of by our technical institutions. There is much need to include the last two pillars in the system.While designing curricula in technical education, emphasis must be given to introducing more courses of humanities and social sciences so that the students may be able to learn more about 'learning to live together' and 'learning to be'.

Shortagaes of Faculty

At present, majority of institutions including IITs are facing acute shortages of competent faculty. Government of India document 'Challenges of Education: A policy Perspective, 1985' estimated twenty to thirty per cent vacancies in the sanctioned staff strength of degree and diploma level engineering institutions. Since 1985, the situation has deteriorated. Bright students have less motivation to take up teaching assignment because industries and other private organisations are offering better salaries and perks. Recently, there was news in *The Times of India* about IIM, Lucknow whose students are offered salaries by Indian firms in the range of Rs. 3.2 lakhs to 9 lakhs. What is the use of talking about inducting them as a faculty, where some of the reputed companies have to return empty handed from the institute. Prof. Debashis Chatterjee said, "We are trying to figure out how do we manage the disappointments emerging out of the some top notch companies returning empty handed." The situation of IITs and other reputed technical institutes are not significantly different from IIMs. The moot question here is : Why should a graduate engineer do postgraduate and then Ph.D. to enter the university as a faculty, when she/he gets much more from industry simply after doing graduation? In most of the institutions, such as University of Roorkee, minimum qualification for a teacher is Ph.D. in relevant field. In several disciplines like computer science, we hardly get a competent person of this qualification. The result is that most of the faculty positions are lying vacant. Certainly the quality of our products is going to be adversely affected in future due to shortages of competent faculty. Hence, to attract the best talent to our institutions, we have to provide better salaries, facilities and environment. The salary structure will have to be made more flexible.

Resource Mobilisation

Resource crunch is another problem of technical education. Most of the institutions of excellence are funded by government budget. Central and state governments are under financial constraints and have to make difficult choice where their investment should go. Recent drive to universalise primary education may shift the focus of government from higher education to elementary education. Moreover educational economists propagate that the rate of return on money invested in primary education is much higher than that on higher education. This is quite often taken as an argument in shifting greater resources towards primary education (Chandra, 1993: 10).

Increasing fiscal deficit of Central Government may be another reason for reduction in government funding to higher education. To reduce fiscal deficit, government may cut subsidy on technical and other higher education. UGC and AICTE are constantly emphasizing on that technical institutions should get self-reliance in financial resources.

The following measures are suggested for resource mobilisation:

1. Faculty members should be encouraged to engage in revenue generating activities such as testing, consultancy, training and organising continuing education programmes.
2. Institutes should also establish training-cum-production centres. They should develop new products and get them patented. In such centres, students would be able to get exposure to practical problems and also would be capable of generating resources for institutes.
3. Fee structure should be suitably revised linking it to the cost of running the institution. However, the interest of poor students needs to be protected through scholarships and bank loans.
4. Institute should make the optimum utilisation of available physical resources such as building, laboratories and other facilities. To generate resources, space can be let out. For example, now in all the cities and towns private computer training centres are mushrooming very fast. If any such centre wants classrooms for teaching, universities/institutes can provide them rooms on rent basis in the evening without affecting the teaching schedule. Similarly we can give our conference rooms on rent to different agencies for organising seminars/conferences, etc.
5. International collaborations in the field of education for developing global pesspective and for raising resources should be attempted.
6. Globalisation and opening up of the Indian economy are recent phenomena which are likely to result in private sector committing itself to research and development in frontier areas on a large scale. Technical Institutions must see the opportunities for involvement in high quality research with potential application to industrial problems for raising resources.

7. Expenditure should be reduced by: increasing teacher-student ratio; weeding out of redundant programmes; reducing the strength of non-teaching staff; and adopting office automation.
8. Efforts should be made to mobilise the support of alumni working abroad for financial assistance for up-gradation of infrastructure and research and Development activities.

Institute-Industry Interaction (III)

The major customers of our products are industries. While designing our products, we have to consider the customers need and satisfaction. Currently industries are spending huge training resources and valuable time in moulding fresh students as more productive human resources. It would be better for the industries to involve themselves in the very process of development of this vital resource so that they can start contributing almost immediately after going to various organisations. For this purpose, institutes should integrate effectively to industries. A number of III activities such as consultancy, testing, R & D and sponsored research projects for new products/process development, faculty exchange and training, guest lectures by experts from industries, continuing education programmes, technology transfer, curriculum development and sharing resources can be identified by institutions for mutual benefits (Tidke, 1994: 32). To understand the practical problems of industries/organisations, faculty members should be given short term assignment in industries. Industry executives should also be invited to deliver lectures on various topic, especially for final year students.

Vision 2020 document prepared by University of Roorkee suggests to establish "a Liasion Centre, which acts as an interface between the university and industry. Such centre should identify the problems of industry and also identify groups within university capable of solving the problems. The document also recommends to university to have a forum, in which faculty members and industry representatives come together to suggest areas of collaborations and interaction. This could be in the form of advisory body comprising some university faculty, representatives from industry, government, association like CII, CCI etc. Such a forum can identify the impediments in industry-sponsored work, suggest remedial measures and new initiatives.

Lifelong Learning and Continuing Education

Learning throughout life is a wonderful idea put forth by the Delors Commission. Due to fast development in science and technology, jobs for life using static set of skills would be less and less available in future. Frequent job changes and upgrading of skills will be the norm in the 21st century. Therefore, constant upgradation in skill would be required to learn throughout life. In future many jobs may eliminate due to change in technology and market demand. For instance, before introduction of computer, typing work was done by manual typewriter, but now manual typing is gradually getting phased out which has reduced the job of manual typist. Hence, to survive in the job market, a manual typist has to learn computer application. In future, the most important skill, which is to be developed among students, is the skill of self-employment and enterpreneurship. The students of tomorrow need to be trained and learnt new skills throughout life. They will, therefore, be required to undergo training and re-training; acquire the skills of employability; develop skills of dealing with entirely new concepts, difficulties and unfamiliar problems; avoid-specialisation at a relatively early age; acquire capability of modifying new information to suit local needs; acquire and development intellectual curiosity and pleasure in learning; be able to think independently; and be able to innovate (Mohsin, 1999:154).

Our technical institutions can provide life long learning through two ways—continuing-education and distance learning. Continuing education of in-service engineers can play a major role in life long learning. We should run regular short-term courses not only on pure engineering subjects but also on management, TQM, entrepreneurship, design tools and software applications. Faculty should constantly upgrade their skills and expertise in relevant areas to train the engineers. They should be given opportunity to go abroad on short-term assignment to clearly focus on faculty development programmes.

Continuing education programmes can also be organised by the universities through distance mode. If big business and industrial firms develop multi-media, tele-conferencing and video-conferencing facilities, institutes of excellence like IITs and University of Roorkee can organise virtual class rooms for the engineers of these firms. This system can be cost effective, flexible and productive.

Summing Up

Indian economy is now moving on a fast track. To maintain the present tempo and to further accelerate the speed, more dynamic, productive, skilled, visionary and committed human resource are required. The onus, therefore, lies on our technical institutions for training the young graduates for facing the challenges of 21st century. To make our products (engineers) more competitive in global job market, technical institutions will have to impart education in a multi-cultural, multi-lingual, and multi-disciplinary environment. Resource generation, globalisation of education, improvement in quality, better delivery system, distance and continuous learning, virtual class rooms through tele and video-conferencing, digital libraries, flexibility in intake, courses, programmes, forging effective linkage with industry, improving infrastructure and its optimum use, flexible salary structure, hiking tuition fees without harming the interest of poor students, collaboration with foreign institutions, and constant development of skills for life long learning, etc., would be the main concerns of technical education in 21st century.

REFERENCES

1. Chandra, A. (1993): 'Financing Technical Education in the Changed Context', *The Indian Journal of Technical Education*, Vol. 16(1), January-March.

2. Government of India (1985), *Challenges of Education: A Policy Perspective.*

3. IAMR (1999), *Human Resource Profile India*, New Delhi.

4. Joshi, M.M. (1999), 'Inaugural Address on Learning: The Treasure Within', M. Mukhopadhyay *et al* (ed) *Learning: The Treasure Within: Implication for Asia*, NIEPA, New Delhi.

5. Mishra, S.N. and T.N. Tiwari (1995), 'Technical Education and RECs: Expectations and Performance', *The Indian Journal of Technical Education*, Vol. 8 (4), and October-December.

6. Mohsin, S. (1999), 'Human Resources Development: Some Challenges', in M. Mukhopadhyay *et al* (ed.)

7. Natarajan, V. and V. Subbiah (1998), 'Quality assurance in Technical education', *The Indian Journal of Technical Education*, Vol. 21 (1), January-March.

8. Ramanujam, P.R. (1999), *Thematic Session: Higher Education* in M. Mukhopadhyay *et al* (ed).

9. Shrivastava, J.P. and R.K. Khare (1998), 'Growth of Technical Education and Unemployment Pattern: Region Imbalances and Remedies', *University News*, Vol. 36(50), December 14.

10. Singh, K. (1999), 'Key Note Address on Learning: The Treasure Within', in M. Mukhopadhyay *et al* (ed).

11. Singh, S.P. and R.K. Agarwal (1999), 'Trade-Technology-Employment Interface: Evidence from Indian Industries', *The Indian Journal of Labour Economics*, Vol. 42 (4, October-December).

12. Tidke, D.J. (1994), 'Managing Institutions of Higher Technical Education', *The Indian Journal of Technical Education*, Vol. 16(4), October-December.

13. University of Roorkee (1997), *Vision 2020.*

22

CHANGING ECONOMIC SCENARIO: MANAGERIAL CHALLENGES

R.L. Varshney

Before discussing the challenges before the managers, it would be useful to have a look at the policy before the changes under discussion.

The areas open to the private sector were clearly demarcated and even in these areas the activities of the private sector were restrained by the operation of Industries (Development and Regulation) Act and the MRTP Act. No major enterprise could be established without a licence and even after establishment, it could not diversify or even expand its activities without a government licence. Even foreign collaboration was not freely permitted. In order to prevent concentration of economic power, the capacities licensed were very often not economic. This led to high cost of production. Because of licencing regulations, those units which got a licence were protected against domestic competition. They were sheltered from foreign competition due to the existence of high tariffs and import controls and thus they virtually operated under a completely sheltered market. As the Monopolies Commission pointed out, industrial licensing did not prevent monopolies. Instead it created ones as a result, there was no incentive whatsoever for cost control and improvement of quality. Not only did the Indian consumers suffer but it also affected the competitiveness of Indian products in foreign markets.

In fact, there was a tripartite vested interest in the continuance of the then existing regulatory framework; the industrialists who were not interested in facing competition from new entrants, the politicians who needed money for fighting elections and used the quota, permit, license leverage to their advantage and the bureaucrats who were intoxicated by the power vested in them. As a former IAS officer pointed out our political system requires a down right corrupt and inefficient administration so that it can operate smoothly. Our political leaders got so much involved in economic administration that, as pointed by Mr. Thomas, former chairman of Hindustan Lever Limited, decisions that could be taken by a joint secretary in 1950s needed Cabinet approval in early 1980s. As a result, most of the time of the managers was spent not in managing their business but in managing the politicians and bureaucrats concerned with their business. Not only private sector companies but also the public sector undertakings had to maintain their liaison offices in New Delhi.

The Recent Changes

Some of the salient features of the new industrial policy are: Abolition of industrial licensing on all but 18 industries with freedom to manufacture in response to market demand, removal of threshold limits of MRTP and dominant undertakings, liberalisation of direct foreign investments provided they are foreign exchange neutral, opening up of areas hitherto reserved for public sector and scrapping up of the convertibility clause in loans obtained from financial institutions. MRTP clearance for merger, amalgamations and takeovers has been eliminated.

Significant changes have also been made in trade policy. The rupee was devalued in July 1991 by 18 per cent and cash compensatory support was abolished. REP licences were replaced by Exim Scrips. But they have also been abolished with the partial convertibility of the rupee. Established exporters have been allowed to open foreign currency accounts and raise external credits. The rupee has been made convertible for current transactions.

These changes in the economic policies are, by and large, in the right direction. In fact, they should have been initiated in the sixties itself as suggested by me in a series of articles published in a number of journals in 1959 and also by C. Rajagopalachari who pleaded for the abolition of quota-permit-licence raj. But unfortunately all those who advocated changes on these lines were declared reactionaries and agents of capitalists. Had these changes been introduced in the sixties, our industries would have become more efficient, improved the quality of their products and devoted their attention to cost consciousness.

I would, however, like to draw the attention to disturbing features of the policy package :

(i) Before allowing external competition in the Indian economy, internal competition should have been introduced so that Indian industrialists could have got some time to prepare themselves to face external competition. If, as a result of liberalization, FERA companies concentrate on selling soaps, shampoos and breakfast foods by promoting brand names under the new trade mark freedom, and expand the production of these goods, with funds raised in India instead of bringing them largely from abroad, the Indian industrialists would find it difficult to stand up to them.

(ii) By eliminating restraints on mergers, amalgamations and takeovers, the Government is virtually providing a green signal for formation of cartels and trusts.

(iii) The absence of any consensus on exit policy is another matter which is causing concern to labour.

(iv) Due to convertibility of the rupee and continued inflationary pressures, the market rate of the rupee continued to decline.

Consequences of the Change

The most significant impact of the change would be that the sellers' market would be replaced by a buyers' market. The barriers to the entry of new competitors have been removed by the removal of the regulatory regime. The Indian industry has so far been tuned to this regulatory regime and passed on the burden of its inefficiencies as also of all indirect taxes to the helpless consumer. Now these shackles have been removed almost completely and private enterprise and initiative will have ample opportunities to play its role and this will mean greater and greater competition in the domestic market.

The emergence of the buyers' market in place of the erstwhile sellers' market has led to significant changes in India's corporate sector. The cost of marketing products has gone up substantially as reflected in higher ad spend. Companies have now been paying more attention to the quality of products. They are also showing a greater responsiveness to customers' complaints. They are now setting up world- scale plants rather than depending upon their ability to corner licences. They are placing greater emphasis on Ressarch and Development. Many of them are now focusing on core competencies and they are not expanding arbitrarily.

Labour unions and workers have realised that labour troubles can permanently disable a company and drive it out of the market. Managements are also making sincere efforts to enlist the cooperation of workers especially in their quality programmes. As a result, employee productivity is higher in terms of value added per employee. Immediately after reforms, owing to keen competition in the domestic markets, many firms decided to seek export markets and exports showed a substantial growth.

I would like to mention at this stage that Indian companies did stand foreign competition well. Many of the multinationals that entered the Indian market with high hopes did not find it easy to compete with wellknown Indian companies.

It is in this context that I will discuss the managerial challenges.

Managerial Challenges for the Firm and its Managers

The firm and its managers have to develop their ability to compete effectively not only to grow but also to survive. It is only under the pressure of competition that a firm would try to improve its product and raise its productivity. Competition itself is not static but is profoundly dynamic in character. To gain a competitive advantage, firms very often add distinct product varieties, adopt multiple distribution channels and cater to several different types of customers. Markets are segmented according to their differing needs and an attempt is made to satisfy those needs. An unadvertised basic shirt and a designer shirt like Charagh Din are both shirts but are sold to buyers with very different criteria.

Firms can develop a competitive advantage to serve a segment that they are capable of serving. In general, the advantage can be acquired or developed either in the form of lower costs or through differentiation of products that command premium prices. Tea City provides an example how premium prices can be charged for a common place product like tea. Hindustan Leaver's Surf competes not on the basis of price but on the basis of non-price factors. Firms can gain and sustain competitive advantage by constant upgradation and improvement of their products. Manufacturers in Ludhiana and Japan have one point of similarity. Both of them have ability to dismantle a product and duplicate it effectively. The similarity ends here.While Ludhiana will continue to produce exact duplicates, Japanese manufacturers will try to improve upon the product. Japanese automakers invaded the US market on the basis of their compact cars and captured about thirty per cent of the US automobile market. But when compelled by the USA to voluntarily restrict their car exports and to overcome the disadvantage of an appreciating Yen, they tried to upgrade their cars and added value to them and thus prevented a decline in the dollar value of their automobile exports.

If your product is better, you can improve your market share even when there is an overall decline in industry demand. Take the case of two wheelers in India. While the overall industry demand has declined, Bajaj Auto increased its share from 60 per cent in 1990 to 64 per cent in 1991 and Kinetic Honda has increased its share from 8 per cent to 11 per cent. But with the advent of new models to target every niche by its competitors, Bajaj Auto continuously witnessed a decline in its market share.

Existence of intense rivalry among the various firms is the most important factor leading to a continuous improvement in products. Intense rivalry causes the various rival firms to improve and innovate. They push each other to lower costs, improve quality and service and create new products and processes. Keen competition between various firms may lead to closure of some but those who remain would be strong survivors capable of defending themselves against foreign competitors and competing with them in their home ground. This is what happened in Japan. While external competition was not allowed, there was no holds barred for internal competition. Japanese companies tried their best to out do each other and in the process improved themselves.

The advent and growth of financial journalism which publishes regularly success stories also induces the managers to excel each other and feel a sense of pride in the publication of news about them and their firms. The financial journals also conducted and publish analysis about the various firms in a particular industry and naturally the major players in that particular industry will not like to be unfavourably commented upon.

To gain a competitive advantage over their rivals, many firms study and evaluate the ever changing needs of the buyers and whatever their needs could be, try to satisfy them. Some examples of successful need perception are : (i) Japanese auto manufacturers perceived the need for a compact car in the face of oil price hike and successfully penetrated the US car market, and (ii) Airbus industry identified a segment of the market that has been ignored by the other aircraft manufacturers - a relatively large plane for short hauls so common in Europe. In fact, many products are generated by acute understanding of the buyers' needs.

Similarly, firms could find out market segments vacated by established industry leaders. Some examples of such vacated areas are: Vacation of 800 cc car by Suzuki, black and white TV by the developed countries, and stoppage of the production of motor cycles by Enfield of U.K.

Thus the emergence of competive conditions results in challenges as also opportunities and it is upto the Indian firms and their managers to devise appropriate strategies to face the challenges and exploit the opportunities. I will now outline some steps which could be taken in this direction.

(1) Cost control-Firms would have to examine their costs if they want to survive. In fact, many firms have started doing so. TVS-Suzuki Ltd. adopted 'Reduce Costs for Survival' as its motto for 1991 and reduced its fixed costs by Rs. 60 lakhs. The work force was also reduced from 2,100 to 1,500.

(2) Total customer satisfaction which depends upon quality, reliability and price. Japanese firms focus on customer needs through quality, Indian firms on the other hand, produce goods of export quality in addition to what is produced for the domestic market. It is high time that this distinction ends. Whatever is produced should be of the best possible quality.

They should also explore the possibilities of

improvement, innovation and upgradation of their products through continuous Research and Development.

(3) Creation of brand image—This would help them to increase their market share substantially. In addition, they should try to identify the market segment or the niche to be catered to. For example, Nirma successfully tried to cater to the low price segment of the detergent market.

(4) Close look at the depth and breadth of the product line Firms should examine whether the various products being produced by them are contributing to the profits or a drag on their revenues. Now that licensing regulations have gone, they should think of diversification suiting to their resources—managerial and financial.

(5) Exports as an additional outlet Intensive competition may lead to unutilised capacities and exports could provide a good wayout. This could reduce costs and improve the overall profitability of the firm. The experience the world over is that saturation of the home market leads to vigorous efforts by firms to penetrate the foreign markets.

Some action is also needed at the Government level. There is a wide gap between the intentions of the Government at the policy formulation stage and the actual implementation thereof. It is therefore necessary to ensure that no hurdles are placed by the tripartite vested interests consisting of the politicians, businessmen and bureaucrats in the effective implementation of the new policies. Further, the Government should ensure three things.

(i) Improvement and strengthening of the infrastructure.

(ii) Stability of Government policies, especially in respect of taxes, both direct and indirect. The high rate of direct taxes leads to a transfer of wealth not from the rich to the poor but from honest rich to the dishonest rich.

(iii) Stability of prices is not merely a reduction in the rate of inflation. This is essential for (a) for sustaining demand and an alround increase in production, (b) to increase the rate of savings and (c) to maintain the competitiveness our exports.

23

SOME SIGNPOSTS IN SOCIAL SCIENCES FOR THE YEAR 2000-2001

Tarlok Singh

Soon after it came into being, the Indian Council of Social Science Research took the initiative for preparing surveys of research in different areas of social science. A large number of leading scholars in each field gave their time freely for this effort and worked together in groups. The result was that in most fields of social sciences a most valuable set of research surveys became available. For a number of social sciences a series of Re-surveys, undertaken at intervals are also available. All these surveys have focused on research without, at this stage, looking into aspects concerning the content, methods, direction and the precise objectives of the teaching being undertaken. Though some attention was given to linkages between each related group of social science subjects, this aspect was not analysed in any depth.

I

Social Science subjects are taught at the higher secondary school level, where the foundations are laid and attitudes and concerns first stimulated, followed by teaching at the undergraduate level, imparted in colleges all over the country, and by teaching and research at the postgraduate level. Interdisciplinary linkages which are of the utmost importance are taken into account mainly at the postgraduate level. From this aspect, the time has come to consider carefully the reorientations that may be now needed regarding the teaching of social sciences at each level, the main social objectives to be stressed, and the manner in which the career requirements of students of social science may be best secured under the prevailing conditions of competing attractions.

In social sciences, while there are areas where pure or theoretical research must be emphasized, in much larger measure, research has an applied character. It is directed particularly to problems bearing on the development of society in its various aspects and phases. The aspects demanding close study and therefore special emphasis both in teaching and in field studies will go on changing in some measure according to developments within society at various levels. The life and activities in a community or group being multi-dimensional in nature while an individual student may concentrate on a limited area, how this area influences and is influenced by other areas of concern or activity within the community has to be constantly stressed. Moreover, in a period in which the influence of science and technology, already powerful, is increasingly becoming more and more dominant, students of social science have to go beyond the traditional curriculum and strive to become more scientifically oriented. Likewise, of course, it has become equally necessary that students of natural and physical sciences and of technology should also become much more oriented towards social concerns and objectives. While there have to be different streams of interest and study both within social science and within natural science, it is important that a sense of unity of all knowledge be imparted to the student at each stage of his or her personal development.

There is no comparison between the limited measure of development in social sciences which took place in India between the First and the Second World War and the vast network of departments in universities, institutes of research, and in postgraduate and degree colleges which has developed since Independence. Yet, compared to the impact of relatively small number of scholars in each area of social sciences on public policy and national thinking before Independence, the role of social scientists at the present time, despite their enormous numbers and much individual learning and expertise, does not stand out as being particularly significant or appreciable. To an extent, economists were an exception, specially during the first two decades of planned development. Periodical consultations with economists still take place, but they do not seem to be making much impact on public policy. In the more recent past, apart from those in political life (of whom some are of course well-equipped to contribute as social scientists or scientists), the greater part of the opportunity for counselling and thinking ahead for a period seems to have passed or is passing mainly to spokesman of the private corporate sector and to senior public servants within the administration aided by their immediate in-house advisory personnel.

While prominent scientists outside Government are continuously sought, by and large, the independent and disinterested contribution of social scientists, as representing a critically important and essential body of knowledge and analysis, does not find much expression. Social scientists as a body need to deliberate on this situation. They may well find that a large part of the answer lies within themselves, in how they conceive their role in the functioning of society and in determining its future. Do they come forward mainly as votaries of individual disciplines and sub-disciplines, working largely in their own clusters? Or, have they an obligation to present from time to time their considered views on major issues of social, economic, political and technological change and to place their views before major segments of public opinion and before the people generally?

In a period of rapid and dramatic change, every major scientific or technological development is producing a whole series of impacts for which those most affected are largely unprepared. Under these conditions, the contribution of social scientists can well be of crucial significance for the future. In the measure in which social scientists as a group live up to such a mission in relation to the future of our society at various levels, they may also win not only greater recognition, but also greater financial and policy support from those in political authority. Objective, dispassionate and in-depth analysis of basic problems by social scientists, acting voluntarily through appropriate groups and associations, ability to anticipate consequences of policies being envisaged or implemented, synthesising their own thinking, warning when necessary and proposing better alternatives, can go a long way to bring social sciences and their exponents into the centre of policy-making at every level. Obviously, these are broad propositions and social scientists will need to refine them and give more concrete shape to them. The object here is to emphasise on the processes involved in which the major initiative lies with social scientists and the groups and associations through which they may function. Also, on their part, they have to insist that, unlike in science and technology where each innovation or group of connected innovations may well proceed more or less autonomously, the interrelations and interdependencies in the functioning of society at each level are much greater and far more complex.

In such areas as money, finance, investment and the like, specially in the context of the modern, organised sector of the economy, experts may be in a position to analyse and advise without having to turn much to other disciplines. But beyond these, in almost every other area, there is a strong interdependence both between different social dimensions and between these and the scientific and technical dimensions. The lead in analysis and formulation and in seeking other interrelations has to be taken invariably by social scientists. Indeed, by their training, they are equipped for such a role and should be prepared to take the necessary initiative and responsibility upon themselves.

III

Three illustrations of what is intended may be cited. India is richly equipped with research laboratories, research institutes and research centres engaged in developing or applying a variety of improved technologies. Many of them have done innovative works of great importance, as, for instance, in respect of leather, glass and ceramics, sanitation, waste disposal, public hygiene and nutrition. Several other areas can be mentioned. However, outside agriculture and health, at the level of the community, the impact does not go much beyond demonstrations of what can be done. The extension links needed remain weak. The community as a whole and the body of workers specially concerned are not able to achieve large-scale technological upgradation. Of course, other conditions have also to be met, e.g., education, training, organizations, credit and marketing support, risk insurance, etc. In each area, appropriate local leaders have to be located, trained and supported.

The second example that may be cited concerns the implementation of the 73rd and 74th amendments to the Constitution concerning Panchayats and Nagar Palikas. Upto the present the main attention has been on the question of elections and organisation and, to an extent still far from satisfactory, on provision of finance and devolution of resources. These are only the first steps. The eleventh and twelfth schedules of the constitution list the various developmental responsibilities which the *Panchayats* and the *Nagar Palikas* are expected to carry out. Considerable knowledge and experience exists already about the implications of each of the responsibilities, how these have been fulfilled in the past and the conditions by way of finance, training, organisation etc. which have to be met, so that the local self-governing organisations may really be in a position to carry out the tasks expected of them. If these are not carried out, Panchayati Raj as a concept will be discredited and disowned. The two amendments and the schedules have a major bearing on Centre-State relations not only in terms of finance and distribution of powers, but also in terms of administrative relations between the Centre and the States and between the State level and *Nagar Palikas* and *Panchayat* institutions. Social scientists have the background and the training to analyse and bring out the issues, so that the right policy decisions are reached. While decisions have to be taken by appropriate agencies of Government, what decisions are reached and how they are carried into effect can be greatly assisted by the work of social scientists. Upto the present, neither at the Centre nor in the States, has the approach of effective devolution and transfer of responsibility been adequately worked out. An example of this is the current view that the Central Government should pass on funds directly to *Gram Panchayats*, bypassing State and district and block agencies.

A third area in which social scientists can make an effective contribtion is the study of decision-making processes by which major policies and programmes are determined within the Government. Examples are abound in which far-reaching decisions are reached without full study of aspects which emerge before long as critical weaknesses greatly undermining gains expected from the decisions taken. Also, while in the past, the word of authority could pass muster, in the changing climate of public affairs, unless those affected are taken into genuine and transparent consultation before decisions are taken or announced, implementation is apt to be thwarted. In particular, when radical changes in policy are in view, workers, supervisors and other staff need to be carried on board. Major policies demand a substantial measure of concensus in their support.

While Governments are now under compulsion to introduce greatly improved management and human resource development methods and practices and to profit from the innovations now taking place in large corporations both in India and the developed countries, their concerns are societal and their criteria will not be precisely those of private or public corporations. Social scientists from several fields—

public administration, political science, economics, sociology, psychology, for instance—have a collective contribution to make to the strengthening and improvement of systems and methods of governance. Nearer the grassroots, there is need also for much education and training of functionaries as well as at the community level. We have a whole set of comparatively new problems and opportunities in relation to which social scientists have much to contribute.

IV

Brief comments which bear on the contribution of social scientists to the making of public policy at the national and state level may be offered, illustratively, in respect of a few other areas for sustaining democratic institutions and processes, it is of the utmost importance that at the base of society there should be progressively greater cohesion and sense of community. These are also the essential foundations for co-operative action in every sphere with the general support of the community as a whole. A society which ensures justice to different segments, e.g., scheduled castes, scheduled tribes, other backward classes, and to the weak and those in need generally, and yet possesses a larger sense of community, can advance rapidly in various directions. Giving what is due to those deprived in the past becomes then the common ethos of the entire society. Conflicts, claims and differences which may arise become capable of resolution without much violence and tension. Through their research, and work with local communities, social scientists should be able to contribute greatly to the integration of society at the base and, thereby, also at other levels. A point to stress here is that in our societies, speciallly in the urban areas, there is an extraordinary amount of unconcern, even callousness, about the needs of others. This is an area in which, through sustained work with the people and through their studies, social scientists can help create conditions to bring in attitudinal changes.

Saubstantial resources are being devoted to poverty alleviation programmes. Much attention and resources are diverted to estimation of numbers below poverty, but too little to the nature and structure of proverty. The time has surely come for social scientists to lead the way to bolder thinking on eradication of poverty, atleast in its starker features, within a decade at the outside. We need now to move away from the notion of 'alleviation of poverty' which has become somewhat of a policy trap, both at the national and state as well as local levels.

Conditions in India vary widely. Much the greater part of poverty is found in regions which can be broadly identified as Poverty Concentration Areas. Poverty at the area level and poverty in relation to particular groups interact and accenturate each other. Through their work, social scientists can do much to present new directions to those who influence the process of policy making. It should be added here that, while the elements of rural poverty have been fairly understood, a whole new set of problems have arisen in relation to urban poverty. This is another area for greater work on the part of social scientists.

As a result of the development which has taken place, it is apparent that the work of society has to be carried out by various agencies in keeping with the capacities which now exist. In other words, there has to be a new and wider scheme of partnership between government agencies, corporate enterprises (both private and public), institutions at local and community level, and non-government and voluntary organizations. The capacities of each of them have to be enlarged and utilized in the larger interest of social advance in the widest sense of the term. Thus, at the community level, the earlier limited concept of utilization of manpower resources has to lead on to the wider notion of development and utilization of all available and potential resources. This is a direction in which social scientists can evolve new ideas and set forth the new possibilities.

Finally, something needs to be said on Globalization, a subject now receiving much attention. From all the new literature that is now available, it is apparent that Globalization is an evolving concept and there is yet no finality about its modes of operation and institutional implications. Social scientists in India do not have to accept all that multinational corporations or international financial institutions or the more developed countries are presently urging on the subject. In India we are in a position to evolve ideas about the concept, institutions and procedures for building up a global order which will be in the interest of India and other less developed countries and will make, at the sometime, for an international order fair to the more as also to the less developed world. Such an international order should make it possible to take advantage of new potentials for technological advance and of flows of resources and knowledge while enabling each society and economy to develop in keeping with its needs and resources and in accord with its basic values.

The main point to stress upon is that social scientists in India now have before them a vast field of urgent and vital work for which they are fully equipped. In partnership with scientists and technologists, they can confidently take their fair share of responsibilities in changing the face of India. They can draw a fair share of the expanding talent among the young and assure them social and economic satisfactions, perhaps not precisely identical with, but certainly as satisfying and self-fulfilling as those which are increasingly becoming available to young people who move into areas of development in technology, management and communications in all their varied forms.

24

YOUTH, EDUCATION AND SOCIAL TRANSFORMATION

S. Kashyap

Dr. Ambedkar and his role in the evolution of constitutionalism and the framing of the Constitution of India is not perhaps known to us. Many misconceptions and myths need to be corrected. Dr. Ambedkar had once told me in the Parliament Library where I then worked as a young research officer that if he had his way, he would be the first man to burn this Constitution and that it was not his. Later, he said the same thing on the floor of the Rajya Sabha and so it is on record. Dr. Ambedkar was a strong votary of uniform civil code. He was against reservations for the Scheduled Castes in perpetuity. He did not want the Scheduled Caste status for some citizens becoming a permanent stigma on Indian society. Above everything else, Babasaheb was for a casteless, classless, egalitarian society and a strong united India.

Dr. Ambedkar's own constitutional proposals were printed under the title "States and Minorities" before his being made the Chairman of the Constitution Drafting Committee. Also, his own draft of the provisions of fundamental rights was very different from the other drafts that were considered and adopted. His strictly time-bound ten-year programme of socialistic reconstruction of society and economic development would, he thought, make reservations unnecessary after the initial period.

The two other themes that occurred to me as apt options for this article were those of: (i) a critique of social justice in the scheme of our Constitution and (ii) a review of the working of the Constitution for half-a-century and the need for reforms. Each of these topics, however, would need a lengthy writing.

I believe that it is my generation that has failed. Our elders had placed before us some ideals and values by imbibing them in their own lives. Their lives presented before us a role model to be emulated and a message to be followed. But, we could not be the role models and provide inspiration to today's youth. Actually, our generation has done such violence to all the ideals and values and presented such an ugly example that we must hang our heads in shame. In education, politics, morality and all other fields, we have failed to do what we should have done and did all that we should have never done.

In a sense, it is also a matter of pity that concern for advising the youth in matters of discipline, character, conduct and observance of duties, is becoming a preoccupation of the older generation. We seem very anxious to advise the youth to develop their morals. We, the elders—the teachers and the parents of today are like Nachiketa's father in the *Kathopnishad*. We do not realise that we are really the guilty generation. We do nothing about our own value system and pay no attention to our own morals, character and conduct. We forget that the youth do not learn from what the teachers and the parents say but from what they do. Before advising, we must assess ourselves, what examples we have placed before them by our own style of lives.

I believe, our original sin, during past fifty years of our republic has been that we have not given due importance to education in the national agenda. Therefore, I would like to express some thoughts on the education scene.

Education has been sadly neglected and has occupied one of the lowest positions in national priorities. Otherwise, there was no reason why in the last fifty years, free and compulsory education to all children below the age of fourteen could not be made a reality or why widespread illiteracy could not be eradicated. As a matter of fact, today India has more illiterates than it had at the time of independence. Among all the countries, we have the largest number of illiterate people.

The dark reality today is that the politicians in the driving seat do not care to listen. They do not need to listen. They have hijacked the ship of the state and emaciated the collective will, the moral elan, the soul of society. They have a vested interest in keeping the people illiterate and uneducated. They do not believe in any values and in sheer self-survival interest, they do not want the people to be educated, much less educated in values and in fighting for them. It seems, therefore, that without changing the valueless political system, it will not be possible to put 'education with a soul' on the national agenda.

The vast majority of our youth are forced to live at sub-human, below subsistence, animal levels. Youth have to decide about their role and responsibility. The new graduates can contribute very meaningfully in the battle for universalization of education. If we have the will, it should be possible to bring about near total literacy and more, within five years. Activist citizenship organisations of the youth could embark upon schemes of education brigades of *satyagrahi* volunteers and constructive workers with each one contributing a year of his life or some hours each week to such a mission. In my humble opinion at the root of all that ails nation today is lake of education in values and of ideal human beings who can constitute living examples before others. But society is commonly run on reward-punishment principle. If values pay–not necessarily in money—they will be adopted. Our politics is not value-based, public life is shorn of all values, no values are respected in social intercourse, in business or in professions. In such a scenario, how can we expect only education to be value-based?

In today's scenario, it is difficult to find those who want to better the world around or to ameliorate the sufferings of fellow humanbeings or even to bother about matters like character building. Qualities of education and training that ensure the growth of such beings are not in demand. The market forces are at work and what is asked for is orientation for securing a paying job and training in the methodologies and techniques for getting things done, for fixing deals and forging ahead. It was an astounding experience when recently a candidate for a job revealed during the interview that he had done a professional course in how to get things done, in other words, he claimed his expertise in bribing others.

Unfortunately today we are living in a world where our minds and hearts are polluted and ideals and values are dead. We face the debris of our dreams of old. The old fashioned wisdom that our elders tried to impart us in childhood said that "when money is lost, nothing is lost, when health is lost something is lost but when character is lost, everything is lost". The position today has been exactly reversed. We have come to believe that character is an easily expendable commodity and that money constitutes the ultimate value.

Competitive consumerism, hedonism, stark materialism and unabashed possessivism have become the yard-sticks of respect in society. No body even talks of our old ideals of *Aparigrah, Asteya, Santosh* and minimisation of wants. Since everything around seems rotten, we tend to withdraw into shells of privatism and make selfishness not only the greatest but the only feasible virtue. The goals become making big money quick, achieving status and living well.

For the last so many years, we are witness to a general erosion in standards of individual and social conduct in various walks of life. There is a general devaluation of values. Crime and corruption are rampant. Character and individuality have lost significance. Worldly success, comforts and vulgar exhibitionism have become the most important concerns. But, we would do well to remember that we cannot build durable islands of safety in the midst of tempests and cyclones all around.

Events and developments in the modern world move at a hurricane speed. Centuries are compressed into years. The most striking development of the 20th century that history will record has presumably been the information revolution characterised by digitalization of information enabling the building of information highways and superways, e-mail, internet, cyber cafes, multi-media and the rest. But information is not knowledge and knowledge is not wisdom.

Wisdom is the ability to discriminate and decide between right and wrong. The objective of true education is to impart such wisdom. Undigested knowledge becomes poison and is dangerous. Learning without the ability of discrimination can be grossly misused.

Sakshara Viprita Rakshasha Bhavanti

(A Spoilt genius becomes a devil)

Wisdom comes from character. Education must develop character along with ability for independent and critical thinking. Education is what remains with us after we forget all the subjects that we might have learnt at the University. Education is a continuous and lifelong process of learning. One can learn even from a fool. In fact, as the Greek thinker Cato said, the wise learn more from fools than fools do from wisemen. Education does not end with leaving the University. It is essentially the process of development of individuality, selfhood and character. To quote Iqbal's famous couplet where he put self above God:

Khudi Kar Ko buland Itna,
Ke har taqdir se pehle,
Khuda Bande se khud puche,
bata teri raza kya hai.

(Take your selfhood to such heights that before determining your destiny, God himself would ask you as to what is your wish). In the words of Swami Vivekananda:

"Education is not the amount of information that is put into one's brain and runs riot there, undigested, all one's life. We must have life-building, man-making, character-making, assimilation of ideas. The ass carrying its load of sandalwood knows only the weight and not the value of sandalwood. If education were identical with information, the libraries would have been the greatest sages in the world, the encyclopodias the Rishis".

Yatha kharas chandan bharvahi

bharasya vetta, ne tu Chandansya.

Vivekananda's message was for an education that produces men who had conquered fear and were full of energy and faith in themselves. His sorrows, disappointments and complaints—he loses faith in everything- in ideals, values, future and friends. The youth would have to give up their defeatism and escapism, fulfil their role, surge forward and assume responsibility. Swami Vivekananda further says:

"What we want is strength, so believe in yourselves.......... make your nerves strong. What we want is muscles of iron and nerves of steel. We have wept long enough. No more weeping, but stand on your feet and be men".

In all humility, I would like to add that if you have faith in yourself, you will find your own answers. We have no answers to your questions. And, if we try to advise you, I for one, would say, please do not follow us. Carve out your own path.

What is needed is a new beginning for national regeneration. India has a destiny to realise and a vision to give to humanity. Nations which lose their vision perish. Societies that fail to transmit to their children their heritage, the quintessence of the accumulated wisdom of centuries and a system of values are relegated to debris. The rubble and the shambles of history and the stories of dead civilizations are a mute testimony to many such fallen stars.

European renaissance was brought about by the effort of about 100 enlightened individuals. Vivekananda also felt that 100 souls if awakened could bring about a revolution. India is a vast country and should easily throw up 100 men and women help regeneration of the country.

"Men, men, these are wanted....................A hundred such and the world becomes revolutionised"

It is a pity that any talk about values and morals as about culture today is considered non-secular. It must be a cause for great concern and anguish that we are gradually getting cut off from the basic truths of our culture. Many of us are not even aware, for example, of the vast reservoir of knowledge in Vedas and Upanishads and in our old traditions.

Thousands of years ago, our common ancestors who incidentaly were neither Hindus, nor Muslims, nor Christians, asked of themselves a question : who am I, where did I come from, what is the aim of life, what heights of excellence can a man achieve?

The Upanishads do not belong to any particular religion, community or group, they are the common heritage of every Indian, in fact of humanity. They teach us that fundamentally there is the same *Atmaan,* in every being. In reality, one is only *Atman.* Thus conceived, there is no high or low. Every member of society is equally important. Everyone has his own place of pride and honour because behind his individuality is his *Atman*—etemal, infinite and immortal. The human personality owes its creative energy and the spirit of oneness and equality to the *Atman.*

How can such knowledge be non-secular. True education awakens the consciousness of the oneness of family, neighbourhood, society, nation and lastly humanity at large. All the walls of high and low are pulled down. In every other man, the individual sees himself. He begins to wish well for everyone as for himself. He feels the pain and sorrow of every to other human being as his own.

Vaishnav jan to tene kahiye,
ji pir parayi jane re.

or as Walt Whitman said :

I do not ask the wounded man how he feels.
I myself become the wounded man.

The sphere of 'I' gets so widened that it comes to encompass within it the entire humanity. The individual comes to feel and realise within himself the whole universe. Once the drop knows that it is water, the drop and the limitless sea are one and the same. This is the concept of Shankar's advait when the sense of the other, of duality disappears.

Real happiness consists not in *bhog* or enjoyment but in *tyag* or sacrifice. Isopanishad speaks of :

Tena tyaktena bhunjitha
(Enjoying life through renunciation)
Yastu sarvani bhutani atmanyevanu pashyati,
sarva bhuteshuchatmanam taton vijugupsate.

or

Yashmin sarvani bhutani atmaivabhudvijanata,
tatra ka moha ka shoka aikatvam anupashyata.

The concept of modern democracy also lays great stress on non-discrimination and participatory equality of all human beings in the system. But, the harsh truth is that in the absence of any education of the spirit, society gets divided on grounds of narrow parochial loyalties based on language, religion, race, caste, region etc. The dividing lines get more and more widened. Social incongruities and tensions keep multiplying. And, we can have no respite from all this unless we seek shelter in spiritual education and its quintessentials of equality, unity and integrity.

But, the *Upanishads* and ancient Indian wisdom do not preach a spiritual education which is devoid of practical training for Life. Education for character building and education for learning the skills for a job or profession etc. cannot be separated from each other. Nor can they be viewed separately. They have all to be accepted as essential parts of the educational process. On the completion of the course of education, at the time of convocation, the *Guru* used to tell his disciples not to transgress truth and *dharma* but at the same time not to ignore their wellbeing or needs of their worldly comforts and prosperity either :

Satyan pramaditavyam,
dharmann pramaditavyam,
kushalann pramaditavyam,
bhutyain pramaditavyam.

Thus, Tatreyopanished does not teach utopian idealism or mere spiritual knowledge. It attaches due importance to the physical worldly needs as well and regards them as essential objects of education. Education may include literacy, knowledge of arts and the physical sciences, training of the faculties of the mind etc. It is natural to expect that education would enable the student to face the ordeals and travails of the struggle of life, to meet his needs and sort out his personal problems, to equip him for a vocation of his liking and enable him to earn his livelihood and the basic comforts of life.

According to *Mundkopanished,* the best education is one that takes us away from the mortal many to the immortal one. It is the name given to illumining the mind and heart of man. It is for carrying us from darkness to light, from falsehood to truth, from death to immortality.

Tamso ma jyotirgamaya,
Asto ma sadagamaya,
Mrityor ma amritam gamaya.

(From the untruth lead me to the truth, from darkness, lead me to light, from death, lead me to immortality)

It is for the growth of the spirit, for character building, and for the integrated development of the human personality to its highest possibilities above the sensory world. It is connected with man's spiritual progress, liberation and development. It is for liberating the spirit of man.

Ya vidya sa vimuktaye

That which uplifts, liberates from ignorance and frees from the shackles of physical limitations, is true education. That is also what the UNESCO report terms as "Learning to Be".

At the beginning of *Kathopanished, Kenopanishad* and several other Upanishads, the usual invocation reads :

Tejasvianvdhitmas tu ma vidvishavahe

(May education light our path)

Each of us is born of immortality. The *Atman* or the *Jyoti* which is within each one of us, is the inexhaustible reservoir of energy and power. It manifests itself through the medium of education. To recognize the 'I' or the *Atman* inside the physical body is the real aim of education and the highest form of learning.

It is quite possible that the present generation may not find the ideal kind of teachers in whom full faith can be reposed or at whose feet or near whom the youth of today can sit, and learn to see the light within and grow through contact communication or through question-answers in the great Upanishadic tradition. It is also a fact that today the youth do not find in their elders any role models to emulate, they find no source of light. There is despair and distress in the scenario around. But I have great faith in the youth of India. The anguished world of today needs the vision and the light that only India of tomorrow can provide. From within the youth, the soul of India would once again rise, awakening would dawn, light would shine, national regeneration would follow.

Darkness may be very deep, but for that very reason, every small candle, every single lamp would shine more brightly. Education is the name of one lamp lighting the other. If every one of us becomes a lamp that lights another, there should be no problem in eradicating ignorance and illiteracy and spreading education at a fast pace.

The path may be difficult but we must march on for there lies the ultimate success and truth-the goal of life.

Utisthat jagrat prapya varannibothat

Kshurasya dhara nishita duratyaya durgam pathastat kavyo vadanti

Arise, awake and stop not till the goal is reached.

Annexure-I
Working Results of Scheduled Commercial Banks for 1995-96 to 1998-99

(Rs. in Crores)

Parameters/ Sub-group	Private Sector Banks 1995-96	Private Sector Banks 1996-97	Private Sector Banks 1997-98	Pvt. Sector Banks (New) 1995-96	Pvt. Sector Banks (New) 1996-97	Pvt. Sector Banks (New) 1997-98	Foreign Banks 1995-96	Foreign Banks 1996-97	Foreign Banks 1997-98	All Banks 1995-96	All Banks 1996-97	All Banks 1997-98	All Banks 1998-99
(I) Income	4332	6389	6438	1000	1968	3012	6096	7008	8697	66058	76226	85849	100078
(a) Interest	3756	4733	5497	835	1639	2386	4960	6212	6783	56082	66484	73733	87370
(b) Other Income	577	656	941	165	329	626	1126	1396	1914	8976	9741	12116	12708
(II) Expenditure	3941	4983	5996	833	1688	2612	5336	6942	8067	64119	71721	79350	95418
(a) Interest	2593	3431	4084	579	1173	1821	3186	3896	4222	37319	44838	50292	60905
(b) Provision and Contengncies	386	434	640	83	201	335	838	1365	1914	9211	7735	8125	9333
(c) Other operating expenses	962	1118	1272	171	314	456	1312	1681	1913	10150	19148	20933	25180
(III) Operating Profit	777	840	1082	260	481	735	1587	2031	2544	10150	12239	14624	13992
(IV) Net Profit	391	406	442	157	280	400	749	668	630	939	4504	6499	4660
(V) Total Assets	36998	44457	55205	9025	16160	25856	47430	56063	65288	599152	672976	795535	950898
					Percent of Total Assets								
(I) Income	11.7	12.1	11.7	11.1	12.2	11.6	12.8	13.6	13.3	10.9	11.3	10.8	10.52
(a) Income	10.1	10.6	10	9.3	10.1	9.2	10.5	11.1	10.4	9.4	9.9	9.3	9.19
(b) Other Income	1.6	1.5	1.7	1.8	2	2.4	2.4	2.5	2.9	1.5	1.4	1.5	1.34
(II) Expenditure	10.7	11.2	10.9	9.2	10.4	10.1	11.3	12.4	12.4	10.7	10.7	10	10.03
(a) Interest	7	7.7	7.4	6.4	7.3	7	6.7	6.9	6.5	6.2	6.7	6.3	6.4
(b) Provisions & Contengies	2.6	1	1.2	0.9	1.2	1.3	1.8	2.4	2.9	1.5	1.1	1	0.98
(c) Other operating expenses	1	2.5	2.3	1.9	1.9	1.8	2.8	3	3	2.9	2.8	2.6	2.65
(III) Operating Profit	2.1	1.9	2	2.8	3	2	3.3	3.6	3.9	1.7	1.8	1.8	1.47
(IV) Net Profit	1.1	0.9	0.8	1.9	1.7	1.5	1.6	1.2	1	0.2	0.7	0.8	0.49

Source: Reports on Trend and Progress of Banking in India for the years 1995-96 to 1998-99.

Annexure-II

Increase in Profits of Scheduled Commercial Banks in India during the Year 1995-96 to 1998-99

(Rs. in Crores)

Sl. No.	Sub-Group	1995-96			1996-97			1997-98			1998-99		
		Operating	*Provisions and Contingences*	*Net Profit*	*Operating*	*Provisions and Contingences*	*Net Profit*	*Operating*	*Provisions and Contingences*	*Net Profit*	*Operating*	*Provisions and Contingences*	*Net Profit*
1.	SBI & A. Associates	4458	2908	1650	645	–312	857	275	–478	753	–84	–910	–994
2	Nationalised Banks	4440	2995	1445	816	–1789	2605	1102	–20	1122	388	1166	–1554
3.	Public Sector Banks (1+2)	8808	6803	3096	1361	–2101	3462	1376	–499	1876	304	256	560
4.	Private Sector Banks (Old)	858	448	410	81	62	19	242	206	37	–291	160	–131
5.	Private (New) Banks	485	199	286	235	116	119	253	134	119	–55	–53	–2
6.	Foreign Banks	1999	1212	787	413	374	39	512	648	–36	–605	–668	63
	Total	12240	7662	4578	2090	–1549	3639	2384	390	1996	–343	–1393	1050

Annexure-III

Required and Actual Capital Adequacy Ratio as on 1995

(Percentage)

Country	*C.A.R. (National Requirements)*	*Actual C.A.R.*
Argentina	12	18.5
Chile	#8	10.7
Brazil	8	12.9
Mexico	8	11.3
Indonesia	8	11.9
Malaysia	8	11.3
Thailand	8	9.3
India	8	•9.5
Japan	8	9.1
U.S.A.	8	12.8

Note: #Legislation now before Congress.

• Relates only to Public Sector Banks.

Source: Goldstein, 1996.

REFERENCES

1. Ministry of Finance. Government of India: The Narasimham Committee Report: The Banking Sector Reform (1991): I by M. Narasimham.
2. Ministry of Finance: Department of Economic Affairs. Government of India: The Narasimham Committee II Report: The Banking Sector Reforms (April, 1998).
3. Ministry of Finance. Government of India: Economic Survey for the years 1995-96 to 1998-99.
4. Kunal Sen, Rajendra R. Vaidya: *The Process of Financial Liberalisation in India*, Delhi Oxford University Press, 1997.
5. Dr. C. Rangarajan: *Indian Economy: Essays on Money and Finance*, 1998.
6. The World Bank: Annual Report 1997 and 1998.
7. Prof. Sanjiv Ranjan Das, of Harwad Business School U.S.A.: *Money Talks: Competing in the future for Banking and Financial Services*, December, 1998.
8. Indian Banks Association: *Managing Global Banking: Emerging Perspectives and Lessons for India*–15-17th September, 1998.
9. Murrav L. Weidenbaim, Kenneth W. Chilton (Ed.): *Public Policy Toward Corporate Takeovers*, 1990.

Annexure–IV

Status on Sactions

Sanctions by the USA

It was reported in the Economic Survey 1998-99 that under Nuclear Proliferation Prevention Act, 1994, which also includes the Glenn Amendment to the Arms Export Control Act, the US ordered sanctions against India on May 13, 1998. The sanction was not applicable in assistance relating to humanitarian needs, food or other agricultural commodities.

On November 6, 1998, the US President announced partial lifting of sanctions on the basis of authority given to him by the Brownback Amendment passed by the US Congress. The relaxations were offered in the operations of EXIM Bank, Trade Development Agency and OPIC. US Bank activities and Military Education and Training Programmes were resumed.

Further, on 27 October 1999, the US President waived some of the sanctions, for an indefinite period. The sanctions that are waived include:

(a) Activities and programmes of the Export-Emport Bank (EXIM Bank).

(b) Activities and programmes of the Overseas Private Investment Corporation (OPIC).

(c) Assistance under the International Military Education and Training Programme (IMET).

(d) Making of any loan or providing of any credit to the Government of India by any US Bank.

(e) Assistance to the Asian Elephant Conservation Fund, the Rhinoceros and Tigar Conservation Fund, and the Indo-American Environmental Leadership Programme.

(f) Any credit, credit guarantee, or other financial assistance provided by the Department of Agriculture to support the purchase of food and other agricultural commodities.

The effect of the Presidential Memorandum signed on 27 October 1999 is that the following sanctions will remain in effect until the President exercises his waiver authority:

(a) US opposition to the extenstion of any loan, financial or technical assistance to India by an international financial institution (i.e., World Bank, International Monetary Fund and the Asian Development Bank loans).

(b) Prohibition on the safe of defence articles, services, design and construction services, as well as the grant of export license for the export of items listed on the US Munitions List.

(c) Grant of foreign military financing.

(d) Prohibition on the export of specific goods and technology, (i.e., dual use goods and technology).

A press release dated 16 December 1999 from the US Department of Commerce, Bureau of Export Administration indicates removal of 51 Indian entities from the list of entities originally sanctioned in 1998. The entities removed included mainly ordnance factories and scientific research institutions. Removal of the entities will make it easier for them to obtain non-sensitive items and technology from the US.

Denmark

Decisions against any fresh aid. Further, all ongoing projects would be wound up in a phased manner so that they can be transferred to Indian authorities in three to five years. Assistance under private sector is also suspended.

Canada

Ongoing projects will continue. Future programmes will focus on environment; poverty reduction; gender equity; human rights and child labour. No support to new non-humanitarian lending. Ban on defence sales.

Position remains unchanged in respect of others

Source: Ministry of External Affairs.

Annexure–V

New Initiatives for Infrastructure Development

General Measures

- Uniform tax holidays of 15 years for all infrastructure sector projects.
- Creation of Foreign Investment Implementation authority to smoothen flow of FDI into the infrastructure sector.
- The important duty structure for proejct imports rationalized.

Power

- Mega Power Project policy announced.
- Restructuring of SEBs to be encouraged, new transmission and distribution systems to get fiscal benefits given to infrastructure sector.

Telecom

- New Telecom policy announced
  - Domestic long distance calls to be opened up.
  - Department of Telecom Services (DTS) to be corporatized by 2001.
  - DTS/MTNL to enter as third cellular operators.
- TRAI reconstituted through an ordiance.
  - Clear distinction between the recommendatory and regulatory functions of the Authority.
  - Mandatory for government to seek recommendations of TRAI in respect of matters dealing with need and timing for introduction of new service providers and the terms and conditions of license to a service provider.
  - Composition of Authority, i.e., TRAI has been changed.
  - Separate disputes redressal body known as

"Telecom Disputes Settlement and Appellate Tribunal" has been set up.

- Sepecific Targets for Telecom
  - Make available phone on demand by 2002.
  - Encourage development of telecom in rural areas and increase rural tele-density from the current level of 0.4 to 4.0 by the 2010.
  - Achieve telecom coverage of all villages in the country by 2002.
  - Provide Internet access to all district headquarters by 2002.
  - Resources for meeting the Universal Service Obligation (USO) would be raised through a universal access levy, which would be a percentage of revenue earned by all operators under various licenses.
  - Existing license holders of basic and value-added services allowed to switch over to a revenue sharing agreement.
  - Provide high-speed data and multi-media capability using technologies including ISDN to all towns with a population greater than 2 lakhs by 2002.

Roads

- A new cess of Re. 1 per litre on HSD imposed to generate funds, which will be transferred to Central Road Fund. Most of it will be used for development and maintenance of State Roads and National Highway etc.
- Model Concession Agreement for BOT road project more than Rs. 100 crore and less than Rs. 100 crore finalized.

Railways

- Indian Railway Catering and Tourism Corporation (IRTC) Ltd. incorporated as a Government Company with the objective of upgrading and managing rail catering and hospitality.

- Indian Railways have issued Letters of Intent for ownership, operation and management of two luxury trains in private sector.

Civil Aviation

- Restructuring of airports of Airport Authority of India (AAI) through long-term leasing route.

Urban Infrastructure

- Special Package for Housing construction and Services, which will facilitate development of urban infrastructure.

INDEX